# Rainbow Cattle Co.

# RAINBOW CATTLE CO.

## Liberation, Inclusion, and the History of Gay Rodeo

Nicholas Villanueva, Jr.

University of Nebraska Press
Lincoln

The University of Nebraska Press is part of a land-grant institution with campuses and programs on the past, present, and future homelands of the Pawnee, Ponca, Otoe-Missouria, Omaha, Dakota, Lakota, Kaw, Cheyenne, and Arapaho Peoples, as well as those of the relocated Ho-Chunk, Sac and Fox, and Iowa Peoples.

∞

Library of Congress Cataloging-in-Publication Data
Names: Villanueva, Nicholas, author.
Title: Rainbow cattle co.: liberation, inclusion, and the history of gay rodeo / Nicholas Villanueva, Jr.
Description: Lincoln: University of Nebraska Press, [2024] | Includes bibliographical references and index.
Identifiers: LCCN 2024020315
ISBN 9781496230195 (hardback)
ISBN 9781496241801 (epub)
ISBN 9781496241818 (pdf)
Subjects: LCSH: Gay rodeos—United States. | Rodeos—Social aspects—United States. | Gay people—Social life and customs—United States. | AIDS (Disease)—Research—United States—Finance. | BISAC: SOCIAL SCIENCE / LGBTQ+ Studies / Gay Studies | SPORTS & RECREATION / Animal Sports / Rodeos
Classification: LCC GV1834.5 .V55 2024 | DDC 791.8/408664—dc23/eng/20240606
LC record available at https://lccn.loc.gov/2024020315

Designed and set in Whitman by Lacey Losh.

To Ryan Villanueva

# Contents

# Illustrations

# Acknowledgments

This book would not have been possible without generous support from the University of Colorado, Boulder (UCB) and the 2022 President's Fund for the Humanities award. I am grateful for multiple grants and fellowships from the UCB College of Arts and Sciences, which include the Fund for Excellence and the Eugene M. Kayden Research Grant. Additional support from the UCB Center for the Humanities and Arts helped me complete the final revisions. The Department of Ethnic Studies provided annual funding for travel expenses to interview IGRA members and take photographs for this book at several IGRA rodeos over a four-year period. I had tremendous support from my department chair, Arturo Aldama, and the intellectual stimulation of my colleague Jennifer Ho, who encouraged me to push forward with writing my manuscript during challenging times. I appreciate the external support from the Excellence in West Texas History Association, the Borderlands Regional Library Association, the National Endowment for the Humanities Becoming American Grant, and the North American Society of Sports History (NASSH) and its Diversity Award for Emerging Non-Traditional Scholars. It was at the 2019 NASSH annual conference in Boise, Idaho, where I met my editor Robert (Rob) Taylor of the University of Nebraska Press. Taylor found interest in my fifteen-minute conference paper and has been with me from the near-beginning of this scholarly project. Thank you, Rob, for your patience and support.

There are many people associated with the IGRA, and this list could go on for pages. I want to send a special thank you to people who sat down for interviews, shared their historical documents that are not found in an archive, loaned photos for this book, and have become lifelong friends. John Beck and Diamond, Tony Valdez (a.k.a. Chili Pepper), Candy Pratt, Brian Helander, Randy Edlin, Tom Sheridan, Tom Devlin, Michael Andrew Martinez Arenas, Andy Siekkinen, Roger Bergmann, Chuck Browning, Kami Boles, Dan Oldenburg, Janelle King-Neptune, Eliana Cohen, David Hill, Patrick Terry, Carl Schmidt II, Ron Trusley, Paula Scougal, Stephanie Garber, Dan Yenter, Christopher Service, Wade Earp, Tommy Channel, Greg Tinsley, Frank Harrell, Ashley Wilhelm, Tim Smith, Evita Peroxide, Sean Moroz, Michael Vrooman, Mark Allen Smith, Wes Givens, Sandy Bidwell, David Lawson, Greg Begay, Devon Garcia, Jacob Burke, Sammy Simpkin, Mipsy Mikels, Alexander Saites, Gunner Sizemore, Gene Fraikes, Jonathan Roman, Todd Tramp, Ryan Knop, Kurt Harrison-Garcia, Robbie Harrison-Garcia, Jackie Kemp, Brendan Sullivan, Jack Morgan, Amy Griffin, Anthony Michael Lumpkins (Chicken Nugget), Jayme Christensen-Walker, Bruce Casey, Phillip Blakesley, Priscilla Toya Bouvier, Jen Vrana, Kade Jackwell, Charis Loren, Jason Martinez, Alexis Cole, Janet Stange, Doug Tear, Mark Arnold, Kevin Springer, Saul Lozada, Monique Zimbelman, Philip Lister, Jeffrey McCasland, Charlie Colella, Kade Hiller, and Jerry Cunningham. I sincerely thank my IGRA family for all your support.

I want to thank the medical team at Encompass Health and Rehabilitation Hospital of East Valley (Mesa, Arizona). When my dedication to my research led to multiple fractures of my pelvis from a fall during a steer riding competition, you encouraged me to stay positive when I was miles away from home. It is most important that I include family and friends who have been supportive of my sobriety. Most importantly, I want to thank my husband, Ryan Villanueva, and dedicate the book to him.

Finally, I would not be the man that I am today without the love and support of my late mother, Patricia (Patsy) Villanueva. When I close my eyes, I can see you pumping your fist and cheering in the rodeo arena.

# Rainbow Cattle Co.

# Introduction

When I was six years old, I told my father I wanted to be a cowboy, a fireman, and a Dallas Cowgirl cheerleader.

—Wade Earp

The opening quotation from Wade Earp characterizes his identity as a young boy. Heteronormative rules of gender and sexuality are taught, but these are socially constructed and not natural. For boys and young men in the borderlands, the American West, and rural regions of the country, cowboy culture is taught at a young age, and tenets of masculinity are enforced. A significant part of country culture includes the sport of rodeo. Earp is a descendant of Wyatt Earp, the historical deputy marshal of Tombstone, Arizona, and the subject of several Western films. Wade Earp did not grow up to be a fireman or a Dallas Cowgirl cheerleader; he became one of the best rodeo cowboys in gay rodeo history.

In 1976 Phil Ragsdale hosted a rodeo that was a philanthropic event with the purpose of bridging the gap between the marginalized LGBTQ people of Reno, Nevada, and mainstream society. Over the following ten years, gay rodeo organizations formed in multiple states, and in 1985 delegates from Colorado, Texas, California, and Arizona met in Denver and held the first International Gay Rodeo Association (IGRA) conference. It is necessary to inform scholars of LGBTQ studies who are reading this book that "gay rodeo" is often used in place of "LGBTQ rodeo." The reason for this is that the organization today—the IGRA—uses "gay rodeo" exclusively and does not use the phrase "LGBTQ rodeo," although it does not adhere to such usage to deny queer identities. Approaching fifty years of the gay rodeo's existence and nearly forty years as an official international organization, many of the old-timers who helped create these organizations know who they are and what gay rodeo is. They do not feel the need to adopt the more academic and socially acceptable identifiers. For the readers of this book who are members of the IGRA, "LGBTQ" is often used throughout these chapters to confirm my inclusion of all queer identities today. Gay rodeo is inclusive of everyone in the LGBTQ community, people of color, and various religious beliefs; as Greg Tinsley of the Colorado Gay Rodeo Association said, "We even accept 'straight' people, because we don't care who they marry."[1]

Following the first successful gay rodeo in 1976, the LGBTQ community throughout the West learned of Reno's event. Men and women who grew up with rodeo in their lives often hid their LGBTQ identities for some time, avoided being seen with same-sex partners, or falsely claimed to live heteronormative lives. The gay rodeo intrigued gay rodeo athletes who only knew the mainstream rodeo, or "straight circuit," as many IGRA members refer to it. Since 1976 gay rodeo has become an annual event bringing the LGBTQ rodeo community together, and for some it has introduced a subculture that many did not know existed. By the early 1980s, Reno's event had hosted more than ten thousand people. Nevada's libertarian political climate appeared to accept unconventional lifestyles. The people of the state seemed to be accepting of the LGBTQ community to some degree, as the gay liberation movement had brought more men and women out of the closet during the previous decade than ever before. As journalist Eric Marcus wrote: "In contrast to the pre-Stonewall homophile movement, which was driven primarily by people in their thirties and forties, college-aged students were often the ones on the leading edge of gay liberation. . . . And because universities and colleges had so drastically changed during the 1960s, most gay and lesbian students were in no danger of being punished or expelled."[2] The same was true to some degree in many other subcultures of the United States. The 1970s gay liberationists brought the LGBTQ identity out of the closet, making it impossible to avoid. Newspapers from Walla Walla, Washington, to New York City reported coming-out stories of celebrities and politicians, and gay rodeo soon became a western phenomenon.

In 1985 the IGRA became the official gay rodeo association. Through a vast network of rodeo cowboys, rodeo cowgirls, and fans, rodeo became the sport that represented the ideological fight for gay liberation in the American West. Founding president of the IGRA Wayne Jakino stated that the association's goals were "to promote and nurture, through fellowship, the sport of rodeo within the gay community; to foster a positive image of gay cowboys and cowgirls within all communities; to provide anyone with education and training in the production of, and participation in, rodeo; and to participate in the preservation of our Western heritage."[3] These athletes celebrated their rodeo cowboy/cowgirl identities as well as their gender and sexual identities. The IGRA became the gay pride of the American West. By 1995 there were thirty-six chapters representing twenty-seven states, the District of Columbia, and two Canadian provinces. The organization was international in location as well as through the countries of origin of its competitors, and LGBTQ magazines in the United States as well as in Canada, Italy, and Germany covered stories about the sport of gay rodeo.

Mainstream rodeo reinforced a gender ideology that, at times, seemed to limit women from full inclusion. In gay rodeo, men and women compete in all of the same events and defy heteronormative social rules in sport. From the first gay rodeo to today, women have ridden bulls and men have barrel raced. This is not to say that mainstream rodeo excludes women, but gay rodeo is a place that has consistently welcomed women and defied gender ideologies in sport. The empowerment of the IGRA has kept these cowboys and cowgirls true to their rodeo roots. IGRA athletes compete in the same speed and roughstock events featured in mainstream amateur rodeo, but they have transformed rodeo into something uniquely their own with camp events. It is not uncommon to find camp events at amateur mainstream rodeos, but in gay rodeo they are respected as competitive events and are required if athletes want to compete for All-Around Cowboy and Cowgirl titles. A contestant can win a championship buckle at the gay rodeo competing in camp events as well. These are timed events that include team competitions for decorating a steer, dressing a goat in a pair of men's white briefs, and engaging in a wild drag race, which has become the campiest of all three events. Camp events allow LGBTQ athletes and spectators to enjoy the free expression of rejecting heteronormativity in sport, while being included in athletic competition without having to hide their LGBTQ identities. As Katherine McFarland Bruce argues in *Pride Parades: How a Parade Changed the World*, the same is the case with gay pride parades: "At pride, being fabulous is a protest. As counter-protesters loudly condemn the open expression of queer sexuality, participants defy them by turning up the volume."[4]

The camp of gay rodeo indeed turns up the volume of individual expression. The power structure in sport, and specifically rodeo, perpetuates a gender ideology that privileges men over women and reinforces heteronormativity as a requirement for athletes. Gay rodeo has addressed this systemic problem. Readers will learn how the LGBTQ community in the 1980s and 1990s became trailblazers in sport long before the global sporting world discussed topics such as gender identity and rules for participation or watched an openly gay man listen for his name to be called during the NFL draft. Gay rodeo in the 1970s and 1980s preceded these high-profile events and helped foster a more accepting sporting world for future generations of LGBTQ athletes.

Gay rodeos became a space where the LGBTQ community could come together as athletes without fear of homophobia and transphobia, and challenge social boundaries and borders. However, during the rise of this sporting sensation, the community had to fight to save members' lives from a different threat. After the outbreak of HIV became a global pandemic, and the subsequent antigay panic, fear led to an increase in homophobia. AIDS was labeled a "gay disease," and federal funding for AIDS research was abysmal during Republican president Ronald Reagan's administration in the 1980s. The IGRA shifted focus from mainstream charitable organizations toward AIDS-related causes. This book examines how gay rodeo emerged as a safe place for LGBTQ athletes and a necessary humanitarian organization for those impacted the most by AIDS. This research examines how gay rodeo challenged stereotypes about masculinity, femininity, and heteronormativity. Furthermore, it explores how gay rodeo became the predominant gay pride celebration for towns that had never hosted a pride festival. In some towns, a gay rodeo event is the only major LGBTQ celebration ever to occur. With every challenge, members came together to help their own. These athletes and philanthropists have raised millions of dollars since the mid-1970s. The LGBTQ community found strength and support within their sporting venue of gay rodeo.

Mainstream rodeo, like many other sports, is controlled by the dominant group in society. White, Christian, cisgender, heterosexual-identifying, able-bodied men have most of the power in the social world of sport. As women and LGBTQ athletes break down barriers that preclude participation, and as athletes of color who protest discrimination are being heard, this dominant group of the sporting world has lost some of that power. The summer of 2020 was a historic moment for marginalized groups. The Black Lives Matter (BLM) movement made strides toward racial justice after the murder of George Floyd by a white police officer. Protests continued throughout the summer, which have encouraged progress to combat systemic racism in other facets of American culture. NFL commissioner Roger Goodell publicly conceded that he understood that, when athletes kneel during the playing of the national anthem, it is a peaceful protest against police brutality toward people of color and not disrespect of the flag. NASCAR officially banned the Confederate flag at events, acknowledging that it is a symbol that invokes hate. In sport, BLM reignited the conversation about the racist name of the Washington NFL football team and the cultural appropriation of Native American imagery. Summer 2020 was also marked by a global pandemic, with political leaders arguing over who was responsible for flattening a curve or whether a person should wear a mask. The timing of this book is concurrent with these socially progressive ideals and examines the progress that LGBTQ athletes in the sport of rodeo have made in forcing change in society and arguing for their acceptance in sport.

In addition to explaining why the term "gay rodeo" is used rather than "LGBTQ rodeo," cultural terms and gender focus must be addressed. A word used throughout this book will be "country," in its sense as a cultural genre. As Michael Vrooman, an IGRA member since 1993, pointed out, the phrase should not be "country and western," because those are two separate identities: "There's a country lifestyle and there is a western lifestyle."[5] Vrooman laughed and said, "It's not the country and western music awards, it's the Country Music Awards."[6] The IGRA began in the American West and can be thought of as western, but it expanded to the Atlantic coast. A rodeo cowgirl from Hot Springs, Arkansas, is not western, but she might identify as country. And regarding women, several of my chapters are gay male focused—partially because, as with most sports, there remains a socially constructed identity that rodeo is masculine and a sport for men. As a result, primary sources such as rodeo programs contain ads that target men using male homoerotic imagery, subscription information for gay male pornographic magazines, and information about social clubs tailored to men. In the interviews conducted for this book, interviewees agreed that there is a sense of a gay-male-centric atmosphere, but that this is not intentional and that inclusivity is the mission of gay rodeo.

Vrooman suggests that the gay-male-centric environment is a result of the gender imbalance in society and that gay rodeo is not exempt from this. Vrooman believes that men were initially not as aware of the gender disparity with regard to advertising and recruitment of women as they are now. Additionally, he questioned whether, in the early years of gay rodeo, women were involved in the decision-making process and the creation of rodeo programs, which focused on gay men. Vrooman does not recall any women saying that they wished they were better represented, but he does believe that they felt that way. He recognized that Candy Pratt, the current (2021) IGRA president, has been a high-profile leader in the IGRA, and he wished that there were more like her.[7] Gay Rodeo Hall of Fame inductee Amy Griffin explained in her interview that the ratio of men to women might have been a factor in women's visibility in gay rodeo, as she estimated participation to be 70 percent men. Furthermore, she explained that separatism in the LGBTQ community was real during the 1980s, and that women avoided bars that catered to gay men. Yet, in gay rodeo, men and women began to work together during the HIV/AIDS health crisis, particularly in the mid-1980s.[8] Thus, the combination of advertisers in rodeo programs targeting men, the disproportionate number of men to women, and the IGRA's shift in focus to address HIV/AIDS, which had its greatest impact on gay men, can explain why the primary sources reveal more about gay men. With breakthroughs in HIV/AIDS research, charities sponsored by the IGRA in the twenty-first century have diversified and include breast cancer research, domestic violence awareness groups, and animal rescue organizations.

This book aims to recognize the forgotten history of the LGBTQ community. In *Stand by Me: The Forgotten History of Gay Liberation*, Jim Downs argues that the history of gay liberation has been oversimplified to equate "liberation" with "sexual freedom." While that was true for some, the 1970s liberation movement included all members of the LGBTQ community. Downs writes: "An image of gay men as hypersexual began to be promoted in order to rationalize the spread of the virus [HIV], and in the process gay men were turned into the leading protagonists of the 1970s and 1980s."[9] Inspired by Downs, I set out in 2017 to write the history of gay rodeo. As he stated, much of the narrative focused on hypersexual gay men. In archived rodeo programs, I found many images that suggest this about gay men, but these images were used in advertisements with the intention of generating profits. Through dozens of interviews, I heard additional stories about how gay rodeo brought rural county men and women together and liberated them from the heteronormative rules of sport. This book seeks to answer the following questions: What heteronormative rules did the gay rodeo break? How did the gay rodeo reinforce the gay liberation movement? What social and political issues did gay rodeo address in the borderland of the American West? This book follows Downs's lead and reveals a history of gay liberation through the sport of rodeo that began in the mid-1970s, provided a safe space in which LGBTQ athletes could simply be athletes, and evolved into a highly successful philanthropic organization.

On an academic level, the IGRA is understudied. This is surprising given the numerous stories about LGBTQ athletes in the twenty-first century, and several documentaries on the topic that specifically examined the IGRA. In 2005 the documentary *Gidyup! On the Rodeo Circuit*, written and directed by Mitchell Horn, examined the lives of IGRA men and women. In 2014 director Matt Livadary released his documentary *Queens and Cowboys: A Straight Year on the Gay Rodeo*, which followed

Wade Earp's year-long quest for the IGRA Finals All-Around Cowboy title. This intersectional study of LGBTQ athletes, heteronormativity, western history, and sport builds on scholarship from multiple disciplines: ethnic studies, critical sports studies, sociology, and history. Patricia Limerick's *The Legacy of Conquest: The Unbroken Past of the American West* is groundbreaking work that reimagines the American West. Peter Boag's *Re-Dressing America's Frontier Past* examines, like no work before, queer and gender-nonconforming people who lived during the latter years of the nineteenth-century "frontier" West. Patricia Nell Warren's *The Lavender Locker Room: 3000 Years of Great Athletes Whose Sexual Orientation Was Different* and sociologist Eric Anderson's *In the Game: Gay Athletes and the Cult of Masculinity* are fundamental in understanding masculinity, sexuality, and the LGBTQ closet. Until recently, serious academic literature on gay rodeo was long overdue. Published in 2017, D'Lane R. Compton's book chapter "Queer Eye on the Gay Rodeo" serves as a queer theorist examination as well as a self-reflective journey of gay rodeo. Rebecca Scofield, author of *Out Riders: Rodeo at the Fringes of the American West*, and Elyssa Ford, author of *Rodeo as Refuge, Rodeo as Rebellion*, examine marginalized western rodeo athletes, with both books concluding with a gay rodeo chapter. Only recently have scholars like Scofield and Ford brought sophisticated arguments about these marginalized athletes in sport. *Rainbow Cattle Co.* is the first book-length, peer reviewed examination of gay rodeo, and the only book or scholarly article that places it within the context of the gay liberation movement. This examination of LGBTQ athletes of gay rodeo aims to investigate the untold story of those who found a sport that helped them persevere through bigotry and discrimination in society, fight a pandemic that ravaged communities of gay men, and create a sporting community that became an international family. Through their fight, gay rodeo became a political force, a cultural sensation, a resource for people in need, and, as many interviewees have said, a chosen family.

Gay rodeo can be seen as an LGBTQ paradox, juxtaposing gay liberation with heteronormativity by challenging traditional gender roles in the sport of rodeo, while at the same time adhering to commonly accepted ideals of masculinity and femininity associated with being a cowboy or a cowgirl. Moreover, gay rodeo simultaneously challenges socially constructed ideas of masculinity and femininity, LGBTQ culture as urban versus rural, and commonly accepted knowledge about gay pride celebrations. This is not to say that gay rodeo has impeded the progress made by gay liberationists; quite the opposite, gay rodeo represents the diversity within the LGBTQ community. This is a diverse group, and not because they are L, G, B, T, or Q but because they are urban and rural, clog dancers and pop music fans, cowgirls and attorneys, liberals and conservatives. Sociologist D'Lane R. Compton attended gay rodeos, interviewed academics and laypersons, and examined documentaries and online sources, concluding: "A central theme that arose from these sources is that gay rodeo is an event that remains open to numerous interpretations."[10] This interpretation is that gay rodeo has liberated athletes from heteronormative rules of sport, while simultaneously celebrating traditional ideals and values of their rural and western identity.

Timing is everything for the emergence of a cultural phenomenon. The International Gay Rodeo Association thrived in the 1990s. The previous decade had seen gay rodeo transform from individual annual rodeos in western cities to an international association. By the mid-1990s, IGRA chapters hosted gay rodeos from coast to coast. LGBTQ rodeo fans emerged from the silence of the closet, as gay liberation and gay rights movements politicized their marginalization. Music contributed to the rise of the gay rodeo. Country line dancing had long been prominent in western and rural culture. No surprise, then, that this held true in the 1980s at gay rodeo events. In popular culture, the 1980 success of James Bridges's romantic drama *Urban Cowboy,* starring John Travolta and Debra Winger, revitalized the sex appeal of the cowboy image. Travolta played a traditional cowboy with conservative views of family, and Winger challenged those ideals, maintaining that men and women were equals. The film ignited a pop-country music trend. By the 1990s country music had become increasingly popular in noncountry bars and on noncountry radio stations. Pop music fans embraced the folk-sounding country music of Garth Brooks and fell in love with superstar Shania Twain. These two country music artists excited music fans across the spectrum, and their songs were heard in bars and dance clubs across the country. Mainstream bars and popular gay dance clubs introduced country music nights on Tuesday or Wednesday, typically the slowest nights of the week. They attracted country music fans and newcomers, who tested their skills at two-stepping on nights that bars offered lessons. LGBTQ people joined in on this fascination and enjoyed the communal environment of line dancing and the intimacy of the shadow dance. LGBTQ bars and clubs advertised in gay rodeo programs, cashing in on the growing popularity of gay rodeos and introducing their non–country music listeners to the world of gay rodeo. Country music grew in popularity with mainstream American pop music fans, and the gay rodeo association thrived throughout the 1990s as well.

This book examines how LGBTQ rodeo athletes created the IGRA and reinvented the sport of rodeo. Chapter one introduces readers to Phil Ragsdale, founder of the Reno Gay Rodeo in the mid-1970s. It explores Ragsdale's decision to form a gay rodeo to fight the stereotypes of gay men during the 1970s, and how heteronormativity functioned in sports like rodeo. The chapter takes readers from the first gay rodeo, attended by fewer than two hundred people, to the early 1980s, when the Reno Gay Rodeo attracted more than ten thousand spectators. The concluding pages introduce the fear and uncertainty that early AIDS-related deaths caused among the community.

Chapter two explores the coming-out experience in rural communities and the homophobia that threatened LGBTQ people's lives. Using stories told through interviews, this chapter examines case studies such as John Beck, who, after Ku Klux Klan members terrorized him, left his Nebraska town for Denver and became a dominant force in gay rodeo. Beck competed in the early 1980s and continues to compete today. His story of triumph is uplifting, but the terror he experienced is heartbreaking. IGRA members defied social norms in sport and risked their own safety. Numerous interviews of gay rodeo contestants in the 1980s and 1990s reveal the severity of homophobia in the sport of rodeo and the secret life many had to maintain; one said: "I would be dead . . . No question.

They would kill me. Literally. Gay Rodeo and Straight Rodeo do not get along. There are other gay cowboys that compete in the straight circuit, but most of them use aliases like me. It can be very lonely."[11] Chapter two illustrates the challenges that the LGBTQ community took on, which allow young athletes in the twenty-first century to focus more on their sport and less on whether they will be accepted because of their queer identity.

Interest in gay rodeo brought LGBTQ people into the arena, and organizers provided them with print material in the form of rodeo programs. It is truly amazing that, after forty-five years of gay rodeo history, consisting of thirty-five regional organizations that have hosted more than five hundred rodeos, the IGRA archives are missing only eighteen rodeo programs. Chapter three argues that these rodeo programs contain valuable information for country LGBTQ people who may not know about others like them in their community; further, the programs inform readers about LGBTQ culture and educate them on HIV and AIDS. Rodeo programs became a cultural educational tool for the LGBTQ community. From the oldest archived gay rodeo program, in 1979, to 2020, the programs have provided information about gay culture, cowboy and cowgirl culture, and advocacy, and they have identified LGBTQ businesses and organizations, businesses, and politicians who supported the LGBTQ community. These documents functioned as gay culture "how-to" guides and connected the LGBTQ rodeo community with gay rodeo organizations in other states. The documents were road maps to other gay rodeos throughout the year, helping each annual event grow in participant and spectator numbers.

Chapter four argues that gay rodeo has functioned as a gay pride celebration in places where such festivals do not exist. In his 1982 Reno Gay Rodeo program, Ragsdale professed that the gay rodeo was "Western Gay Pride."[12] This chapter argues that gay rodeo is the pioneering gay pride movement of rural America and eventually managed to introduce gay cowboy and cowgirl culture to cosmopolitan urban centers as far east as Washington DC. As a result, gay rodeo brought together a somewhat divided urban versus rural LGBTQ community with a common cause: to have fun, celebrate identities, and raise money and awareness for issues that affected their lives. In small towns and large cities alike, gay rodeo became a political force that contested heteronormativity in the American West and rural communities.

Chapter five illustrates how the IGRA has remained focused on the sport of rodeo, while creating a unique version of its own. This chapter examines the specific events in the rodeo and how they have been altered by the association. First, gendered rules do not exist that prohibit women from competing in all the same events as men. Second, animal welfare has become a significant focus, and the annual convention emphasizes transparency in terms of athlete and animal safety. Finally, the LGBTQ community has placed its metaphorical stamp on rodeo with camp events. Staying true to a liberationist mantra, events like Wild Drag Race have allowed the IGRA to break social rules in sport. These competitions are fan favorites and are entry-level events for anyone interested in competing.

Chapter six explores the complexity of gay men's masculinity and the forced heteronormativity of gay rodeo. I draw upon work by sociologist Eric Anderson regarding "masculine capital," work by Jay Coakley defining gender ideology, and analysis of the politics of masculinity during the 1970s and 1980s by historian Rebecca Scofield, who argues: "The upwelling of cowboy kitsch explicitly linked cowboy masculinity to an emerging desire to reassert American global dominance after the supposed effeminizing effects of the 1960s."[13] Gay rodeo founder Phil Ragsdale claimed that gay rodeo helped break down stereotypes that mainstream society held of gay men. Many commentators, from rodeo organizers to participants, have argued that the term "gay cowboy" is not a paradox. However, gay cowboys have consciously adopted heteronormative ideals about masculinity that are inconsistent with their liberationist goals. Moreover, this chapter is an interrogation of the cowboy aesthetic as a form of drag, thus demonstrating how masculinity is fluid and socially constructed.

Chapter seven can be described as the *Brokeback Mountain* of this book. Relationships are the focus, and how gay rodeo has provided like-minded cowboys and cowgirls opportunities to find their life partners, who share a love for western culture and rodeo. The chapter concludes with an understanding of the complexity of relationships and dating for some gay men and argues against the hypersexual narrative that existed for the 1970s liberation movement. Chapter eight then addresses HIV and its impact on the gay rodeo community, and the fight against AIDS and societal prejudice. This chapter discusses the social stigma of an HIV diagnosis, how society initially responded, and how political leaders failed to act aggressively in the domestic battle against AIDS. Moreover, it illustrates how gay rodeo organizers fought with local community members who attempted to shut down gay rodeos because of the AIDS panic.

Finally, the conclusion examines the future of gay rodeo, its longevity, and the volunteers who were there during the early years and continue to push forward over forty years later. Gay rodeo philanthropy, through the rodeos and royalty members, raised money to fight the AIDS pandemic and support the LGBTQ community when the U.S. government failed them. Royalty members are the philanthropic members of the IGRA. They include drag queens and drag kings who perform in their local communities to raise money for charity and bring awareness to their local gay rodeo associations. The primary focus is on Tony Valdez, a.k.a Chili Pepper, a Latinx rodeo competitor and royalty drag queen who raised thousands of dollars in the fight against AIDS. This chapter further explores how Valdez disclosed his HIV-positive diagnosis with the IGRA as a means of opening the conversation with those reluctant to share, or ashamed to share, their HIV-positive status. In December 2019 Valdez shared a personal archive of papers, letters, and photographs from his gay rodeo history with this author, which was an indispensable resource for this book.

*Rainbow Cattle Co.* is not a comprehensive history of gay rodeo, and it is not a queer theorist's study of the LGBTQ community. This historian's intention is to inspire further interest in and examination of the IGRA. With the dozens of gay rodeo organizations that have been active and the meticulous recordkeeping of past events, historians can write a history of the Colorado Gay Rodeo Association or the Texas Gay Rodeo Association, or a book on gay rodeo in the Bible Belt. Biographies on the people who created this organization, such as Brian Helander, Candy

Pratt, and John Beck to name a few, can serve as inspiration for future leaders. People like Wade Earp, who explains in chapter four that he never thought anyone would call him a hero, had a story told in a full-length documentary—*Queens and Cowboys*. Now that the Autry Museum of the American West reopened after several years of closure, its collection of historical documents can provide scholars with countless stories of gay rodeo. The IGRA donated thousands of pages of records to this archive. Through interviews, newspaper and magazine articles, and archived primary documents, the story of the gay rodeo is remembered on the following pages. Gay rodeo interviewees share a spirit of togetherness unparalleled by that of any other sporting organization. Gay Rodeo Hall of Fame inductee Amy Griffin explained that IGRA members look after each other and help each other in life and in the arena of competition.[14]

The following chapters examine the gay rodeo, contestants, and fans. *Rainbow Cattle Co.* reveals a history of the LGBTQ community that paved the way for social progress in sport and society and is a long overdue historical examination and recognition of the IGRA. IGRA members have experienced discrimination from local community members who protested their events, and they have been the targets of death threats for being gay in rural America—and they came together to help members of their community battling HIV/AIDS. This book promises to deliver an academic examination of gay rodeo culture, capture the history of the gay rodeo and pride that is missing from the narrative of the American West, and entertain readers with real-life stories of rodeo cowboys and cowgirls, kindness and charity, activism and struggle, lifelong friendships, and true love. Quoting Peter Falk from the movie *The Princess Bride*, as he has to explain to a young and skeptical Fred Savage that the book he is about to read to the boy is worth his time: there is "fencing, fighting, torture, revenge, giants, monsters, chases, escapes, true love, miracles . . ."[15] *Rainbow Cattle Co.* promises to deliver wrestling, wild drag, speed events, giant beasts, narrow escapes, true love, and, yes, miracles. Hang on, gay rodeo readers, it's going to be a wild ride!

# 1 A Rodeo to Call Their Own

## The Origin of Gay Rodeo

With only one large arena, "wild" cows and calves running loose, no holding pens, no chutes, IT WAS RODEO TIME! There was three categories–1. King of the Cowboys (Male), 2. Queen of the Cowgirls (Female), and 3. Ms. Dusty Spurs (Drag) . . . And, rather than trying to be like a professional rodeo, we still like to maintain it for ALL! Men and women compete in ALL events, equally. Be it the professional, amateur or the "novice," maybe it's easier to sum it up as a "Western Gay Day."

—Phil Ragsdale

The history of Gay Rodeo is a forgotten piece of the gay liberation movement in the American West. In 1976 Phil Ragsdale imagined an event that would bring men and women together who identified as lesbian, gay, bisexual, or transgender (LGBT) to enjoy a part of western life that was almost exclusively identified with heteronormative sport, history, and popular culture. Similarly, music, film, and television targeted their heteronormative social lyrics and storylines toward an opposite-sex coupling audience. Thirty years later, on Valentine's Day, 2006, Country Music Hall of Fame artist Willie Nelson released the song "Cowboys Are Frequently, Secretly Fond of Each Other." Nelson timed this release to express his support for the LGBTQ community and gay marriage. The song debuted on Howard Stern's radio broadcast and became available on iTunes shortly thereafter.[1]

The lyrics, by Ned Sublette, were written in 1981.[2] The song remained "in the closet" for twenty-five years, but two factors were instrumental in the recording and release of the song in 2006. First, the critical acclaim for the 2005 movie *Brokeback Mountain*, Ang Lee's epic romantic drama about two gay sheepherders, demonstrated that twenty-first-century American popular culture was ready to accept intimacy between men as love on the movie screen. Twenty-five years earlier, Arthur Hiller's film *Making Love*, the first gay-themed film to include an on-screen kiss between two men, had been a box office failure.[3] During the 1990s Hollywood films with gay male protagonists began to earn positive recognition with movies such as *The Birdcage* and *Philadelphia*. However, they either emphasized campiness with drag queens or dramatized the AIDS pandemic within gay society, thus reinforcing stereotypes that gay men are effeminate or HIV positive. *Brokeback Mountain* challenged American audiences to understand cowboys and the American West in an unconventional narrative with great success. *Us Weekly* and *Vanity Fair* both ranked the film among the top twenty-five romantic movies of all time. *Time Out* ranked the film as sixth, beating out fan favorites like *When Harry Met Sally* and the blockbuster *Titanic*, surpassed only by classics like *Annie Hall* and *Casablanca*. Even though many conservative communities banned *Brokeback Mountain* from their theaters, limiting it to a 60 percent nationwide release (compared with hits like *Titanic*, *Pearl Harbor*, and the 2013 version of *The Great Gatsby*, which were widely released), *Vanity Fair* reported in 2013 that *Brokeback Mountain* ranked twelfth "among the highest-grossing romantic dramas of all time."[4]

Additionally, Nelson was motivated to release his cowboy ballad for his manager and longtime friend of thirty years, David Anderson, who was gay and had come out two years earlier.[5] In an interview with the *Dallas Morning News*, Nelson declared: "The song's been in the closet for [over] 20 years. The timing's right for it to come out."[6] Hollywood and the country music world provided mainstream America with examples of LGBTQ actors and songs that were no longer marginalized; instead, they became the focus. With the recent success of college and professional athletes opening up about their LGBTQ identities in the high-profile and high-revenue sports of football, basketball, and soccer, an examination of LGBTQ athletes and the sport of rodeo is long overdue.

When, in 1981, Ned Sublette wrote the song Nelson later made famous, the gay liberation movement had already made great strides in bringing

LGBTQ people out of the closet and into the public spotlight. The 1969 Stonewall riots in New York City twelve years earlier had been pivotal. And gay liberation was not exclusive to the major cities of New York, Chicago, and San Francisco. In Reno, Nevada, for example, a group of cowboys led by Phil Ragsdale organized an event known as the Reno Gay Rodeo in 1976. In the 1970s LGBTQ communities nationwide operated through an "imperial court system," whereby local communities elected people to a "court" that organized fundraising efforts for various charitable causes. These fundraisers were creative ways to get involved and connect with mainstream society, which had constructed divisive walls separating the LGBTQ community from other people.[7] Ragsdale, a rodeo athlete, had the idea to host a gay rodeo with events for men and women and a royalty celebration that would raise money for the Muscular Dystrophy Association. Gay rodeo is an overlooked part of the 1970s gay liberation movement. The goal of rejecting heteronormative social rules in sport was advanced in the American West by country LGBTQ rodeo athletes, and it became a powerful force in the community nationwide, becoming an international spectacle by the 1990s.

Ragsdale initially encountered resistance, but Reno business owners eventually welcomed the new visitors from around the country as these visitors boosted the local economy. The timing of this analysis of the Reno Gay Rodeo is pertinent to the emergence of openly gay athletes in mainstream sports. Scholars have argued that closeted athletes who came out as LGBTQ after their careers ended have had a significant presence in collegiate, amateur, international, and professional sports since the 1970s. This examination of the intersectionality of athletics and gay liberation identifies the factors driving this emergence, the tension between inclusion and exclusion in Reno, and the social stigma associated with same-sex relationships, which led conservative opponents to fight against the inclusion of the LGBTQ community in mainstream society. Through their struggles, LGBTQ cowboys and cowgirls in Reno created an event that became an international sensation.

In the late 1980s the International Gay Rodeo Association (IGRA) formed. Through a vast network of rodeo cowboys, cowgirls, and fans, rodeo became a location where gay participants exemplified the ideological fight for gay liberation in the American West and disrupted stereotypical beliefs about gay men. These men and women celebrated their rodeo cowboy identities, gender identities, and sexual identities during these events. The Reno Gay Rodeo, thus, became the gay pride celebration of the American West, as discussed in greater detail in chapter four. Moreover, the rodeo helped break down stereotypes of gay men and challenged popular cultural assumptions about masculinity and femininity. These stereotypes, which are typically rooted in fear, are the basis for homophobia, which emerged as a topic of popular discourse on homosexuality in the 1970s. While homophobia has existed in some form for millennia, people were now openly talking about it and condemning the gay lifestyle. The Reno Gay Rodeo attempted to bridge the marginalized LGBTQ community with the mainstream Reno community through philanthropic efforts to give back to the community and confront the American West's homophobic milieu. However, after the AIDS outbreak and the subsequent antigay panic, fear led to an increase in homophobia across the country, and the Reno Gay Rodeo Association began to focus much of its philanthropy on LGBTQ-related charities. Thus, as mainstream society distanced itself from the LGBTQ community, the community pushed back and found strength and support within LGBTQ organizations and within its sporting venue of gay rodeo.

The Reno Gay Rodeo typified Nevada's particular version of the American West. Nevada's libertarian political climate and reputation as a state that had legalized prostitution and gambling were part of a culture that cultivated the creation of gay rodeo, which held a similar social stigma. Nevada's version of the American West embraced the classic masculinity of the rodeo cowboy and became a place for gay liberation at the same time. These "ruggedly handsome men," historian Chris Packard declares, "epitomize the strong, silent type that for more than 150 years" have been "associated with the freedoms of wide-open spaces in the American West."[8] Packard examines the relationship between the cowboy and his sidekick—the cowboy's "partner and loyal friend"—and "the erotic affection that undergirds their friendship."[9] This chapter uncovers the

A Rodeo to Call Their Own

bonds among gay rodeo cowboys and cowgirls, a chosen family, and how gay rodeo liberated them from social rules in sport. Moreover, the gay rodeo disrupted the traditional, romanticized image of male masculinity, and it emerged in society as homophobia increased and gay liberationists became more visible in popular culture. Gay rodeo empowered these athletes and their spectators and disrupted a power structure that reinforced a gender ideology that privileged men over women and preached heteronormativity in rodeo.

## GAY COWBOY/COWGIRL IDENTITY

Most Americans can trace their image of cowboys to Hollywood Westerns. When we envision a cowboy, John Wayne or Clint Eastwood typically comes to mind. These films developed costumes and music that typified the cowboy, his sidekick, and the villain. Native Americans were often the enemy in Western movies, with a Hollywood-created drumbeat pattern that audiences heard shortly before they appeared. Late nineteenth-century cowboy literature sensationalized by northeastern publishers churning out frontier cowboy stories of Seth Jones and Nick Carter dominated the American West's narrative.[10] The reality of these men was a life of male companionship. Men sought solace with other men who ventured west. Cowboy identity and its origin, as it turns out, are much more complex than first imagined.

Latinx rodeo athletes know that Anglo-cowboy identity emerged in the American West from their heritage in the region. The nickname "buckaroo," for example, evolved from the Spanish word vaquero.[11] Its origin is from the word vaca, which is Spanish for cow, and the suffix "means one engaged in working with cows," the original cowboy.[12] To an NFL football fan, the word "cowboy" draws upon a different image, possibly that of tight end Jason Witten, who played for "America's team" in Dallas. Even among cowboys, there is debate over true cowboy identity, leading ranchmen to dismiss rodeo men as hardly "real" cowboys, even though they are at a far higher risk of injury than competitors in any other sport. Contact sports are likened to masculinity; thus, masculinity requires a degree of violence to reaffirm toughness. The potential for harm in a rodeo, with an injury rate of 89 percent, exceeds that of any other competition, based on a study of collegiate rodeo athletes. This high percentage of injury, coupled with the mystique of risk that often encourages rodeo cowboys to deny that an injury has occurred, is seen as an "occupational hazard endemic to the sport."[13] Often, rodeo athletes laugh off the threat to their safety. Cowboy images may differ in meaning, but one thing remains constant: the word "cowboy" exemplifies the romanticized masculinity of the American West, and scholars Christopher Le Coney and Zoe Trodd believe that "rodeo is a space where American masculine identity is performed."[14]

Phil Ragsdale, the founder of the Reno Gay Rodeo (also known as the Comstock Rodeo and the Reno National Gay Rodeo), knew that mainstream society believed that the phrase "gay cowboy" seemed to be a contradiction, which is similar to arguments made in Eric Anderson's study of gay athletes and hegemonic masculinity.[15] Gay men in sport are a paradox because they "comply with the gendered script of being male," yet they "violate another masculine script through the existence of their same-sex desires."[16] The same rationale is valid for gay cowboys—their script is a narrative of hard work and strife on the frontier, dressing the part with their Stetson hats and Levi's jeans, but, as Willie Nelson so poetically sang, "they are secretly, frequently fond of each other."[17] Historically, as far back as ancient Greece, the act of sex between men was not disruptive to heteronormativity. Notably, Greek soldiers engaged in sexual intercourse. "Sexual relations between men were viewed as an experience that intensified masculinity because it left women out of the equation."[18]

A similar philosophy was true in the United States during the Great Depression. Colin Johnson maintains that hundreds of thousands of men left small towns and farms in search of work. Johnson states, "These men created an expansive homosocial world in which cross-dressing and eroticized horseplay were seen as largely unremarkable pastimes pursued in the context of an emergency work relief program that had, ironically, been created primarily to preserve their endangered manhood."[19] Historical periods reveal other homosocial aspects within labor camps.

"Laboring rural men, regarded sex between men as acceptable if women were nowhere to be found."[20] In reality, the concept of heterosexual sex being the orthodox union in society is relatively new in world history.[21] In his groundbreaking study of gay men in the twentieth century, George Chauncey reveals that same-sex encounters between men did not jeopardize a man's heteronormative identity if he maintained his marked masculinity. For example, in New York, an undercover agent questioned a seaman who had engaged in sex with young male prostitutes, known as "punks." The man seemed to brag about having sex with teenage males, and the power dynamic between the man and the boy marked his masculinity when he told the investigator that the punk satisfied him the same as a woman could. Chauncey argues that the openness of the seaman in talking about his same-sex encounter with a stranger "suggests that he did not expect to lose much, if any, status because of it."[22]

More recent research reveals that the pinnacle of orthodox heteronormativity has passed, and that sexual flexibility among men who identify as heterosexual, or "straight," is becoming more common. Sociologist Eric Anderson explains this through examples of mutual masturbation between young men, that since 2010 there has been "an increase in the percentage of young men that have masturbated with another friend."[23] Anderson believes that the decreased stigmatization of homosexuality in society coincides with the decreased stigma attached to men masturbating together.[24] Moving beyond masturbation, sociologist Tony Silva explores a subculture of heterosexual-identifying men in rural Texas that have sex with other men. Silva's concept of "bud-sex" is a relatively understudied topic within the academic discourse on men who have sex with men (MSM). These men internalize that their mutual understanding is that they are relieving sexual urges, "helpin' a buddy out," without an attraction to each other. Silva explains that this reinforces their heterosexuality and rural masculinity.[25] Thus, comparing sexuality and society today with that of the gay rodeo world of the 1970s, we can appreciate *heteroflexibilty* as a new way to understand the ever-changing social construction of masculinity. A counternarrative existed for gay rodeo cowboys in the 1970s when they created a space to celebrate masculinity and reinforced hegemonic masculinity. The sporting arena of the Reno Gay Rodeo presented a "hegemonic model as the heroic ideal of modern manhood" for gay men in the American West. Ragsdale believed this had become a space where they could challenge the dominant narrative of the 1970s that gay male identity was unmasculine.[26]

Gay male identity emerged in popular print media in 1950, when prominent journalists reported on the "lavender scare," the purge of ninety-one "suspected homosexuals" from the State Department, led by Senator Joseph McCarthy from Wisconsin. McCarthy believed that gay men and lesbians were a security threat; if a man working in the State Department was living a secret gay life, McCarthy maintained that he could be blackmailed by Communists for classified information.[27] Guy George Gabrielson, Republican national chairman, reported to the *New York Times* that, like Communists, "sexual perverts" were a threat to the American people. Gabrielson stated: "Perhaps as dangerous as the actual Communists are the sexual perverts who have infiltrated our government in recent years. The State Department has confessed that it has had to fire ninety-one of these. It is the talk of Washington and Washington Correspondence Corp. The country would be more aroused over this tragic angle of the situation if it were not for the difficulties of the newspapers and radio commentators inadequately presenting the facts while respecting the decency of their American audiences."[28]

Gabrielson's concluding remarks illustrate the media's caution about openly discussing same-sex intercourse or LGBTQ people as newsworthy topics in the 1950s. While the media and popular culture influenced public opinion about gay men and lesbians as threats to society, scholarly literature emerged that explored the perception of gay men as hypersexual and overtly effeminate. George McCall and J. L. Simmons argued in 1966 that gay men were believed to be introverts and perverts. Eugene Levitt and Albert Klassen asserted in 1974 that public perception of gay men included concerns that they were mentally ill, "perverted and lonely."[29] Further, dominant public perceptions, according to sociological and psychological studies, saw gay men in one of five categories: "closeted, flamboyant, feminine, cross-dressing, and activist."[30] Gay rodeo cowboys

A Rodeo to Call Their Own

challenged these notions, and Ragsdale's initial plan for the rodeo was to raise money for local charities, to bring the LGBTQ community into Reno society as civic participants. Yet, when allowed to speak with the press, he almost always made a point of commenting that the rodeo was "a good way to show that the gays aren't strictly stereotyped as limp wrists."[31] Ragsdale did not fit the effeminate stereotypes, either—he was a rugged-looking man who usually sported a scruffy "days' growth" of a beard.[32]

## THE FIRST GAY RODEO

Early Anglo-cowboy rodeos began as bragging rights on who could "stick to the back of an ornery bronco or catch that calf with the least amount of trouble."[33] Today, cowboys and cowgirls continue to brag about which state should take credit for the first organized rodeo: "The Professional Cowboy's Rodeo Hall of Fame credits Colorado's own town of Deer Trail (located approximately fifty miles east of Denver). Other records report Pecos, Texas, offering the first money in 1883, and Prescott, Arizona, was first to charge admission to spectators; and Stanford, Texas, hosts the oldest cowboy reunion with thousands of spectators each July."[34] Gay rodeo members are proud of their tradition, and the Colorado Gay Rodeo Association (CGRA) members boast that CGRA is the longest continuously running gay rodeo association in the world.

Early in 1976 Phil Ragsdale began his mission to host the first gay rodeo. The Washoe County Fairgrounds manager, a "very understanding and liberal individual," agreed to host the event, scheduling it for October 2, 1976.[35] Ragsdale faced many challenges locating ranchers willing to rent out livestock. As soon as Ragsdale disclosed that the interested civic group was the Reno LGBTQ community, ranchers quickly refused involvement. Ragsdale contacted Reno farmers and ranchers, not lying about the gay rodeo but not initially disclosing the participants' LGBTQ identity either, or he approached each stating that he represented a civic group trying to raise money for local charities. He approached his first rancher, explaining that he wanted to rent some of his livestock to put on an amateur rodeo for the Senior Citizens' Annual Thanksgiving Day Feed. He told him it was a "local civic group." The rancher told Ragsdale he was sure there wouldn't be any problems loaning him the livestock needed. The rancher was amused with the thought of Drugstore Cowboys/Cowgirls putting on a rodeo. The rancher then asked, "Exactly what group is putting this event on?" To which Phil replied, "The Reno Gay Community." At this, the rancher began finding many excuses for backing out of his oral commitment.[36]

Thirty-six ranchers repudiated Ragsdale before he secured the location. On Friday, October 1, 1976, the night before the inaugural event, Ragsdale traveled sixty miles east of Reno to purchase the livestock at auction in Fallon, Nevada. Shortly after he arrived, he found a posted sign that read, "Auction Every Wednesday." He asked office officials about securing stock, and they referred him to a local rancher. By 10:00 p.m. that evening, Ragsdale had bought the animals with his own funds, and he overcame the challenge of acquiring transportation shortly before midnight. Saturday morning the livestock arrived: ten "wild" range calves, five "wild" range cows, one pig, and a Shetland pony.[37] At the end of the one-day event, a donation of $214 was made to the Muscular Dystrophy Association in the name of "Gay People."[38] The following year, the Reno Gay Rodeo raised $3,400 due to increased interest from out-of-state LGBTQ visitors. Ragsdale donated $1,200 to a senior citizen Thanksgiving Day dinner, $1,200 to needy families at Christmas, and the remainder to the Muscular Dystrophy Association.[39] A decade after the first gay rodeo in Reno, Denver, Oklahoma City, Phoenix, and Dallas hosted regional gay rodeos, with the first national finals held in the San Francisco Bay Area. By 1986 the multicity rodeo had raised over $300,000 for local and national charities. Reno's one-day rodeo event expanded to two days, and unofficially a weeklong celebration, culminating in the rodeo on the weekend and the Saturday night "Stand by Your Man" celebration dance.

Challenging the stereotypes of the 1970s proved a difficult task. Pop culture had few gay icons or role models. Historically, gay actors lived closeted, secret lives, and gay characters on television were often cast in a comic or an unflattering light. The 1969 Stonewall riots marked a turning point in the gay liberation movement. The movement urged lesbians and gay men to reveal their identities and eradicate any sense

A Rodeo to Call Their Own

of shame by celebrating who they were during festivals, such as gay pride parades. These parades were scheduled annually in June, in honor of the June 1969 Stonewall riots. However, with this new and increased exposure came a backlash, and new stereotypes and negative popular culture references emerged.

The term "homophobia" had never been used before 1965. Psychologist George Weinberg coined the term, as he began to examine homosexuality in nonclinical settings. Weinberg argued that homophobia "was a phobia about homosexuals. . . . It was a fear of homosexuals, which seemed to be associated with a fear of contagion, a fear of reducing the things one fought for—home and family. It was a religious fear, and it had led to great brutality as fear always does."[40] Politically, Senator Joseph McCarthy likening Communism to homosexuality created an additional fear about American manhood during the Cold War.[41] Out of such fear came anti-LGBTQ violence, driven by an abhorrence for same-sex relationships and unconventional gender identification. Eventually, this anti-LGBTQ violence became known as "gay bashing."

Anti-LGBTQ violence often went unpunished throughout the 1970s and 1980s because police failed to protect victims or were the perpetrators of these crimes. Closeted victims rarely faced their attackers in criminal and civil courts because they feared that family, friends, or employers would learn about their LGBTQ identity. Law professor Teresa Eileen Kibelstis explained: "While victims may want to prosecute their assailants, they are too vulnerable as homosexuals in American society to be exposed in this manner."[42] The increase in these crimes was linked to increased exposure of LGBTQ people in society. As gay liberationists became more vocal, violent backlash resulted. This was true not only during the 1970s and 1980s. In the early 2000s, as proponents of same-sex marriage successfully fought for the passage of laws granting this right, hate crimes against the LGBTQ community peaked.[43]

For the Reno Gay Rodeo participants, anti-LGBTQ violence was a serious concern. After the 1976 rodeo made national news, the press paid more attention to the planning of the August 1977 event. Gay rodeo provided a sense of security within the confines of its fairground, where gay cowboys and cowgirls were pulled out of the closet and into the competition arena. David Renier competed in his first gay rodeo in 1985 and continues to compete today. In an interview, historian Rebecca Scofield asked him what it was about the gay rodeo that made him want to "invest." Renier said: "It definitely was a place that made me feel safe and secure and able to be the authentic me."[44] Many of these men would have remained in secrecy without the gay rodeo. Bull rider Patrick Kelly stated that he could not come out in mainstream rodeo (the "straight circuit") out of fear for his safety. He said that he did not feel safe competing until the Reno Gay Rodeo. Texas cowgirl Pam White noted: "In rodeo, we not only run the risk of serious injury just by participating, but we're also exposed to deliberate injury. I don't think there is anything worse than a redneck cowboy."[45] Ragsdale was concerned about "redneck action" that might occur outside of the fairgrounds and hired security for the festivities.[46] While he believed that the Reno population was becoming more open minded toward gay men and lesbians and that many had cultivated a "live and let live" philosophy, his concern with "gay bashing" was warranted, and he believed that the potential for antigay violence increased when "redneck cowboys" got "a few drinks under their belts."[47] Ragsdale reiterated that the event was geared to represent the opposite of gay stereotypes; more importantly, he said that "gays do not want to create a problem. We do not want protesters spurred by the Anita Bryant thing."[48]

According to Weinberg, homophobia is a fear that gay men and lesbians are a threat to "home and family." Sociologist Eric Anderson differentiates homophobia from what he refers to as "homohysteria."[49] During the late 1970s, the actions of singer and former Miss Oklahoma Anita Bryant epitomized that very concern that the LGBTQ community was a threat to "home and family." A born-again Christian and publicist for Florida orange juice, Bryant led the "Save Our Children" campaign to overturn a 1977 Dade County, Florida, ordinance that prohibited discrimination based on sexual orientation.[50] Bryant's campaign was successful, and on June 7, 1977, Dade County voters repealed the anti-discrimination ordinance. After hearing the news, Bryant and her husband, Bob Green, danced with glee. Bryant believed that the original nondiscriminatory mandate would allow gay men and lesbians to appear as role models and recruit children, a belief that exemplifies Anderson's delineation of homohysteria.[51] In response to her efforts, supporters of the legislation fought back, and a boycott of oranges and orange juice went into effect. Gay and gay-friendly bars took screwdrivers, the vodka and orange juice beverage, off the menu and replaced them with the "Anita Bryant," a mixture of vodka and bitter apple juice.[52] Probably the most famous incident of blowback against Bryant was when a man smashed a pie in her face during a press conference in Des Moines, Iowa.[53] At the 1981 Reno Gay Rodeo, John Calendo, a writer for *In Touch for Men*, overheard men talking about boycotting Coors beer. Even though Coors placed advertisements in the *The Advocate*, an LGBTQ magazine, the men shared a rumor that the owner of the brewery gave money to Bryant and her efforts with the Moral Majority.[54]

Antigay prejudice played out in the media as a response to the very cause of the gay liberation movement, namely individuality. Gay rights proponents saw "coming out of the closet" as a way to express their individuality and reject what heterosexual, cisgender society typified as "normal." At gay pride celebrations, the diversity of the LGBTQ community was on display. Women rode through the streets on motorcycles wearing black leather jackets, drag queens paraded through towns with colorful sequined and feather-lined dresses, and gay men lined the parade route shirtless with their arms around their male partners. By the late 1970s these annual June parades had become weekend news stories in cities coast to coast. Rather than focusing on successful, openly gay elected officials, such as Harvey Milk of San Francisco, riding in a convertible during a pride parade, the reports often focused on nudity and cross-dressing, or a trend seen as far worse, the leather subculture in gay male social groups.

In 1979 Hollywood producers began filming a controversial film in New York City called *Cruising*. The LGBTQ community condemned the movie, which focused on the dark underside of gay life in New York. The film depicted gay men as sadomasochists who were leather-clad and sexually violent. The LGBTQ press argued that the movie would sway public opinion to believe that all gay men looked and acted like those in the film, a misperception that could lead to further violence.[55] Hollywood continued this trend beyond the 1970s and 1980s, depicting LGBTQ people as sadomasochistic, violent, and mentally deranged, with "sexually perverse" villains such as the pre-op transgender serial killer in *Silence of the Lambs* (1991), Sharon Stone's lesbian character in *Basic Instinct* (1992), and Matt Damon's infatuated and insecure young man–turned–sexual predator in *The Talented Mr. Ripley* (1999). The negative image of leather-clad gay men arose from a subculture of sexually experimental men who found freedom of expression within the gay liberation movement. However, the 2005 documentary *Gay Sex in the 70s* further distorted the reality of the gay liberation movement by equating liberation with hypersexuality. Historian Jim Downs explains that the film simplified the 1970s gay liberation movement and "flattened the history of the 1970s in order to rationalize the spread of HIV."[56] The reality was that the 1970s was more complex than that. Downs insisted that some gay liberationists were political theorists who critiqued democracy because of their oppression, and who formed their own churches when their local places of worship dismissed them.[57] Likewise, gay rodeo liberated LGBTQ rodeo athletes from heteronormative subjugation in their sport during the 1970s.

The Reno Gay Rodeo exemplified these celebrations of individuality and, in its early years, was often referred to as the "gay pride" of the American West. The arena had male and female participants, and the overall winners were crowned King of the Cowboys and Queen of the Cowgirls. Today, winners are referred to as simply All-Around Cowboy and All-Around Cowgirl. Additionally, there was a drag queen winner of the event honored with the title Miss Dusty Spur. (Previous winners have included Misty Michaels [Steve Rogers], Magnolia Spirits [Buddy Sojourner], and a Latina, Chili Pepper [Tony Valdez]. [fig. 1])[58] At the 1980 National Reno Gay Rodeo, organizers changed the name of the categories to All-Around Cowboy and All-Around Cowgirl, but continued to refer to the drag queen winner as Miss Dusty Spur.[59] The campiness

A Rodeo to Call Their Own

Fig. 1. Chili Pepper rings a cowbell during grand entrance of the Greater Northwest International Rodeo, Saturday, September 11, 1993. Credit to Therese Frare, Frare Davis Photography.

of the competition, the exaggerated costumes, and the overabundance of makeup transformed the western man into the "saloon vixen" of the "Wild" West. The costuming was a deliberate attempt to transform the participants visually, which is similar to the unconscious "queering of the cowboy," suggesting that straight "rodeo cowboy's masculinity is not straightforward."[60] From the "impractically tight pants to the garishly colored shirts and chaps with bright fringe . . . at the rodeo, the more a man exaggerates his masculine performance, the more he feminizes himself through the addition of gold belt buckles and meticulously pressed shirts."[61] Thus, maybe the gay cowboy is less of a paradox than Ragsdale first believed. Regardless, the individual expression of Miss Dusty Spur pageant competitors was part of the foundation of gay liberation.

The Reno Gay Rodeo became a big business for Reno establishments. Businesses owners paid for advertising space in the rodeo program handed out to spectators at the event, hoping to cash in on the visitors in town looking for a good time. Businesses used homoerotic imagery of men to attract their attention to these ads. Advertisements for gay men's bars often featured an image of a rugged cowboy, usually exaggerating his male anatomy. An adult toy store, Sweet Pieces, offered a 15 percent discount on all purchases with proof of a rodeo ticket.

Private clubs, a.k.a. baths, exclusively for gay men advertised their locations and hours of operation, typically 24/7. Advertising was not exclusive to Reno businesses, however. By 1980 the programs announced gay-friendly hotels, gay bars, and gay baths located in cities like Denver, San Jose, San Francisco, and Houston. Reno travel agents paid for ad space and quickly learned where the popular destinations were for gay men, to earn commissions from their travel bookings. Rodeo programs became a "how-to," "where-to," and "all things gay" instruction manuals for rural gay men and lesbians who had ventured to Reno to escape from their heteronormative isolation in rural western communities. Additionally, the programs included mail-in order forms to subscribe to gay advocacy magazines and pornographic material. Near the end of many archived Reno programs, an advertisement for Budweiser can be found with the message: "The only official National Reno Gay Rodeo Beer!"[62]

A Rodeo to Call Their Own

## THE COWBOY AND COWGIRL FIGHT

By the early 1980s the Reno Gay Rodeo had grown in popularity among anyone who could profit from the event. The Sands Hotel and Casino became the host hotel. The rodeo program featured a letter from Mayor Barbara Bennett welcoming rodeo participants and fans to Reno. She closed her letter with the following statement: "On behalf of the citizens of Reno, best wishes for an exciting and successful event" (fig. 2).[63] However, in the coming years, gay rodeo cowboys and cowgirls continued to struggle against conservative bigotry, while simultaneously working for inclusion in society with their rodeo. The comradery became an asset as they came together to fight an even more significant challenge, the fight against HIV/AIDS.

Not all citizens of Reno welcomed gay cowboys and cowgirls to their city, however. As early as 1977, the year of the second Reno Gay Rodeo, protesters sought to shut down the event. "It's an abomination," minister Kevin Linehan declared as he tossed a pink flyer announcing the rodeo. On the flyer was a drawing of a rugged cowboy with hairy arms and legs, and one notable distraction—the cowboy also had breasts. Linehan argued that due to the attention Reno drew from the 1976 gay rodeo, masses of gay men were moving from San Francisco to Reno. That same year, the Universal Fellowship of Metropolitan Community Churches opened an LGBTQ church in Reno, a development Linehan called "the work of Satan."[64]

Linehan believed that he had firsthand knowledge, because he admitted he had found Christ in 1972 and had subsequently denounced his own homosexuality, believing in "cure" through prayer. Linehan stated: "We feel God loves gays and hates homosexuality."[65] This Christianesque lingo professes to "love the sinner, hate the sin."[66] Linehan published *Such Were Some of You: The Spiritual Odyssey of an Ex-Gay Christian* in 1979, in which he encouraged closeted gay men to "come out" and find God—not other gay men.[67] Other like-minded Christian organizations joined the protest over the next seven years. Groups like the Pro-Family Christian Coalition gathered hundreds of protesters, wrote letters to the governor,

# City of Reno

POST OFFICE BOX 1900 • RENO, NEVADA 89505 • (702) 785-2000

June 30, 1982

TO: PARTICIPANTS IN NATIONAL RENO GAY RODEO

Once again it is indeed a pleasure to welcome the Comstock Gay Rodeo to the "Biggest Little City in the World", Reno, Nevada, July 30, 1982, through August 1, 1982.

When spectators and participants are not at the fairgrounds, they will find a multitude of other interests to whet their appetites; we are only 30 minutes from historical Virginia City and our State Capitol Carson City; the unique Atmospheriur Planetarium is only a few blocks from downtown Reno and we believe you will agree that our entertainment, food and gaming are among the finest in the world.

On behalf of the citizens of Reno, best wishes for an exciting and successful event!

Sincerely,

Barbara Bennett
Mayor

Fig. 2. Mayor Barbara Bennett's welcome letter, 1982 National Reno Gay Rodeo program, p. 4. Credit to Frank Harrell and the International Gay Rodeo Association Archives, gayrodeohistory.org.

and published editorials in the *Reno Evening Gazette* denouncing these activities as immoral, against God, and a threat to children. However, their efforts were mostly unsuccessful. Publications like Lineham's altered the discourse about homosexuality. Sociologist Craig O. Stewart suggested that "ex-gay" testimonies allow Christians to "reframe gay men and lesbians 'as tragic, rather than dangerous; to be pitied, rather than vilified.'"[68]

Political figures weighed in with their disapproval of the gay rodeo. Republican governor Bob List faced negative press when his lieutenant governor, Myron Leavitt, went on record stating, "I'm strongly opposed to queers using public property," further advising that they should "go elsewhere like California."[69] Governor List himself regretted that Reno hosted the gay rodeo because he believed that it led Americans to think of Nevada as the gay rodeo capital. List denounced the use of the word "queer" by his lieutenant governor but supported a ban on the use of public property by the Reno Gay Rodeo Association, leaving it to the public to decide who it believed was a public threat.[70] The proposed ban on the use of public property by the rodeo echoed a nearly century-long argument against "homosexuals" that began with the early-twentieth-century exclusion and deportation of immigrants deemed "sexual deviants," based on the assumption they were a "public charge." This was a federal immigration policy dating back to the 1917 Immigration Act.[71] The proposed ban in Reno illustrates the citizens' rights historically denied to LGBTQ people, and the Reno Gay Rodeo Association challenged these proposed restrictions. Two months after Leavitt's and List's statements, Patrick Kelly, president of the Pacific Coast Gay Rodeo Association, announced plans to host a gay rodeo in San Francisco. He was quick to point out that Leavitt's comments had not inspired his endeavor.[72] Gay liberationists of the 1970s had a growing political voice, and they were quick to respond to attacks by conservative politicians.

The Reno Gay Rodeo attracted gay men from throughout the western states. Initially, the event was not entirely embraced by all LGBTQ competitors. Todd Ruhter, born in Hastings, Nebraska, was thrilled when he first heard about the gay rodeo. Ruhter began his rodeo training as a boy on his family farm. As an adult, the thought of meeting a boyfriend who was a rodeo cowboy as well excited him—"Yes, all right! I'd love to meet somebody in a gay rodeo."[73] After competing in his first gay rodeo, Ruhter was reluctant to fully endorse the event, as it proved campy with a "humorous sideline." Ruhter explained, "I'm learning to get into that, but it makes my teeth itch a little bit. If rodeo is not done traditionally, the way I'm used to it, I shy away from it. Where I grew up, rodeo was serious stuff—fun, but not campy fun. Everybody who was worth anything rodeoed. If you were a cowboy, you were cool. We always said, 'Cowboy is as cowboy does.' It isn't necessarily a big hat and big boots. It's what you do and how you think."[74] For Ruhter, gay rodeo lacked authenticity, and he acknowledged that he was more attracted to "straight cowboys" because of this.[75] However, for many men and women, gay rodeo celebrated a subculture within the LGBTQ social world with which they identified. Gay rodeo is where many of them found their life partners, which is discussed further in chapter seven.

The Reno Gay Rodeo inspired LGBTQ rodeo athletes throughout the western United States to organize rodeo associations and host regional rodeos. Denver hosted the first Rocky Mountain Regional Rodeo in 1983; Simonton, Texas, forty miles west of Houston, hosted the first Texas Gay Rodeo in 1984, and Phoenix followed in 1986. By the turn of the century, there were gay rodeos from coast to coast in the United States, and in Calgary, Alberta. Reno served as a host city for the final time in 1984. These offshoots of the Reno Gay Rodeo would keep the tradition going and continue today. However, the gay rodeo community would witness devastation and great losses as a result of the AIDS pandemic.

The LGBTQ community of Reno and across the United States faced an incredible amount of discrimination in the early 1980s, as HIV, the virus that causes AIDS, was discovered and became associated with gay men in society's mind. AIDS, first identified in 1981, appeared to target young gay men initially, as they began to exhibit rare, opportunistic infections. "Outbreaks of Pneumonia among Gay Males Studied" and "A Pneumonia That Strikes Gay Men" were the titles of two early news items about the virus that appeared in the *Los Angeles Times* and the *San Francisco*

*Chronicle*, respectively, in early June. By the Fourth of July weekend, the *New York Times* reported in a headline, "Rare Cancer Seen in 41 Homosexuals."[76] The press first referred to the disease as "gay cancer" and then GRID (gay-related immune deficiency).[77] The Centers for Disease Control and Prevention briefly called it the "4H disease" because it appeared only to affect Haitians, homosexuals, hemophiliacs, and heroin addicts. In Reno, Ragsdale and other gay rodeo organizers faced an uphill battle to host another event in 1985.

The Pro-Family Christian Coalition was at the forefront of shutting down the Reno Gay Rodeo. The group claimed that the event "menaces the public by threatening to spread AIDS."[78] A growing number of Reno citizens feared that among the twenty thousand gay visitors from around the country, many could be carrying the deadly virus. As people slowly learned more about the disease and how it spread, false information, fueled by fear, likewise spread among the public. Unknown to many during the early years of AIDS, the virus could not be transmitted in the air, by basic physical contact, or even by kissing. Yet social distancing meant distancing from gay men in society. Some concerns led dentists to turn away patients they suspected of being gay, and people worried that they might be at risk of contracting the disease while dining in a restaurant staffed with gay cooks and servers. Homophobia and antigay attacks increased as a result of the HIV/AIDS panic, as the number of infections rose from several hundred to ten thousand cases diagnosed by the summer of 1985. AIDS researchers charged that homophobia and prejudicial policymakers delayed AIDS research. Walter Batchelor of the American Psychological Association in Washington DC argued that the Department of Health and Human Services purposely ignored efforts to fund AIDS research. He claimed that "the money goes down a dark hole because of homophobia."[79] Intensifying the gay panic, the right-wing weekly *Human Events* speculated that infected patients might deliberately attempt to spread the disease by contaminating the nation's blood supply to force Ronald Reagan and his administration to more aggressively seek a cure.[80]

As the Reagan administration continued to adopt a contemptuous approach toward the AIDS epidemic, and as society grew concerned and suspicious of gay men, the gay liberation movement witnessed setbacks. Reno Gay Rodeo organizers initially wanted Reno Nevadans to look past stereotypes and accept these cowboys and cowgirls, but now they faced new and more devastating challenges. During the first seven years of the Reno Gay Rodeo, organizers donated money collected from the rodeo to the Muscular Dystrophy Association. In 1983 organizers allowed members from each state to give 50 percent of the money they raised through their Mr., Ms., and Miss royalty competitions to a "gay charity of their choice," recognizing the need to help members of the LGBTQ community affected by AIDS.[81] By 1986 the Texas Gay Rodeo Association had raised over $70,000 for charity, in only three years, through its royalty participants.[82] AIDS activists became increasingly argumentative with the mainstream media, as they grew critical of religious and political conservatives. The gay rodeo community reorganized its philanthropic mission to benefit its own "in-need" individuals. After 1983 rodeo associations mostly selected charities directly related to helping people living with AIDS. Phil Ragsdale learned that he was also infected with the virus, and he died of AIDS-related complications on the first day of Gay Pride Month in June 1992.[83] However, even in his absence, gay rodeo continued to thrive and became an international organization.

## EMERGENCE OF THE INTERNATIONAL GAY RODEO ASSOCIATION

In 1981 Wayne Jakino, Ron Jesser, and seven others formed the Colorado Gay Rodeo Association (CGRA). At the 1982 Reno Gay Rodeo, the CGRA had more than four hundred representatives, including forty-three competitors and a drill team. Attendance surpassed ten thousand in Reno that year, with television personality Joan Rivers as the grand marshal. In 1983 the CGRA brought the gay rodeo to Denver, which became the second city in the United States to host a gay rodeo. The CGRA is currently the longest-lasting continuous gay rodeo in the IGRA. Furthermore, 1983 witnessed the formation of the Texas Gay Rodeo Association, and the following year California's Golden State Gay Rodeo Association emerged. Cowboys and cowgirls from around the world, representing more than fourteen countries and totaling more than twelve thousand in attendance, helped the gay rodeo emerge as an international success story for the LGBTQ community.

The International Gay Rodeo Association (IGRA) emerged during the 1980s; the organization became not only a source of athletic competitions but also a philanthropic organization, a political force, and an LGBTQ cultural celebration. Gay rodeo organizers created events that were unique to their rodeo. In addition to roughstock events like bull riding and chute dogging, riding and speed events were included. Moreover, trailblazers of the rodeo sport like John Beck created "camp" events unique to gay rodeo such as wild drag racing, which is discussed in conjunction with its cultural significance in chapter five. From the 1980s to the time this book was written, in the 2020s, gay rodeo has provided the LGBTQ community with a space to celebrate their identity and love of a sport in a safe environment.

The Reno Gay Rodeo of 1984 would be the last. However, on September 1, 1985, four regional rodeo associations met in Denver and formed the IGRA. Founding members came from the Colorado, Arizona, Texas, and Golden State (California) associations. The IGRA emerged as the gay rodeo governing body, which standardized rules for all affiliated rodeos to ensure fair and equitable guidelines for judging as well as "the safety of our competitors and the well-being of the animals used in this sport."[84] Wayne Jakino, known as the grandfather of gay rodeo, became the first president of the IGRA. At the association's first convention, members added a seat at the table for the Oklahoma Gay Rodeo Association, for a total of five organizations. Three new regional rodeo organizations were seated at the second IGRA convention in 1987: Kansas, Missouri, and New Mexico. That year witnessed the first IGRA finals; today, it is commonly referred to as "finals." In 1990 the IGRA convention seated nine represented state organizations, and the following year the IGRA consisted of seventeen regional rodeo organizations representing three divisions in the circuit.[85]

In 1993 a small group of men from Omaha, including founding member Philip Lister, formed the Heartland Gay Rodeo Association (HGRA), which included Nebraska and Iowa. In 1993 they were seated at the annual convention as an official IGRA association. The HGRA hosted seven regional rodeos from 1997 to 2003 and its final official gay rodeo in 2006.[86] The HGRA held its first regional rodeo at Christensen Field in Freemont, Nebraska, with weekend events scheduled to begin with the "Hi & Howdy Party" at DC's Saloon on Thursday, June 26, and conclude with the 8:00 p.m. awards ceremony, in the New Tower Ballroom at the Quality Inn, on Sunday night.[87] Philip Lister explained that, during the weekend events, a tornado touched down near the rodeo grounds. Participants took shelter in a nearby Quonset structure with athletes and fans from a church softball game in the same complex. Lister recalled that late-night television personality Jay Leno mentioned the gay rodeo and the tornado during his opening monologue. In Omaha, a popular local radio personality duo was fond of the HGRA's sporting event and promoted upcoming gay rodeos with featured spots. Lister explained that, in later years, the event was held at the Sarpy County Fairgrounds in Springfield, Nebraska: "The radio hosts would call the sweet lady who worked for the chamber of commerce and interview her about the gay rodeo coming to town. She was so sweet and always mentioned how nice we were and how we always cleaned the rodeo grounds up after the weekend was over."[88]

## CONCLUSION

An examination of the early years of gay rodeo during the 1970s gay liberation movement demonstrates how the community defied social rules in sport. This social history of sport reveals the lives of men and women who were marginalized and discriminated against but who nevertheless fought to celebrate their LGBTQ cowboy and cowgirl identity. The challenge to overcome social and political opposition to ensure inclusion for LGBTQ people exemplified their hard work, as they concurrently embraced their country identity. By 1992 the IGRA was a philanthropic success, serving hundreds of charitable organizations. The Texas Gay Rodeo Association alone reported $64,371 donated to twenty-seven charities.[89] During the early years in Nevada, the gay rodeo presented Reno with new images and a new cowboy and cowgirl narrative for local society to see and read about in their newspapers. After the release of *Brokeback Mountain*, scholars examined the film and its contribution to LGBTQ culture. Judith Halbertam concluded: "It should be no real surprise that it [the Western film genre] has finally been recognized for what it was all along: a very, very queer thing."[90] Gay rodeo disrupted LGBTQ stereotypes and reinforced the gay liberation movement's goals, which celebrated the uniqueness and difference of the LGBTQ community—a diverse group of calf ropers, bull riders, drag performers, and community activists who created a rodeo to call their own.

# 2  Rough Riding

## Coming Out and Homophobia

> The church thought we were sinful.
> The health field took us as sick.
> The capitalist saw us as unemployable,
> and the nuclear family mistook us for a birth defect.
>
> —Morris Knight

Is homophobia a disease? At least it was defined as such by American psychologist George Weinberg when he introduced the word in the early 1970s.[1] One can appreciate using the word "disease" to describe homophobia because our initial reaction is to fight it, seek a cure, and eradicate it from our world. Nevertheless, when thinking of the word "disease," we wish for all those things because of the care and love we have for the afflicted. This presents a challenge to people who are targets of homophobic actions and words. When we search for a cure for breast cancer, we wear pink ribbons and pray for those fighting for their lives. If homophobia is a disease, what color ribbon would the inflicted wear? Black, for the hatred in their soul, or red for the bloodstains on their hands? For LGBTQ people, homophobia often presents itself as hatred toward them. At times, religious conservatives argue that it is not hatred; instead, their actions respond to "God's will," which they claim condemns homosexuality.[2] Following natural disasters or catastrophic events, the news media reveals hateful rhetoric by a faction of the conservative far right, claiming that it was punishment for a city's "tolerance of homosexuality," for instance in New York City after the 9/11 terrorist attacks or New Orleans following Hurricane Katrina.[3] More recently, the COVID-19 pandemic has led these religious extremists to condemn the LGBTQ community, and this tendency is not only a U.S. problem. Honorary Patriarch Filaret of the Orthodox Church of Ukraine, one of that country's most famous religious figures, said that the pandemic was "God's punishment for the sins of men, the sinfulness of humanity . . . same-sex marriage."[4]

Homophobia, like racism, sexism, and xenophobia, is something that is taught. In some social worlds, the lessons are taught by clergy members or politicians. In the world of sport, homophobia is taught at an early age. "Smear the Queer" is a pickup football game where a football is tossed into the air, and the person who catches it is the "queer." All the other participants then seek out the young player and tackle, or smear, the youth. Thus, homophobia and violence coexist in the game, and this transcends to society. While there are several aliases for the name of the game, such as "Throw-up Tackle; Crush the Carrier; Throw Them Up, Bust Them Up; Muckle; and Rumble Fumble," many football players today remember the game as "Smear the Queer."[5] In an interview with Hall of Fame coach Tony Dungy, wide receiver Julio Jones explained that he played the game as a kid. Dungy went on to ask if that was where Jones learned to be so tough, "and Jones replied, 'most definitely.'"[6] Dungy spent much of 2007 raising money to fight marriage equality in the state of Indiana, where he was an NFL head coach. He publicly stated that he would not sign openly gay defensive player Michael Sam because all the attention might be a distraction. The "distraction" excuse was popular among NFL draft committees, but this Christian faithful was lying. "Dungy's lie was proved when he publicly said he would welcome Ray Rice onto his team. Wife-beater Rice would attract far more questions and media than Sam, yet Dungy would embrace him with open arms just as he did with dog-killer Michael Vick (who incidentally had the distraction of a reality show following him) when he was released from jail . . . That outward homophobia and clear disdain for gay people has led many to openly wonder whether Dungy's son, who killed himself in 2005 (may he rest in peace), was gay."[7] These open attacks by Dungy against the LGBTQ community perpetuate the hate and is evidence of why LGBTQ athletes remain in the closet.

Hatred for the LGBTQ community is so intense within some social worlds that some Christian conservatives believe that if God does not eradicate them, individual citizens should take up the challenge with intimidation and violence. In June 2019 an American pastor, Grayson Fritts, went so far as to say, "Just as much as God loves, God hates."[8] He ended a Sunday sermon saying, "Put homos to death."[9] In a local news media interview, Fritts explained: "Here's how it should work . . . The Bible says the powers that be are ordained of God and God has instilled the power of civil government to send the police in 2019 out to these LGBT freaks and arrest them. Have a trial for them, and if they are convicted, then they are to be put to death."[10] Fritts was a Knox County, Tennessee, police detective when he was not preaching from the pulpit on Sundays. The county prosecutor investigated seven allegations of misconduct and anti-LGBTQ bias but only filed charges for one, and it was later dropped. Fritts has since retired.[11] American gay rodeo cowboys and cowgirls often come from conservative towns in the West, the Midwest, and the South. In rural, isolated communities, a church is not only a place of worship but a center, or heart, of the town. These social worlds are populated mainly by similar, like-minded people: white, Christian, native born, English speaking, and not LGBTQ identifying. Thus, their beliefs are communal, and stereotypes about LGBTQ people are difficult to challenge.

Symbols such as hand gestures and flags have taken on meanings used to intimidate the unwanted. Hate has permeated symbols such as the Confederate battle flag. A gay rodeo might seem to be an unusual place to see this flag on display in protest of the event, but it happened at a gay rodeo in Dade County, Florida. Jack Morgan remembers the occasion, during which he and other rodeo participants were met at the arena's entrance by protesters waving Confederate flags. "I remember our first rodeo in Florida was in Dade County. We didn't find out until Friday, going to registration, that the authorities were involved. We didn't know this at the time, because there was a threat of a bomb and gun violence. Letters were sent [to local authorities] that they would kill us as we were going into the arena grounds. . . . That was the most fearful I have ever been . . . ya know, seeing the big, lifted trucks with the Confederate flags . . . that was pretty terrifying going to the grounds on that Friday in Florida."[12]

There are arguments for and against publicly displaying this flag. Some argue that the flag represents heritage, while those against it believe that the symbol is hateful. Exploring the Confederate battle flag's anthropology reveals that its message began as heritage, or remembrance of Confederate soldiers and civilians who died during the Civil War. However, the flag displayed today was never the official flag of the Confederacy; it was "the battle flag of the Army of Northern Virginia."[13] Around the turn of the twentieth century, it was uncommon to find the flag on houses or in front yards: "Until World War II, the flag had been used almost exclusively in Confederate memorial activities, such as reunions and monument dedications. . . . The emergence of the Confederate battle flag (elevated in popular perception to the Confederate flag and erroneously dubbed the 'Stars and Bars') as a fixture in American popular culture occurred in the 1940s."[14] The flag became a symbol for states' rights and was honored by "Dixiecrats," politically active men and women who fought integration and opposed the civil rights movement.[15] Shortly after that, students at the University of Mississippi unofficially adopted the flag. The flag was popular on southern college campuses, as many of these students attended the Dixiecrat political convention in 1948. Historian John M. Coski contends that during the three years following the convention, "a full-fledged 'flag fad' swept the entire nation."[16] Today, southern popular culture and some University of Mississippi alumni argue that it is a symbol that honors college students who fought and died in the Civil War. They claim that, in 1861, all but four students from the university perished in the war. These men are known as the "University Greys."[17] The flag lost the semblance of heritage and became a symbol to invoke hate when segregationists began bringing them to civil rights rallies in the 1950s and 1960s. Decades later, this flag, which many people believe to be a symbol of treason, appeared at a hotel in Oklahoma City where President Barack Obama was staying in 2015. Later, supporters of Donald Trump brought this flag to his rallies, from 2015 through 2020, in cities like Kansas City and Tulsa, advocating a candidate and then president who is on record making racist comments. Trump has referred to Mexicans as murderers and rapists, called Senator Elizabeth Warren "Pocahontas," and labeled COVID-19 as the "China virus."[18] On January 6, 2021, an insurrection occurred at the U.S. Capitol and rioters attempted to disrupt the electoral confirmation of President Joe Biden. During the chaotic scene, two flags were prevalent among the rioters—the Confederate flag and flags with the word "TRUMP" on display. The flag undeniably embodies hate. Thus, protesters, knowing that the flag is a symbol of abhorrence, brought it to the gay rodeo to terrorize participants.

Sport is another microcosm or social world that is controlled by a similar demographic of society's dominant group. National Football League games display an immense American flag spanning the entire length of a one-hundred-yard football field. Black athletes might appear to be a powerful force in many professional sports, such as American football and basketball, because of their numbers. Latinx athletes make up more than a quarter of all Major League Baseball players. However, white, Christian, native-born, heterosexual-identifying men control sport and hold most of the power over athletes and teams. League commissioners and team owners are from this dominant group. When San Francisco 49ers quarterback Colin Kaepernick drew multiple media outlets' attention because he refused to stand with his hand over his heart during pregame performance of the national anthem, they responded by transforming his message from a peaceful protest to an unpatriotic display. Fans of the NFL primarily identify with the dominant group as well and reacted with more anger about the nature of his protest than about the reason for his protest: racial profiling, police brutality, and the death of Black men at the hands of white police officers. Members of the dominant group in the sporting world regarded Kaepernick's actions as disrespecting the flag.[19] Sociologist Erin C. Tarver explained: "Understanding many white football fans' responses to football players' protests against police brutality requires recognizing the historical and contemporary role of football fandom in managing racial and gendered anxieties."[20] Ironically, one can drive from Nashville to Knoxville for a University of Tennessee football game and spot more orange flags displaying the letter T and Confederate flags than the Stars and Stripes.

Flying the University of Tennessee flag has become a ritual every game day. According to sport sociologists, there are six components to "inventing a tradition" in sports: costumes, sporting pastimes, institutions, anthems, symbols/flags, and rituals.[21] These are all socially constructed by people who do not realize that they are politicizing sports. What does a military flyover have to do with football? Millions of taxpayer dollars are spent each season for these five-to-ten-second spectacles. In baseball, the seventh-inning stretch was once a moment when fans visited the restroom before the conclusion of the game, purchased their final beer, and joined strangers to sing "Take Me Out to the Ballgame." Now, "God Bless America" is played at most ballparks, with people standing at attention with their hand over their heart. The spectators fail to realize that organized sport, like organized religion, is a form of social control. If it were not, then questioning the greatness of either would not earn countless worshippers' condemnation. Many people believe in the "great sports myth" that sport builds character, is a safe activity to keep youth out of trouble, and promotes healthy bodies and minds. The great sports myth is embedded in society. The myth contends that sport is "essentially good and that its purity and goodness are transferred to all who participate in it."[22]

Sport and Christianity have merged in the United States, a situation that is challenging for LGBTQ athletes to maneuver. Once again, the dominant group in sport is mainly Christian and does not see that when athletes wear biblical scripture on their bodies or uniforms, they are making a political statement. Like religious groups, sporting worlds can foster hate and homophobia. This chapter examines the personal stories of coming out in the religious conservative social world of rodeo and rural America. It examines homophobia and hate crimes against LGBTQ rodeo athletes in the American West and identifies how homophobia has functioned as a tool of oppression. However, these men and women have fought the injustice, allowing LGBTQ people greater freedom and protection today.

The dominant group reacts to fear of the "other," dehumanizes marginalized groups, and has used its power to take civil and human rights away from women, people of color, and LGBTQ people. A homophobic response to gay rodeo evolved during the decades that followed its emergence. As with the marginalized groups previously mentioned, national and global events influenced the reasoning for this oppression. During the 1970s, as the LGBTQ community liberated themselves from heteronormativity, politically conservative social groups saw them as a threat to children and the moral fiber of the United States. Beginning in the 1980s, conservatives grew in number, and religious conservatives became a powerful voting group within the Republican Party. The rise in conservativism during the 1980s in the United States was a reaction to second-wave feminism (which appeared to disrupt the "traditional" family); anti–Vietnam War protesters, who appeared un-American; the counterculture, which shocked older generations with their use of recreational drugs and sexual experimentation; and a gay liberation movement that embraced the word "pride" to celebrate diversity. As the LGBTQ community gained traction in politics and in fighting anti-LGBTQ laws and public policies, the battle for their freedom waged on.

In the late 1990s, pop culture slowly began to recognize LGBTQ people in a more positive light. Cable networks produced hit shows about the LGBTQ community, such as *Queer as Folk*. Major networks like NBC featured programs such as Emmy Award–winning *Will & Grace*, with two of the lead male actors portraying gay men. The new millennium soon brought hope with Ang Lee's love story about two gay cowboys (sheepherders), *Brokeback Mountain*. Medical research on AIDS led to a new class of drugs that showed promise in treating HIV as a chronic condition similar to diabetes. Nevertheless, homophobia, discrimination, and violence against the LGBTQ community continued, with voters amending state constitutions to ban same-sex marriage. In Indiana, a court case ruled in favor of a baker who had refused business to a gay male couple.[23] In Wyoming, the murder of gay college student Matthew Shepard revealed the dangers of being openly gay in rural America.[24] In the social world of sport, many LGBTQ athletes still feared coming out and chose to live in a world of "don't ask, don't tell." Sociologist Eric Anderson argues that "athletes [who] espoused homophobia" are not "agents in their disgust of homosexuality. Rather, they were socialized into it."[25] For many LGBTQ rodeo athletes, there were dangers associated with coming out in a religious conservative environment.

## COMING OUT GAY COWBOY/COWGIRL

In a 1981 interview for *In Touch for Men* magazine, Dave Wilson explained how the gay rodeo helped him come out, not just to others, but to himself. Wilson explained that he had known he had gay tendencies since he was very young: "I tried to get them out of my mind. I hid it, hid it for years. I was married for five years, was in the army. Of course, I wasn't gay in the service even though I kinda wanted to be. . . . To myself. I actually came out a few months before the rodeo. I came out officially in Portland. . . . But it wasn't really complete until I came here. That's when I came out to myself and said, Yes, I am. . . . And here I finally met men like myself, who I could sit down with and rap about horses and cows."[26] Wilson's coming-out experience highlights the support system that gay rodeo provided people who were struggling with openly identifying with their sexuality or gender identity.

Gay rodeo has provided a judgment-free space to come out of the closet. In the early years of gay rodeo, contestants who also competed in mainstream rodeo feared being identified at gay rodeo events. At the Reno Gay Rodeo in 1977, a contestant who only identified himself as "Bill" to the press said that he was "scared to death" of being identified.[27] Bill, a professional rider from Wyoming, stated: "If they find out on the rodeo circuit I'm gay, my career will be ruined. It took a lot of courage to be here, and I'm still nervous."[28] Even with these doubts and fears, Bill carried the U.S. flag into the arena on horseback during the grand entry ceremony.[29]

In the early years of the Reno Gay Rodeo, contestants wore their competitor numbers on their backs with either red or white numbers. The arena announcer informed the audience that it was only permissible to take photographs of contestants with white numbers. The official reason was to protect any professional rodeo rider's identity while that person was competing in a non-sanctioned rodeo. If identified competing in such an event, a professional rodeo contestant can lose their official standing. John Calendo of *In Touch for Men* magazine speculated that it was also a way to protect any participant who was not out of the closet from being photographed.[30]

Not all gay cowboys and cowgirls have a coming-out story, because they fear the reaction they might get from family and friends in their hometowns. Harry, a horse trainer from Colorado, explained that he began doing rodeo when he was twenty. Throughout his life, he remained in the closet and never entered a single gay rodeo event; he even avoided attending them. Thirty-six years after the first gay rodeo, the sixty-three-year-old man attended his first gay rodeo in Colorado, the Rocky Mountain Regional Rodeo. Initially, he feared that someone would see him at the event, and a friend warned him of such a possibility. Four years later, at the same rodeo fairgrounds during our interview, Harry explained that he was not worried about that anymore. He remained somewhat closeted and chose to remain anonymous for this interview. However, coming out can mean something different to everyone, and an argument can be made for Harry that having the courage to simply attend a gay rodeo entails a degree of coming out.[31]

Coming out is not necessarily a before-and-after process, and it is not always chronological. Some people come out to friends and not family, or family and not colleagues. Psychologist and gay rights activist Robert Eichberg helped establish an annual day during which LGBTQ people are encouraged to reveal their identities. National Coming Out Day, on October 11, is an annual liberation celebration.[32] Eichberg argued that coming out is a cumulative process that begins with trusting oneself to process one's identity internally, then sharing this experience, and finally living openly and freely. He identified three stages in the coming-out process: personal, private, and public.[33] Not only time but place matters when coming out. International Gay Rodeo Association (IGRA) members' coming-out stories reveal that gay rodeo helped them accept their identities and openly express themselves. Gay rodeo discredited societal stereotypes of effeminacy about gay men, which, as boys, they had been taught and had believed. Conversely, gay rodeo men debunked the notion that a man with an abundance of masculine capital, cultural capital discussed in chapter six, could not be gay. For some of these men and women, when they attended their first gay rodeo, something felt familiar to them. Even though he had never attended a gay rodeo before, one gay rodeo cowboy described it as a homecoming.[34]

Gay rodeo archivist Roger Bergmann, a charter member of the Golden State Gay Rodeo Association and an attendee of the first IGRA convention in Denver in 1985, was born and raised in Kalispell, Montana, in the northwest corner of the state. He and his parents regularly attended a local Methodist church. His father owned a business, and both of his parents were conservative and registered Republicans. However, his aunt was once recognized as Montana's Democrat of the Year; thus, "family didn't talk politics at the card table!"[35] Bergmann was the equipment manager of his high school's varsity football team for three years. One of his first homoerotic encounters occurred while traveling with the team. The only sophomore among a group of junior and senior players, Bergmann roomed with the players in hotel rooms and explained: "Nothing significant ever happened." One night, however, he glanced to his left while they were all watching TV and caught one of the juniors masturbating. "He quickly pulled up the blanket though he knew I had seen him. I lost my interest in TV for the rest of the night!"[36] Like many gay youths learning about their sexual desires, Bergmann thought that he was just curious and never really thought that his focus on the incident meant that he was gay. His curiosity led him to find satisfaction by admiring male physiques, by cutting out the wrestling team's newspaper photos. Bergmann said, "Their uniform was just wrestling tights from the waist down. I got to see bare skin from the waist up, but I was 'just curious!'"[37]

Bergmann might have found other young men attractive, but he did not act on his feelings nor identify as gay. Sociologist Amin Ghaziani identifies three questions that social scientists routinely ask in order to determine whether a person is lesbian or gay: Are you gay? Are you attracted to people of the same sex? Do you have sex with people of the same sex? A given individual might answer "yes" to having had sex with someone of the same sex and answer "no" to being gay. Alternatively, an individual might answer "yes" to being attracted to someone of the same sex, yet "no" to having physically acted on this attraction. This last combination of answers was the case with Bergmann. Psychologist Rich Savin-Williams assessed that, based on the variation of yes and no responses among a sampling of interviewees, the prevalence of homosexuality among the general American population ranged from 1 percent to 21 percent.[38]

Bergmann graduated from high school in 1967 and explained that he had little information about LGBTQ culture at that time. He recalled only having three dates in high school. His first date was when he took a girl to the movies shortly after earning his driver's license, and his second and third dates were with the same young woman, who accompanied him to his junior and senior proms. She lived in a town about ten miles away and, likewise, had no other dates.[39] His only knowledge of any LGBTQ activities came from Spokane, Washington, news outlets, which typically reported someone arrested for dressing in drag. He was not interested in drag and, thus, believed that he must not be gay.[40] Bergmann was largely in denial about his thoughts of men and his same-sex desires during his late teens and early twenties. He never acted on his attraction to men until his first experience in 1981. Sexual liberation for some gay men during the late 1970s and early 1980s led many to openly meet other men and experience sexual freedom, which gained greater acceptance in larger U.S. cities. However, during these same years, an unknown and unidentified deadly virus was spreading via sexual intercourse. Bergmann explained how he was not sexually active at this time, and he revealed a sense of relief for his reluctance to act on his desires:

Every summer during my college years I worked on a cattle ranch operating a piece of equipment called a "swather," which cut the hay before [the hay was] tied into bales by the "baler." The first two summers, the rest of the "hay crew" were high school kids; fifteen to seventeen years old, who traveled about fifteen miles back and forth every day from town. The third summer, the ranch owner had fixed up a barracks, so all the crew stayed at the ranch. At age twenty with five high school kids and a shower room with four showerheads, sorry, as much as I wanted to do something . . . luckily, nothing happened! After college, I moved to Bishop, California, where I worked for the California Division of Forestry as a conscientious objector to the Vietnam War. We built campgrounds, [blazed] trails, did fishery projects, and fought wildfires. Eighty men [lived] in the barracks with open bathroom stalls and ten showerheads in one room . . . but nothing happened! When I went to Reno, San Francisco, or Los Angeles, I would seek out [video] arcades to watch gay porno and go to gay cinemas and buy gay magazines. Then I would get a guilt trip and throw the magazines away, and the next day, wish I hadn't thrown them away.[41]

Bergmann suppressed acting on any same-sex desires until he was in his thirties. In January 1981 he went to an arcade in Reno, where he and another man had a sexual encounter. He began to test if his desire to be with other men meant that he was gay. The following month, on Valentine's Day weekend, he went to San Francisco to experience the gay culture. "I was determined to go to a gay bar to figure out if I was just curious. First, I went to a gay cinema in the 'Tenderloin' area of the city. After three hours of movies, I asked the concessions guy for directions to a gay dance bar. He sent me to the 'I-Beam,' located on Haight Street near Golden Gate Park. As I approached the entry, I was a nervous wreck. The movie *Cruising* had just been released, and I thought my body would be found in an alley, and my mother would wonder why I was there."[42] *Cruising* was a 1980 thriller/drama about a serial killer in New York City who sought out his victims at gay clubs.

Bergmann overcame his nerves and entered the I-Beam after paying a cover charge of two dollars, with his hands "shaking wildly" as he handed over the money.[43] He then walked up a short flight of stairs. It was early, about 9:15, and no one was on the large dance floor. He found an adjacent room with several pool tables, where there were about fifteen to twenty men: "I immediately relaxed and knew I was home. Yes, I went home with someone that night, but it was a one-night stand. This was 1981, and just a few months later, the gay newspaper *Bay Area Reporter* was writing stories about this unknown disease that seemed to be killing gay men. My sister was three years older than me and chose to go to college at San Francisco State University. If I had known I was gay, I would probably have followed her to San Francisco, and I probably would be dead now."[44]

The experience was liberating for Bergmann, and within three months, he accepted that he was gay. He told his best friend and his wife after staying late following a party at their house. "I quietly told them to sit down because I had something to tell them. When I told them I was gay, they both said that it was not a problem. Then his wife began to laugh and said she thought I was going to tell her that I heard some gossip about her."[45] Shortly after that, he told his sister and her husband, who lived near San Francisco. Once again, he did not experience a problem, but he was still nervous about coming out. It took another three years before he told his parents. Even though he was thirty-four years old, they said it was probably just a phase. This response is typical of a parent who is in denial about their son or daughter. Amanda Denes and Tamara D. Afifi explain that some parents go through a grieving process that includes "shock, denial, guilt, anger, and acceptance. . . . Researchers have pointed out that it is not uncommon for parents to 'pretend that their child's self-disclosure never occurred,' or deny their child's coming out by writing it off as 'experimenting' or a rebellious phase."[46] Bergmann's coming-out experience was a nearly two-decade journey. He never really talked to his father about being gay after coming out, although his mother would ask how he was doing. For the rest of their years, he had a great relationship with them, and he took his second boyfriend to meet them in Montana: "We went sightseeing with my parents, and out to dinner with many of my other relatives in the area."[47]

For many LGBTQ people, coming out happened after years of suppressing their desires, hiding, and denying their identity. Gay rodeo cowboy Paul Vigil explained that the first person he came out to was his wife.

The two shared their love with two children. When Vigil came out, their children were ages four and two. He explained to his wife that he loved her but that he was not sexually attracted to women. He recalls a lengthy conversation: "We talked about it for what seemed like forever."[48] The following day he went to the New Mexico Gay Rodeo in Albuquerque, and his wife outed Paul to his parents. In the end, Vigil's parents were upset that the marriage was ending, but they wanted him to be happy more than anything else. His brothers and sisters were just as accepting, even though one brother found it hard to believe because Paul did not fit any of the gay stereotypes and competed in rodeo. Coming-out stories such as Vigil's provide us with a window into societal beliefs and stereotypes of gay men during the 1980s.

Paul Vigil dispelled his brother's stereotype of gay men that assumed a rugged rancher could not possibly be gay. Before coming out and prior to competing in gay rodeo, Paul competed in mainstream rodeo. He wrestled steer and went to college on a rodeo scholarship. When he began competing in gay rodeo, Paul continued steer wrestling and competed in calf roping and several speed events. Nevertheless, masculinity and femininity are not something that Paul is concerned with: "I accept people no matter how they identify."[49] Paul competes in IGRA royalty as Priscilla Toya Bouvier and is Miss International Gay Rodeo 2019.

Cowboy couple Jeffrey McCasland and Philip Lister shared their coming-out stories. Lister explained that he knew he was gay from a young age. Isolated from gay culture in a small town in Kansas, Lister believed that he was different from other boys but never understood how or why. Lister accepted his gay identity during his senior year of college. Shortly after that, he came out to his supportive parents and family. Described as always being "incredibly supportive and loving," the family accepted Lister's first partner, Patrick, and were a fantastic support system for him when Patrick died of lung cancer.[50] Similarly, Jeffrey came out to a compassionate family. "Jeffrey's parents and family have been very supportive of him being gay. Jeffrey's Dad grew up around horses, and both of Jeffrey's parents thought it was great that he was involved with horses and the rodeo."[51]

Gay rodeo cowboys and cowgirls shared their coming-out stories for this chapter, and through these experiences, we can learn more about homophobia and stereotypes in rural America. Some of these stories tell of experiences that ended with relatively favorable outcomes. These positive experiences might happen when family or friends realize that LGBTQ people are within their social world. When family members learn that their son, daughter, brother, or sister has an LGBTQ identity, then false narratives and stereotypes are challenged and reevaluated. Despite these encouraging outcomes, homophobia and transphobia remain severe threats to the health and safety of LGBTQ people living in rural America; the latter part of this chapter explores this unfortunate truth.

Although these coming-out stories paint a progressive picture of rodeo culture and rural America, there remain many heartbreaking stories of families that are unaccepting of LGBTQ siblings or children. Bull rider Deanna Trujillo-James experienced homophobia within her own family. Trujillo-James, a Latina, grew up with a large extended family while being raised by a single mother. When Deanna's mother learned of her romantic interest in women, the two became estranged.[52] She eventually met and then married Judy James, "a gay rodeo promoter, who grew up watching rodeos with her father in Wyoming."[53] James "ran away from home at 17, after her parents found her love letters to another woman."[54] The family attempted to intervene, but sadly their encounters ended with her father pointing a gun at her head. Years later, James attended a rodeo with her father. It was one that she recalled going to with him as a child. James brought Deanna with her and remembered, "The greatest joy in my life is that father got to meet Dee [Deanna Trujillo-James] and accepted her."[55] Trujillo-James's mother had long hoped that her daughter's interest in women was a phase, but today she is more interested in introducing her daughter as "a gay cowgirl. She loves educating people."[56] As for the small towns they visit on the rodeo circuit, these rural communities are beginning to accept gay rodeo, but possibly more for economic reasons: "When we show up, people shout, 'Gay cowboys are here!' We bring in a lot of business to these small communities."[57]

One of the earliest founders of gay rodeo, John King, explained his coming-out experience. King was in a relationship with a man who was much younger than he, and the man eventually started doing drugs. The two did not share the same values, and when King attempted to end their relationship, the man threatened him with a list of eight things he would do to King. After two weeks, King believed it was a bluff and acted. King recalled:

Well, he proceeded to do many of them. And one of them was calling my father and waking him up at 3 o'clock in the morning and not only telling him about my sexual, in those days we called it preference, not your orientation, and described some explicit sexual acts and how much he enjoyed it. And my father never got over it. He cut me out of the will, and put a provision that I could not stay in the family farmhouse, I couldn't sleep over night there . . . I thought that was the end of the world but within a couple of days I realized I was walking around with a bounce in my step, it was like having a mill stone removed.[58]

King's ex-lover went as far as running through his place of work announcing that King was his lover using sexually explicit language.[59] King went on to become a successful businessman in Denver with his country gay bar, Charlie's, and its locations in Phoenix, Chicago, Las Vegas, and Puerto Vallarta, Jalisco, Mexico (Paco's Ranch).

One of the youngest IGRA members interviewed was Anthony Lumpkins, also known as Chicken Nugget. Lumpkins explained that his coming-out process was not completely under his own control, and when he was sixteen years old, a group of high school boys jumped out of the back of a pickup truck and brutally beat him, breaking several of his ribs. In an interview for Rebecca Scofield's "Voices of Gay Rodeo" digital archive, Lumpkins told how his parents reacted when they learned he was gay. He explained that his mother appeared indifferent; she was not upset with him, but she did not seem to embrace the idea either.

His father initially rejected Lumpkins and tried to kick him out of their house. It was his grandmother who intervened and told the family to sit down and watch the movie *Prayers for Bobby*. Lumpkins explained, "I don't know if you've ever seen it, but it's oh, my God . . . And at the end of the movie, all of us were crying. And my dad came up to me and he hugged me and said, 'I would never want to see myself do that to you.'"[60]

## THREATS AND INTIMIDATION

Hate and homophobia have led citizens to protest gay rodeo and attempt to ban the event from public facilities. The dominant group in the sport of rodeo is composed of white, heterosexual-identifying, Christian men with high-ranking community standing, and this group attempted to shut down an event in Reno. Nevada's lieutenant governor, Myron Leavitt, agreed that protesters had a valid concern in preventing Phil Ragsdale from hosting the 1981 Reno Gay Rodeo because he believed that the LGBTQ community did not have the right to use the arena, saying: "Queers shouldn't be allowed to use public property."[61] Leavitt went on to say that he strongly opposed the use of the arena by LGBTQ people because "if you give them the fairgrounds, you're condoning their lifestyle, and I don't think we should do that." The county commissioner argued that the decision was not about gay rights, that it was more about the community's right to oppose the gay rodeo because it was detrimental to its image.[62]

Ragsdale struggled to secure a stock contractor for the first Reno Gay Rodeo in 1976. John King, the owner of the popular country gay bar Charlie's, recalled the challenge to find an arena for the first Colorado Gay Rodeo Association (CGRA) rodeo in 1983. Officials from the Arapahoe County Fairgrounds never returned his calls. On the final call, King said that they deliberately hung up on him. The Denver Complex was not an option because it was too expensive. The situation appeared to be more positive with Dave Stahl, director of the Boulder Valley Pow Wow Grounds. All that was necessary was for Stahl to get board members to agree. Four days went by, so King went to Stouffer's, a bar frequented by Stahl, where he and a group of men sat at the bar, wearing expensive gray Stetsons. Unfortunately for the CGRA, King reported that "two men on

Rough Riding

his board were so vehement against renting to us, they turned down the application."[63] They settled on Coal Creek. It was not an ideal location or facility, but the CGRA became the first gay rodeo organization outside Nevada to host a gay rodeo.

In Fallon, Nevada, a legal challenge trying to ban the gay rodeo occurred in 1988. David Lantry, who had rented out his facility to the IGRA for its second annual IGRA Finals Rodeo, worried that he would be out more than $5,000 if the protesters were successful in shutting down the rodeo. However, the cancellation of the rodeo would be an estimated loss of $20,000 for the IGRA. Fallon residents rallied against the gay rodeo community. A sheriff's patrol car blocked the entrance to the property. Lantry's father and nephew came to care for animals on the ranch, and officers told them that they would be arrested for being "homosexual" if they were on the property. Residents interviewed for the *Reno Gazette-Journal* believed that it was the right thing to do. Thrift store employee Austine Eason agreed with canceling the event because she did not "care anything about them. Period."[64] Service station owner Dave Cornmesser said that he did not have a problem with a gay rodeo; he just did not want it in his town. He was afraid that LGBTQ people might stay, buy a horse, or even a house, arguing that "in 10 years, my property might be worth nothing."[65] John Beck arrived at the rodeo grounds the morning before the start of the rodeo. At 5:45 a.m., three cars pinned his vehicle against the rodeo gates. Pointing guns at Beck's head, these reckless police officers asked him what he was doing at the fairgrounds. When he told them he was there for the gay rodeo, they explained that a judge had granted the request to shut down the rodeo. With one signature, the gay rodeo did not open its gates that year. Beck recalled the officers saying that there would be "no faggots in this county," and they arrested Beck on charges of being gay.[66]

At that time, systemic homophobia existed in police departments across the country. The 1969 Stonewall riots in New York City were in response to harassment by the NYPD. In San Francisco, violence against the LGBTQ community in the 1970s went mostly unpunished by law enforcement. Gay rights advocate and preacher Raymond

Broshears remembers the abuse of LGBTQ people in the Bay Area. San Francisco has a history of being a gay-friendly center for the LGBTQ community. However, the reality was that as gay men moved to San Francisco in large numbers, gangs often targeted these new residents. Broshears claimed there were numerous unsolved murders of gay men that "crooked cops" never investigated. "In the Tenderloin, Broshears witnessed the violence against and misery of the gay and [transgender] community: police looking to pad their arrest numbers, straight teenagers who thought it was fun to beat up drag queens or gay men, or sociopathic assailants like the 'Doodler,' a serial killer believed to be responsible for 14 murders of gay men in the mid-70s. Danger lurked everywhere—and corrupt police officers, Broshears believed, were part of the problem."[67] Elisa Rleigh, a close friend of Broshears, described a typical night in the Tenderloin: "Young gay men and drag queens would go out to the bars, kids would come to harass them—throw bottles or smoke bombs or beat them up—and the police wouldn't do anything. If you called the police, it was like, 'OK, figure it out yourself.'"[68] For LGBTQ people, Phil Ragsdale's vision that the gay rodeo would be a safe place became a reality.

Lesbian bull rider Char Duran competed alongside gay men in rodeo for twenty years. Duran rode her first horse after moving to Colorado from California in 1995. She prefers the gay rodeo over competing in a mainstream women's rodeo association because of the widespread sexism and homophobia she encounters in the latter. There is a gender ideology that plagues the social world of sport. The belief system argues that humans are either male or female. It defines masculinity and femininity and emphasizes that men are physically stronger and more rational than women, heterosexuality is the accepted form of unions, and other expressions are deviant and abnormal.[69] This ideology in sports led to the exclusion of women from much of twentieth-century participation, and the exclusion of LGBTQ athletes altogether. In mainstream rodeo, this belief historically prohibited women from competing in all the same events as men. This was not true for all mainstream rodeos, but it was never the case with gay rodeo. Lesbians and gay men openly participating in these regional rodeos exposed an underlying homophobia, which led to intimidation or physical violence. Duran explained, "Every one of us has a sad or scary tale of being treated differently—and sometimes downright shitty—from being part of rodeo. . . . if not because of being gay, then because of being a woman. Neither one is particularly welcomed with open arms on the straight circuit, that's for sure."[70]

Roger Bergmann remembers that in 1993, while on a bus full of gay rodeo officials and contestants for the first Northwest International Gay Rodeo, the group encountered a hostile environment when they approached the rodeo arena. The small town of Enumclaw, Washington, was hosting the 1993 event. When gay rodeo brought LGBTQ people to rural America, a clash of culture often occurred. Mainly due to ignorance and immaturity, gay rodeo is not always welcome in these "one-horse towns," Bergmann explained.[71] Once their transport arrived in Enumclaw, a beautiful town with spectacular views of Mount Rainier, about twenty-five protesters accosted the group. The protesters consisted mostly of men in their late teens and early twenties who shouted obscenities and bigoted slurs, calling the athletes "faggots and queers."[72] They were waving obscenity-filled signs. Bergmann remembers that he and his fellow passengers did not let it dissuade them from entering the rodeo park, stating: "We all just waved and laughed."[73] The protesters attempted to vandalize the buses by scattering nails in the parking lot. However, they picked the wrong location in their haste and actually "screwed up a straight event instead of the gay rodeo."[74] Bergmann explained that, in a demonstration of goodwill, members of the gay rodeo helped members of the other event clear the nails out of the parking lot before they had to be at their rodeo. They did not see the protesters on Sunday. Bergmann laughed and said, "I guess they were all in church!"[75]

Bergmann's sarcasm demonstrates how many of the gay rodeo participants responded to discrimination with humor. Homophobia was not a laughing matter. Rodeo participant Amy Griffin explained that law enforcement officials were on the scene at that very same rodeo because rumors circulated that a sniper was in the wooded entrance to the rodeo grounds. Threats were made in the days leading up to the event, and as the contestants, judges, and fans arrived, there was concern that locals armed with weapons were targeting the LGBTQ visitors.[76]

## HOMOPHOBIA, HATE, AND THE KKK

This chapter began with coming-out stories from rural America that mostly had a positive ending, followed by stories of discrimination and hate. The reality for some LGBTQ people is that they lived with constant fear. Tragic events validated these concerns. On the night of October 6, 1998, Matthew Shepard, a twenty-one-year-old gay University of Wyoming student, met two men in their early twenties at the Fireside Lounge in Laramie. Aaron McKinney and Russell Henderson lured Shepard out of the bar and offered him a ride home. The two men took Shepard down a remote, rural road with the intent of robbing the young man. What followed was a brutal murder. Shepard was tied to a barbed-wire fence, tortured, and beaten so severely with a pistol that his skull was fractured. The investigation revealed that his face was almost entirely covered in blood except where his tears had washed away the stain. A jogger found Shepard eighteen hours later, initially mistaking him for a scarecrow. The motivation for the murder is still a matter of uncertainty. In *The Book of Matt: Hidden Truths about the Murder of Matthew Shepard*, Stephen Jimenez, who had worked on a 2004 segment about Shepard on ABC's 20/20, theorized that McKinney and Shepard secretly met up at times for sex. A witness for the perpetrators said that Shepard had made sexual advances toward McKinney, which she later recanted. Shepard's death became a national news story and a source of pain and unification in the LGBTQ community to fight against hate and remember the young man. As the LGBTQ community came together to fight discrimination and anti-LGBTQ violence, hate groups reacted to this political message.

Historically, groups like the Ku Klux Klan are synonymous with murder and hate. The early KKK is often incorrectly remembered as solely an anti-Black hate group. However, the KKK was more of a political group than anything else in origin, and they protested anything and anyone that might disrupt their preferred social order. Moreover, the KKK is often remembered as a southern organization. However, every state in the continental United States had a KKK chapter at some point in its history. Founded on December 24, 1865, in Pulaski, Tennessee, this fraternal organization was founded by southern men following their defeat in the Civil War. Klan members organized to maintain a white, male social order that the abolition of slavery and the Fifteenth Amendment's eventual passage would certainly disrupt. Following the Fifteenth Amendment's ratification, which provided Black men with the right to vote, Klan organizers terrorized white northerners who traveled into the southern states to register Black voters. The politics of white nationalism was, and remains, the core of the Klan's message.

The Klan had periods of near extinction in the first decades of the twentieth century, but this trend reversed course, and the Klan enjoyed a massive surge in membership in the 1920s. Following the release of D. W. Griffith's film *The Birth of a Nation* in 1915, the Klan reemerged as a civic group that professed "100 percent Americanism" and celebrated their Christian faith. Klan parades up and down Main Street in cities across the United States were a common event by the mid-1920s. Their white nationalist ideology excluded Jews, Catholics, immigrants from southern and eastern Europe, and Mexicans in the southern borderlands. Members were male (until the Women of the Klan formed), white, and Christian. Enforcement of their white nationalist beliefs was carried out through intimidation, vandalism, and violence, including lynching. Furthermore, by the latter half of the twentieth century, KKK members targeted gay men and lesbians.

John Beck did not come out of the closet through a chosen path. When the residents of his hometown of Crete, Nebraska, learned of his gay identity, he had reason to be concerned.[77] The state had an eighty-year history with the Klan. During the 1920s it was common for KKK members to march in parades on July Fourth, in their hooded dress, carrying a U.S. flag while on horseback and setting a large wooden cross on fire. Thousands gathered in towns such as York and Scottsbluff, Nebraska, for Klan rallies and parades. Membership numbers are estimated to have reached forty-five thousand (there were over four million members nationally by 1925) only one year after the first Nebraska Klavern was established in 1921. By mid-decade, there were eleven Klan chapters in the state.[78] Social and political issues motivated KKK terrorism. As society changed throughout the twentieth century, so too did the target of Klan members. By the 1980s the Klan had a new group of Americans to target—the LGBTQ community.

By the late twentieth century, Klan members had adopted the Confederate flag, and they maintained that they were "100 percent American" and a Christian organization. In 1986 KKK members protested the gay pride parade in New York because the parade route passed by several cathedrals.[79] In Chicago, thirty uniformed Klan members chanted "White Power" as they protested Chicago's Pride festivities. They were met by counterprotesters shouting, "No Nazis, no KKK, no fascist USA," and "White supremacy, we say no. KKK has got to go."[80] Three counterprotesters were arrested for a minor scuffle. One of the men said as the police took him into custody: "When I saw that guy saluting Adolf Hitler, I lost my temper."[81] Eighty-five police officers, dressed in blue riot gear, were prepared for the demonstrations to turn violent. When the event ended without a significant incident, the police escorted Klan members to the nearest expressway. All the men were from towns outside of Chicago, yet they had traveled into the Windy City to disrupt the gay pride celebration.[82]

Historically, when the Klan is abundant in a region of the country, it has included politicians, law enforcement, and clergy. During the Freedom Summer of 1964, Andrew Goodman, Michael Schwerner, and James Chaney were murdered by Klan members in Philadelphia, Mississippi. Alan Parker's 1988 movie *Mississippi Burning* is loosely based on these events. The lynch mob that gathered to kidnap and murder the men included a salesman, Samuel Bowers; a truck driver, Jimmy Snowden; and a local minister, Edgar Ray Killen. One common thread among this group was Klan membership. Murder charges were not brought up, only the offense of violating the victims' civil rights. All but Killen were convicted, and seven men were sentenced to three to ten years in prison. In an 11–1 jury decision, Killen was exonerated because one juror stated that she could not send a preacher to prison. In

2007 Killen was tried for and convicted of manslaughter, and he spent the final years of his life in prison.[83] In Nebraska, Beck did not have the security of law enforcement officials, and the Klan had infiltrated power groups in his community.

John Beck, a gay rodeo pioneer who began his gay rodeo career in the early 1980s, continues to challenge himself and compete in gay rodeo. The challenges that Beck fought in the early 1980s could have ended his life. Beck was not fearful of a bucking bronc or an angry bull, but he feared for his life at the hands of angry men who believed that being gay was a sin, and they wanted him out of the town of Crete, and out of the state of Nebraska. Beck's coming-out story reveals the dangers of being openly gay in rural America during the early 1980s. However, before his coming out, John was married to a woman.

John and Betty Beck appeared to be a rural Nebraska love story. John, from a well-established farming family, and Betty, a former Miss University of Nebraska, lived together in Crete, Nebraska. However, John Beck had desires that he could no longer suppress. John is not alone. Jason Large examined closeted gay men and found that many of them married women shortly after high school to avoid any suspicion that they might be gay. One interviewee explained: "I met my wife-to-be in the ninth grade, graduated, and married her at age twenty-two. . . . Back then, if you weren't married or seeing someone, you were considered queer—you were strange, a freak."[84] In 1980, after four years of marriage, Beck no longer denied his attraction to other men. It was that summer that he met a handsome cowboy named Harley Rowe. Beck and Rowe exchanged flirtatious smiles, but both knew that this was a dangerous adventure if pursued. Rowe then invited Beck out to the pool hall in town after Beck finished unloading his corn around 5:30 p.m. They met up four or five times, shot pool, and drank beer. One night, Rowe made his move, and Beck willingly accepted. The two had about six sexual encounters before Beck broke it off. However, he knew that his marriage with Betty had to end. Like many gay men and women attempting to conform to a heteronormative lifestyle, John knew that his suppressed feelings and identity could no longer be kept secret.[85]

Later that year, Rowe showed up at John and Betty's house on Hallow-
een night. Betty prepared dinner, and John went outside to speak with
Rowe. Rowe sat in his Ford Galaxie convertible dressed in full drag. John
went out to the car as Betty asked, "Who's out there?" John replied that
it was the real estate lady who was trying to sell them the neighboring
property. The hospitable Betty shouted for him to invite her in for dinner. John realized that the man was "drunk as a skunk."[86] Rowe was so
intoxicated that he broke a heel off his stiletto and took both off. He
stumbled into the house with bare feet and joined the two for dinner.
Beck remembered that he made himself the most potent rum and Coke
of his life. Rowe excused himself from the table to use Beck's bathroom.
Rowe entered the bathroom with a woman's appearance and, after re-
moving his makeup and wig, exited looking like a man. Rowe quickly left
the property as John had to explain to Betty who the man was. Enraged,
Betty grabbed a butcher's knife and chased John around the house. She
spent the evening destroying their home. She broke nearly every window, busted off all the kitchen cabinet doors, and ordered John to leave.

John lived in a hotel for a couple of months until the divorce was final.
Betty's parents showed up at his home with fifteen pickup trucks to haul
off all their possessions. The men were instructed to take everything, including his clothes. John called the local sheriff, who arrived and blocked
the trucks on the property, stopping them from taking everything. John
slept on the floor for months to follow. And the sheriff's support on
that evening was the last Beck received in the town of Crete. Betty had
a sister who knew almost everyone in town. Beck explained, "She was
a nasty bitch. Betty's sister went and told the entire town."[87] Then the
harassment began and continued for a year.

The network of hate spread. At the Farmers Home Administration,
after making an $84,000 deposit into his family's farm account, he was
turned away from seeking any personal funds for his livelihood. The man
stated, "Figure out how you are going to pay your bills."[88] At the nearest
gas station to his home, the attendant refused to sell him gas, saying,
"We don't sell gas to faggots."[89] Matters became much worse when his
brother called him in the middle of the night, saying that the Ku Klux

Klan wanted Beck. When his cuckoo clock struck 4:00 a.m., John made his way to his parents' house. His mother was confused: "I don't know what's wrong with this Goddamn family. Is it drugs? Is it money?" John told his mother that she needed to sit down as he told her the truth. "No," he explained, he was gay, and the entire town knew. John realized that after the 1981 crop season, he would have to leave Nebraska.[90]

That was not soon enough for members of the Nebraska KKK. Over the next few months, the harassment escalated to terrorism. Beck learned that the safest way to live was by protecting himself. "For a year and a half, I slept with a gun."[91] These Christian men turned John's life into a living hell. First, they set his barn on fire. When the inspector showed up, the man stated that it was an electrical fire. When John's machine shop, a sixty-foot by two-hundred-foot structure he had built himself, burned to the ground, the same inspector declared that it was an electrical fire. There was one problem with this assessment; the shop was not wired with electricity. In the most deplorable act of violence, the men threatened Beck with a note affixed to his collie puppy, Lassie, that read: "Move or die." John knew that it was time to leave. The next night, John went to the door to call his little companion inside for dinner. When he opened the door, he saw his lifeless puppy staring up into his eyes. Lying there, covered in blood on the porch steps, wearing her little red scarf, the dead puppy clearly demonstrated that the KKK of Nebraska were cowardly terrorists, hell-bent on ridding their community of Beck. Telling this story nearly forty years later, John teared up and said, "Those bastards killed her."[92] Beck called the sheriff when he found a bloody message on the windshield of his Chevy Chevelle that read, "Move or die. You're next."[93] Underneath Beck's car, the police found a bomb. Beck knows with certainty that some of the homophobic men who terrorized him were associated with the Nebraska Ku Klux Klan.

John shared a conversation he had had with his grandmother when he was eighteen and she was ninety-nine. She said that she knew, when his parents brought him home from the hospital, that he was something special. He believes she knew at that moment that he was gay. She stated that when she saw him, she knew that his life was "going to be very different." On his final night before leaving Nebraska for Denver, Beck had dinner with his parents. John said that he would never forget his last evening in Nebraska; his mother made potato soup. That night, he slept on the floor of his trailer, not knowing what would happen in the months and years to come. What followed was nearly forty years of gay rodeo. Beck moved to Denver and later became an influential member of the Colorado Gay Rodeo Association. Beck has won more buckles than any other gay rodeo cowboy; he has competed in every IGRA finals competition except for 2006, when a barrel racing injury prevented his participation; and he won three gold medals at the 1990 Gay Games in Vancouver, Canada, for barrel racing, pole bending, and the flag race.[94] The Gay Games, an event that occurs every four years, similar to the Olympics, added rodeo events for the first time that year. The IGRA is responsible for introducing gay rodeo to the Gay Games and to the international sporting world.

## CONCLUSION

Whether in the early twentieth century, the early 1980s, or 2020, hate and threats of lynching are used to maintain a social order that privileges the dominant group. The threat of lynching remains a concern in the United States in the twenty-first century. Three University of Nebraska football players protested racial injustice in the United States by kneeling during the national anthem before a September 24, 2016, football game against Northwestern University in Evanston, Illinois. Senior linebacker Michael Rose-Ivey, DaiShon Neal, and Mohamed Barry peacefully protested anti-Black violence by taking a knee. A firestorm of racist comments and death threats by University of Nebraska fans and a member of the university board of regents followed their peaceful protest.

Rose-Ivey publicly addressed the fans on September 20, 2016, with an impassioned statement about his experience following that game: "Some people believe DaiShon, Mohamed, and myself should be kicked off the team or suspended. While some say we deserve to be lynched or shot just like the other black people that have died recently . . . Another believed that since we didn't stand for the Anthem that we should be hung before the Anthem for the next game. These are actual statements we received from fans."[95] Head coach Mike Riley offered support for his players and stated: "Obviously, this is a choice they have made for personal reasons and that's the beautiful thing about the United States that they can do that."[96] Higher up in the university administrative ranks, Regent Hal Daub voiced his frustration with the players, fueling the hateful rhetoric of some Husker fans. Daub stated, "It's a free country, they don't have to play football for the university either . . . They won't take the risk to exhibit their free speech in a way that places their circumstance in jeopardy, so let them get out of uniform and do their protesting on somebody else's nickel."[97] Rather than addressing the racist comments made by students and fans, and rather than acknowledging the death threats these young men received, one of the first questions Daub asked was if these were "scholarship" athletes. If so, he believed that he had the power to remove them from the team for not following the dominant sports ideological script associated with the national anthem.

Whether it be for social justice or out of hate, every message needs people to disseminate a group's mission. When a group of white supremacists counterprotests Gay Pride celebrations or Black Lives Matter events, it is difficult for many Americans to tolerate such hate speech. When marginalized groups are outspoken about discriminatory laws or unjust profiling, Americans who are not directly affected by these matters are beginning to lend their support in growing numbers as allies. As hate groups increase the volume of their bigoted rhetoric, they are unknowingly creating more allies for marginalized members of society. Americans are forced to pick a side, and often equality and peace triumph over discrimination and hate. At the beginning of this chapter, Jack Morgan described a scene at a Florida gay rodeo where protesters decried the event and waved their hate symbols. Morgan went on to say that the way the organization handled it was remarkable. Many of the protesters were teenagers and young men. Gay rodeo associations began to reach out to high schools and area football teams. They had players work the parking lots, charging admission for a space and letting these local teams keep the money as donations toward players' and cheerleaders' uniforms. Morgan said that gay rodeo associations turned a homophobic situation into a philanthropic one for the local community. Schools began contacting gay rodeo associations to run their parking lots.[98]

The social stigma that comes with being a member of the LGBTQ community continues to leave them the targets of bigotry and violence. However, phrases like "Boys don't cry," "Take it like a man," and "Nice guys finish last," are getting more scrutiny. An increase in political power and a positive presence in U.S. popular culture have led to greater acceptance as well. LGBTQ prime-time actors and professional athletes coming out of the closet in higher numbers than ever before, and Democratic presidential candidates in 2008, 2012, 2016, and 2020 recognizing LGBTQ rights, are encouraging signs. While the Republican Party continues its support for "conversion therapy," and for marriage as exclusively a union between a man and a woman, at national conventions, LGBTQ advocates can count a growing number of conservative allies within rodeo communities, examined in chapter three. Gay rodeo has empowered LGBTQ athletes to create a space of acceptance and inclusivity in towns densely populated by the dominant group of sport. These athletes have created a safe place for LGBTQ athletes to compete and celebrate with the person they love. For many of these men and women, gay rodeo was the first large gathering of LGBTQ people that they attended. Some spectators were new to rodeo as well. Rodeo organizers helped them learn about rodeo and LGBTQ culture through rodeo programs. These programs helped them overcome concerns about their identity, provided subscription information for LGBTQ advocacy magazines, and listed future rodeo dates. These programs, examined in chapter three, became "how-to" guides for the newly outed as well as still closeted LGBTQ people who attend gay rodeo.

# 3 Gay Rodeo Programs

How-To Guides about LGBTQ Culture

To kick off the weekend, take my advice! Contestants and Officials—
get your A-game on. Royalty Teams and Entertainers—get your face
on. Spectators and Media—get your excitement on. Everyone—get
your gratitude on for the Sponsors and Volunteers that Support IGRA
and WGRF.

—Candy Pratt

On page six of the 2018 IGRA Finals Rodeo program, IGRA president
Candy Pratt gave "a big Texas welcome to sponsors, volunteers, spectators, royalty teams, officials, and contestants in the rodeo program."
As readers will observe, many of the primary sources used throughout
this book are gay rodeo programs. Research for this chapter examined
421 archived programs, averaging twenty-five to thirty pages each, and
studied how they became a culturally educational tool for the LGBTQ
community. From the oldest archived gay rodeo program in 1979 to 2020,
the programs provide information about LGBTQ culture, cowboy culture,
and advocacy and identify organizations, businesses, and politicians that
have supported the LGBTQ community. Many social and cultural issues
relevant to gay rodeo have been recorded in gay rodeo programs. Patrick
Terry boxed up all of the IGRA's archived materials, drove them to Los
Angeles with Tommy Channel, and donated the twenty-two boxes to the
Autry Museum of the American West.[1] The archive has been closed since
2018 for its relocation, and COVID-19 most certainly further delayed
reopening, but this archive will provide valuable resources for future
gay rodeo research.[2] When thinking about the rodeo programs, Terry
said, "You can get a lot of information, a lot of stuff that I learned over

the years that I didn't even know occurred. And finding out more and more, and I'm still finding out more and more, about gay rodeo that existed before [the Colorado Gay Rodeo Association] or IGRA were created."[3] From the early 1980s, IGRA rodeo programs have been a tool to educate readers on LGBTQ culture, and they have indeed taught some newcomers how to be a gay cowboy or cowgirl. By 1982 nearly all rodeo programs addressed these three themes: LGBTQ culture, rodeo culture, and allies. The LGBTQ cultural section of this chapter examines the literature on entertainment and social groups. Then, a discussion of rodeo culture illustrates how the programs have taught readers the history of gay rodeo, the rules, the lingo, and how to dress the part of a cowboy or cowgirl. Allies are important, and rodeo programs include messages from politicians and business owners who support the LGBTQ community. Finally, these programs have led readers to support networks and advocacy groups that openly discuss the dangers of drugs and alcohol and provide support for mental health as well as HIV/AIDS resources. Examining gay rodeo programs chronologically tells the story of where gay rodeo members have stood as an LGBTQ community. These programs document the evolving position of the IGRA with respect to social issues that have affected the community.[4]

A cultural historian might look at these programs and see how they functioned as a tool to educate readers on the abovementioned topics. However, it is important to recognize that for rodeo organizers, the program was a guide to their rodeo, their IGRA chapter, and their city. Most programs began with a letter by the IGRA president, followed by a letter from the host chapter's president, a list of members of the board of directors, a presentation of the grand marshal, mention of royalty members and what they accomplished, a list of event volunteers, and the event dates. A critical examination reveals that these programs, whether intentionally or not, educated readers about LGBTQ culture with their advertisements. It is essential to understand that gay rodeo spectators, in the early years in Reno, were mostly from rural western towns. These men and women did not live in large cities with highly visible LGBTQ communities or neighborhoods. Many of the real cowboys and cowgirls

Gay Rodeo Programs

could skip the section of the program about rodeo lingo and event rules, because this was their culture. Finding advertisements for LGBTQ-friendly vacation destinations like Puerto Vallarta and all-LGBTQ cruises and subscription information to LGBTQ print media were important because readers could not find this information in their local papers. In 1982, when the Reno Gay Rodeo increased from the modest 125 participants in 1976 to over 10,000, the rodeo program provided directions to local LGBTQ bars and social clubs. In the 1980s and 1990s these historical treasures were a necessity.

## LGBTQ CULTURE

Rodeo programs provided information about the host city. Their pages included advertisements for restaurants, bars, community theaters, dance venues, gyms, and charity events. This chapter does not argue that dance clubs and bars typify LGBTQ culture. However, they were popular among LGBTQ patrons in that, once inside such a venue, these guests were with others like them in a safe environment. Thus, many of the advertisements were from the entertainment industry. The oldest gay rodeo program available in the archives is from 1979, the fourth Reno Gay Rodeo, and it provided everything visitors needed to know if they were looking for LGBTQ entertainment and nightlife in the city. The 1979 program opened with a message from Phil Ragsdale, the founder of the Reno Gay Rodeo:

> A dream becomes a reality, and I'm glad to be a part of it. . . . This is the fourth year of the Reno Gay Rodeo. We're sure it will prove to be better than last year and be even greater next year. We are learning and gaining experience each year. The Reno Gay Rodeo is for Gay people first, Charity second, and to anyone who wants to come and have a good time alongside us. The Rodeo is for all Gay people, be it Macho, Lesbian, or Drag. Let's show Gay Pride.[5]

Ragsdale created a cultural celebration that continues today. What he might not have known at the time was that these gay rodeo programs were important cultural artifacts that helped LGBTQ people feel a sense of community and find a safe place to openly identify as LGBTQ and celebrate their queer cowboy and cowgirl identities.

Rodeo spectators visiting a city used the program to help them find exclusively LGBTQ establishments—restaurants, bars, and baths. Bathhouses were popular with gay men in the 1970s and part of their gay culture. One advertiser, Club Baths, was located throughout the West, in Reno, San Francisco, Oakland, Sacramento, Portland, and Salt Lake City, although in Utah the establishment was known as Jeff's Gym. On the final page of the program, Club Reno Baths, a gay men's bathhouse, announced their location, that they had "private rooms, sun deck, Japanese pool, [and] steam room," and that they were open twenty-four hours each day.[6] Reno Gay Rodeo programs provided directions to lounges, bars, and venues that featured live country music and dancing. Ragsdale included a hand-drawn map on page 9 with LGBTQ business locations.[7]

These rodeo programs were simple at first, providing a schedule of events and local community support for visitors. As the rodeos grew in attendance size, the number of advertisements increased. The Bum Steer, an after-hours establishment in Phoenix, described its business as a place to meet a man's man, with a "Leather, Levi, or Western" dress code.[8] To an out-of-town visitor, the Denver Swim Club, with its unassuming name, would not be easily identified as a bathhouse. However, the ad in the 1994 Rocky Mountain Regional Rodeo program made it clear that the "swim club" provided gay men with a public place to meet other men in an intimate environment described as having the cleanest facility, best music, and hottest men.[9] At times, the ads bordered on being pornographic. The 1995 Golden State Rodeo program contained two ads with full or partial nudity. Page 19 featured an image of a cowboy wearing only his hat and backless chaps in an adult bookstore advertisement.[10] For closeted gay men and others who lived in small, conservative towns, the person in charge of marketing for these businesses knew how to attract their attention. Using a more discreet image, the Triangle, a Denver bar, displayed a similar picture of a cowboy exposed by backless chaps with his rear covered with the message "Censored! To See More, Visit Us at the Triangle!"[11] Less discreet advertisements included Chicago's Jackhammer Bar, with the message "Ride 'em, cowboy," informing rodeo visitors of a male wet underwear contest on Sundays at 7:30 p.m., illustrated with a man wearing only a black cowboy hat.[12] "Sex Sells" is a phrase that has long been used as an advertising ploy, and homoeroticism was a successful technique to sell services to gay male readers. Oklahoma City's 1996 Great Plains Regional Rodeo program advertised a housekeeping service—"Man-Maid House Cleaners"—that offered to send an attractive, muscular man to one's house to clean while being almost nude.[13] Whether gay men were aware or not, they were quickly learning through these rodeo programs that, to some, being a gay man meant denying a conservative lifestyle.

Today there are dating apps for almost every lifestyle. Technological advances have changed traditional meetings in public, either unexpectedly or as prearranged by friends, to virtual introductions. Apps like Grindr or Scruff, in the LGBTQ community, are now used as icebreakers, rather than having to approach another person and introduce oneself. Since the turn of the twenty-first century, internet chatrooms and dating websites have evolved into real-time, and real-distance, mobile applications. In the 1980s and 1990s, technology played a role in the form of telephone chat lines. These allowed men and women to meet while maintaining some anonymity by calling a phone number, with a toll charge per minute. This was important to LGBTQ individuals if their hometown environment was hostile to them or if they were not out of the closet or comfortable entering a gay bar. Whether LGBTQ rodeo visitors used the latest technology of their time or used old-fashioned "one-liners" to meet people, the rodeo programs provided them with knowledge of how and where to accomplish this. As a result, relationships were formed through the gay rodeo that would not have been made otherwise in cities like Wichita, Little Rock, and Albuquerque.

In 1999 a gay cowboy or cowgirl interested in the rodeo could start the year by attending the Roadrunner Regional Rodeo in Phoenix in January, take trips to Tucson and Las Vegas in March, travel to rodeos in the South and Midwest throughout the spring and summer months, and attend as many as three different gay rodeos in September, for a total of seventeen host cities in one year. At each of these rodeos, newcomers were introduced to LGBTQ culture through rodeo programs. While attending Rodeo in the Rock in Little Rock, Arkansas, people learned about upcoming regional gay rodeos in Los Angeles and Atlanta. The rodeo program became a roadmap for cowboys and cowgirls, many of whom had full-time jobs outside of ranching and used their vacation weeks for gay rodeo. It was inevitable that travel agents advertised in rodeo programs, and the vetting process usually awarded the ad space to organizations that clearly gave back to the community rather than merely profiting from gay rodeo.

In 1982 the Jean Beaton Travel Agency took out a full-page advertisement in the Reno Gay Rodeo program. Beaton Travel knew their target audience and featured an image of a cowboy in tight jeans holding a small suitcase (fig. 3). Readers of the program not only learned about the local agency, they saw ads for LGBTQ-owned establishments in other cities inviting them to experience Houston, San Antonio, Cedar Springs (Texas), Denver, and the Sunset Point Resort in Clearlake Oaks, California.[14] The Starlite Resort Motel, also located on Clear Lake, advertised its sandy beach, private sun deck, and outdoor activities like waterskiing, sailing, or just an afternoon at the pool. Both ads for the Sunset Point Resort and Starlite Resort Motel included a man wearing only a speedo-type swimsuit while waterskiing. Visitors could finish their evening with a night at the Cabaret cocktail lounge in nearby Glenhaven. Hosts Chuck, Scotty, and Bill offered an oasis for dancing to disco music.[15]

Within the travel industry emerged RSVP Vacations, a travel company that arranged large group events at exotic destinations. RSVP became known in the LGBTQ community for their cruises. A 1993 advertisement in the Golden State Rodeo program for the Los Angeles competition invited readers to a "gay cruise," November 20–27, to the Mexican Riviera over the U.S. Thanksgiving holiday week.[16] The company worked with cruise lines like Royal Caribbean and Carnival and eventually became so popular that they sold out an entire ship's cabins and had waiting lists. John King, owner of a Denver bar called Charlie's, opened Paco's Ranch in the popular LGBTQ travel destination of Puerto Vallarta, Mexico. The

Fig. 3. Jean Beaton Travel Agency, 1982 National Reno Gay Rodeo program, p. 23.
Credit to Frank Harrell and the International Gay Rodeo Association Archives,
gayrodeohistory.org.

Calgary 1999 rodeo program led readers to Puerto Vallarta. Two men and two women took out ad space to rent out condos in the tropical paradise town: "Escape to Puerto Vallarta—to a warm sunny gay-friendly destination in affordable Mexico."[17] The following year, the same advertisers, listing under the name Dale Scott, Tourcorp, held a drawing for one-week accommodations in Puerto Vallarta at the conclusion of the "Farmer's Daughter" performance at the rodeo.[18]

LGBTQ attendees of the rodeo learned more from the programs than just where the local bars and baths were; they were introduced to LGBTQ literature and popular culture. Gay rodeo attendees might attend only one or two rodeos each year, but they learned from the programs what cable channels televised LGBTQ-related shows and how to get monthly print material mailed to their homes. In the 2001 Alberta rodeo program, an ad provided information about a distributor who sold the complete British TV series *Queer as Folk*. This cable series, eventually re-created for an American audience, became a pop cultural success with the LGBTQ community. Like viewers of the popular cable show *Sex in the City*, fans went to viewing parties with their friends at popular gay bars, and closeted men and women could watch these shows privately in their homes if they subscribed to HBO or Showtime. Additionally, rodeo programs provided subscription information for advocacy magazines like the *The Advocate*, LGBTQ western magazines such as *Roundup* (the magazine had two versions of its name: *Roundup* and *Round Up*), publications from larger cities like *Out Front* (publishing in Denver since April 1976), and regional LGBTQ publications.[19] *Family and Friends Magazine* advertised in the Diamond State Gay Rodeo Association's 2001 Rodeo in the Rock program. The magazine stated that it was for gay, lesbian, bisexual and transgender readers, and they could receive a free copy by writing to their Memphis office or by sending an email request to their AOL account.[20] Even the pornographic magazines provided useful information to readers. In the 1980s, when few mainstream publications discussed LGBTQ issues or HIV/AIDS, these magazines offered important information about legal rights and social services for the community.

Gay men's pornographic magazines, such as *Manhunt* and *Honcho*, were advertised in the rodeo programs. These might seem insignificant to some readers, but these magazines published articles that addressed topics of importance to gay men that mainstream magazines like *People* dismissed or found too shocking to print. These publications reported on gay rodeo and the many charities the IGRA supported as well. Such magazines were not limited to the United States; gay rodeo was featured in international LGBTQ magazines in Germany (*Männer*, *Aktuell*, and *Duich*), the Netherlands (*Expreszo*), Italy (*Pride*), Spain (*EGF and the City*), and Canada (*Gay Friendly Canada*). These magazines often included national hotlines for LGBTQ people to call for mental health support, suicide prevention, and HIV/AIDS awareness. While mainstream print media avoided addressing these vital health issues, these taboo publications addressed socially stigmatized topics.

These magazines are important in other respects as well; had it not been for *Honcho*, much of the easily accessible archival information about gay rodeo might not exist in digital form. In a 1995 issue of *Honcho*, Frank Harrell found an advertisement for *Roundup* magazine. Harrell subscribed to the gay and lesbian cowboy magazine, learned about gay rodeo, and has attended gay rodeos across the country ever since. This cowboy loves history and is skilled with digital archival work. After Frank and his partner, Tom, moved to Castle Rock, Colorado, Frank eventually found himself in possession of the IGRA archives. Using his computer and server, Harrell registered the domain gayrodeohistory.org. The website, live on July 26, 2011, has become an impressive digital archive. Less than a year later, in March 2012, roughly thirteen thousand scanned pages of rodeo programs, magazines, and photographs were up on the site. On January 18, 2018, Tom passed away in the night. Frank continues his quest to record the history of gay rodeo and lives full time in a new fifth-wheel trailer and truck, traveling to as many gay rodeos as he can.[21] As for the digital archive, Patrick Terry said that Harrell "took it to yet another level. A level that I never even envisioned would happen, and it's just been absolutely wonderful, and it's made, it's brought Tom and Frank and myself so close, we are so close, it's been amazing."[22]

Rodeo programs explain the royalty competition, inform readers about the importance of their fundraising, and introduce the people whose annual efforts as a Mr., Ms., Miss, or MsTer. raise thousands of dollars each year for charity and gay rodeo. The programs include their photographs and personal biographical information. Chili Pepper, who was named Miss Texas Gay Rodeo Association (TGRA) 1992 and later Miss IGRA 1993, welcomed rodeo fans in the 1992 TGRA program. She explained how royalty members traveled throughout the country meeting other royalty members to raise money for charities and expressed that she looked forward to seeing everyone again now that she had been crowned Miss IGRA for 1993. She sent a special thanks to her mom and dad for their love and support. Most importantly, Chili Pepper recognized them for attending the finals in Phoenix: "The experience of sharing the Miss IGRA competition as Chili Pepper and rodeo competition as Tony Valdez with my family is truly the definition of unconditional love and support."[23] Mr. TGRA, Terry Neal, also recognized Chili Pepper, saying that she made all his work throughout the year worth his effort.[24]

## RODEO CULTURE

Readers of gay rodeo programs were introduced to the popular western magazine the *Roundup: The Gay and Lesbian Western Magazine*. *Roundup* covered LGBTQ issues more comprehensively than most other publications but focused primarily on men. Its third issue featured Candy Pratt and Greg Olson on the front cover for winning All-Around Cowgirl and All-Around Cowboy at the 1993 IGRA Finals. *Roundup* featured articles about the All-Around Cowboy and All-Around Cowgirl winners, country music artists, advocacy for HIV/AIDS resources, and LGBTQ travel. The magazine included letters to the editor, along with responses:

> Dear Roundup,
>
> I picked up issue #4 at the newsstand the other day and thought it looked pretty good, except for one thing. Why, I wonder, do you always list the cowgirls before the cowboys in the "Roundup

Standings" section? If you're trying to be politically correct, then why don't you also list everyone's full and real name instead of initials and obviously phony names like "Panda Bear"? You can't be p.c. and defend the closet. If these people feel free to enjoy the hard work that those of us who are out of the closet have done by competing in a gay rodeo, perhaps they should help further our acceptance rather than enjoy the benefits and take none of the risks. What gives?

Bill S.
San Diego, CA[25]

The editor responded that "top billing" isn't much of an issue and that assuming that these men and women are in the closet is not completely factual, stating: "Many contestants do use their full names, whether they seem real to you or not. Read the Roger Bergman interview for a little more insight. By the way, why didn't you sign your full name in your letter?"[26] Letters such as these provide a window into concerns for LGBTQ visibility.

In 1985 the Colorado Gay Rodeo Association (CGRA) hosted its third Rocky Mountain Regional Rodeo. The gay rodeo program served as a guide for thousands of attendees on how to be an authentic cowboy or cowgirl. For men and women from ranches and rural western towns, hats and boots are naturally part of their daily attire. For many newcomers to gay rodeo and gay western life, the Rocky Mountain Regional Rodeo provided an opportunity to role-play a cowboy by obtaining, or performing, a new identity. For women, it was an opportunity to appear tough as well as comfortable with a more rugged appearance than was generally accepted in their daily life, where society demanded "appropriate" femininity. For gay men, taking on the masculine identity of John Wayne, to whom they had been introduced in their childhoods and who epitomized the authentic masculinity idolized by their fathers, was within reach. Whether this identity shift would continue when they returned to their urban Denver lifestyles remained a conscious decision. But for one weekend, or more if they traveled the gay rodeo circuit, an LGBTQ person enamored with western culture could take on a romanticized identity.

The gay rodeo programs provided instructions on how to be a real cowboy or cowgirl. In the 1985 Rocky Mountain Regional Rodeo program, Paul's Liquor, on East Colfax Avenue in Denver, took out a quarter-page ad and provided their suggestions on how to be a real cowboy: "You can't be a real cowboy without the proper accessories. You need boots. Lizard skins are the best. And you need spurs, [you] can't be a real cowboy without spurs on your boots. You also need a red bandana, 501 jeans, and a flannel shirt, no matter how hot or humid it is (Remember, real cowboys don't sweat). And ideally, you'll need a horse, but realistically, a Chevy s-10 will substitute just fine."[27] As men and women who were not born into ranching or rodeo families read through the programs, they quickly learned how to dress the part, even if they never entered the rodeo arena. Advertisers like Prestige Ford in Garland, Texas, mostly targeted gay men. Prestige Ford's ad featured an attractive man with a day's-long scruff and attempted to sell F-series trucks to genuine cowboys, and men interested in gaining the attention of one: "Haulin' horses or haulin' butt . . . Roamin' the wide, open spaces or roamin' the streets . . . Good Lookin' . . . lookin' good . . . or just plain lookin' . . . If you're a cowboy (or just want to look like one), you need a truck from Prestige Ford!"[28] These men and women became part of the rodeo through a performance of cowboy drag.[29]

To understand cowboy drag, it is essential to understand "drag" first. There are drag queens, men performing as women; and there are drag kings, women performing as men. In the early twentieth century, female impersonators became part of popular culture at vaudeville shows. As the word "gay" evolved from indicating a lack of inhibitions to homosexuality, by the mid-twentieth century, female impersonators performed in nightclubs that had earned scandalous reputations because their young patrons crossed the boundaries of heteronormativity. Female impersonators became associated with the "gay" community. In 1969, during the Stonewall riots in New York, drag queens in attendance became a powerful voice in the demonstrations.

An example of this today is the award-winning RuPaul's Drag Race, a reality TV show in which drag queens compete each week to win the season's title of America's Next Drag Superstar. RuPaul's Drag Race is analogous to the rodeo. The contestants compete against each other in several events, such as the Library and the Snatch Game, as well as on the runway. Cowboys and cowgirls compete in their own sets of events, which will be examined in chapter five. While the drag queens put on extravagant dresses and do up Texas-size hair, cowboys wear Stetson hats and their biggest buckles. In rodeo, the bigger the buckle, the better. The similarity between the wardrobes of cowboys and drag queens is uncanny. Both activities involve competition as well as performance for the fans. For rodeo cowboys who grew up in this environment, Levi and Wrangler jeans have always been staples of their wardrobe. However, newcomers from the city, who mostly wore Jordache, Lee, and Guess jeans in the 1980s and 1990s, needed help learning how to look like real cowboys, and rodeo programs became their cultural instruction manuals.

Cowboy drag is not a criticism of cowboy or cowgirl attire; it is a critique of the look. One might say that an authentic cowboy is born on the prairie and raised alongside cattle, living Theodore Roosevelt's preferred "rough and tumble" life.[30] Then there is the urban cowboy or cowgirl who is from the city but embraces their inner country self. Michael Vrooman remembers riding around his family's property on horseback, as a child, with his father. As an adult, he lives in Denver, and he has never owned a horse but wears his cowboy boots almost every day. Vrooman explained: "Even though I might not be classified as your typical cowboy because I am not out there on the ranch or the range, that doesn't mean that I don't have it in my heart and it's not part of my spirit."[31] Judges and other volunteers claim their cowboy and cowgirl identities through their active participation in gay rodeo, which includes production, facilitation, and implementation of the rodeo. These men and women claim cowboy and cowgirl identities in different ways, and at the rodeo few people question their authenticity.

Some men are attracted to the rugged cowboy appearance and have no connection with the country lifestyle. They might want to be seen as the hypermasculine cowboy. Thus, the advertisements in rodeo programs with tight jeans, leather boots, and black Stetson hats lead them to see these items as markers to claim such an identity. These men need guidance, and gay rodeo programs provide this with advertisements for stores that can help them look the part. The list of regional rodeos printed in the programs provides a schedule for them to follow the circuit and meet up with other men who share the same physical attraction to the cowboy appearance. Gay bars advertise their locations and genres ("country" or "leather"), informing these men where they can go during the rodeo, and after the rodeo leaves town.

Rodeo programs and certain local publications became "how-to" guides for gay rodeo novices. Closeted gay men and women read the advertisements and shop the stores that can help transform them into rugged westerners. Newcomers might look the part as cowboys or cowgirls, but they need to learn the dialogue as well. These programs include sections on rodeo lingo as an educational tool for understanding the weekend event, and for the urban cowboy, it is useful in developing their cowboy drag personas.

The 1981 Reno Gay Rodeo had ten events, from roughstock Bull and Bareback Bronc Riding to camp events such as Steer Decorating and Wild Cow Milking. The program explained the rules for each event and how they were scored and defined terminology such as "fishing," "honda," and "flank." By 1989 programs included examples of rodeo lingo that helped attendees look and talk like people "who could make it into a Marlboro ad."[32] First, an aspirant should have a "Cowboy Cadillac," a pickup truck "equipped with gun racks, four-wheel drive . . . and more miles on dirt roads than highways."[33] Newcomers read the pages and learned that "covering" meant that a cowboy or cowgirl had ridden their bronc, steer, or bull long enough to earn a qualifying score.[34] As one program puts it, "Let's Rodeo, means to have fun, enjoy the rodeo, and root for your favorite athlete."[35]

Many authentic cowboys can spot cowboy drag immediately. In a 1981 interview for *In Touch for Men* magazine, Dave Wilson explained how he could recognize if a man was a real cowboy. First, he noticed the way he walked, then the way he dressed, and finally how he put his hat down. As for walking, Wilson explained that these impostors don't move quite right. This might be caused by not wearing cowboy boots daily. As for their dress, "Cowboys wear one brand: Levi Strauss. A cowboy will sell anything he has to get a good buckle. A cowboy's buckle is his image. You go to a horse show, that's the first thing everybody looks at. . . . The third thing is the hat they wear. Wearing it back on your head is fake. It's sexy to show your forelocks; that's what everybody wants to do. But the cowboy hat has a big brim for a reason. To keep the rain from going down your neck and to keep the sun out of your eyes. . . . The big give-away is how they set that hat down. The way to put a cowboy hat down is to turn it upside down and put it down on its crown; so, you won't disturb the fold of the brim."[36]

For weekend cowboys, or anyone attending who wants to grab hold of a cowboy or cowgirl and swing them around the dance floor, dance lessons are necessary. Gay bars in rodeo host cities advertise lessons. Country-western gay bars like Charlie's offer lessons each week on designated nights. For instance, at Charlie's in Chicago, Monday was once designated as "Virgin Night," with two-step lessons and line-dancing lessons with drag queens Stina and Crystal.[37] Because Mondays were usually slow nights, newcomers to country culture could practice so that when the weekend arrived or, even more important, the Windy City Rodeo oc-curred, they were ready to strut the dance floor in their boots and buckles. Charlie's in Chicago has become known for Friday and Saturday night line dancing, and two-stepping from 9:30 a.m. to 2:30 a.m.[38] Discussed in greater detail in chapter four, gay rodeo's rise in attendance, number of chapters, and rodeo events has coincided with an increased interest in country music in U.S. popular culture. Stars like Shania Twain and Garth Brooks helped popularize country music, and even LGBTQ people who had no prior interest in dating cowboys or cowgirls attended these establishments because they had become fashionable.

During the 1988 Los Angeles gay rodeo, rodeo organizers held dance lessons during the day on Sunday so novices could participate in the dance party following the rodeo awards ceremony later that evening. The program announced: "At the Golden State Country Fair '88 there will be some of the best doggone classes in clogging, line dance, square dance, partner dance and funning sets. If you have never danced before, or if you want to brush up on your steps, this is your chance to learn and join the dancing fun." Line dancing can be intimidating to watch, but if you want to rope yourself a real gay cowboy, you must learn the steps. Then, the night could end with a partner dance like "shadow dancing." This intimate dance, reminiscent of the waltz, follows a similar pattern with one modification: the dancers are not facing each other. One person is facing forward with their partner behind. The partner in the back reaches around the forward partner, pressing their chest into the other's back, circling around the floor in a waltzing pattern.

## ALLIES

Allies are important in breaking down the social barriers that limit the activities of LGBTQ people in society. Their involvement can take many forms. For instance, NFL player Chris Long was an outspoken ally who defended Michael Sam, the first openly gay professional football player. He defended Sam against people who thought that Sam should not even be in the locker room. Long also defended Colin Kaepernick shortly after the 49ers' quarterback began his peaceful protest against racial injustice by kneeling during the pregame playing of the national anthem. He stated that, unfortunately, it would take white players like him defending such actions—which is the definition of an "ally" in such circumstances— before the intense backlash might end. In cities that host gay rodeos, allies have come in the form of local businesses that support the event. The 1979 Reno gay rodeo program advertisements identified where rodeo participants and spectators could socialize in the evening after the rodeo events. Not all these establishments were considered gay bars. Silver Barons, a lounge and casino still operating today, did not have an LGBTQ connection, but they welcomed rodeo visitors with an advertisement that stated: "So Many Men . . . So Little Time . . . Next Year I'm Getting a Motorcycle," with an image of a cowboy racing through the prairie on his way to Reno.[39] More than twenty businesses were recognized on page 4 of the 1979 program because of their support of the rodeo. Bartenders Terri, Bruce, Jimmy, and Natalie of the Exchange Lounge invited spectators to their upscale establishment, which featured fine wines, imported beers, and drinks with fresh fruit. Paul's Lounge, open twenty-four hours, welcomed Reno Gay Rodeo fans with their ad for disco and gambling. The Trapp, another bar that offered cocktails and gaming, placed an ad featuring a shirtless man standing in the entryway of a saloon wearing a cowboy hat. All these businesses displayed little concern that non-LGBTQ patrons would take offense at these visitors.

The gay rodeo in Reno grew in numbers of participants and spectators after the first rodeo in 1976. Small local businesses and major international corporations alike attempted to cash in on the event. Gay rodeo programs featured advertisements trying to earn gay rodeo business, volunteer support, and votes. Political support in the Reno rodeo program came as early as 1982 in the form of a letter from Mayor Barbara Bennett, briefly mentioned in chapter one, addressing rodeo visitors. Bennett welcomed everyone to Reno and boasted about the city's entertainment, food, and gaming, as well as its planetarium. Bennett also encouraged visitors to take a thirty-minute drive to historic Virginia City, for a unique experience. Debra Danburg, Texas state representative for District 137, located southwest of Houston, wrote a letter supporting the 1984 Texas Gay Rodeo. Danburg wrote: "A hearty Texas welcome to all participants, friends, and guests of the first annual Texas Gay Rodeo."[40] Likewise, Houston city council member George Greanias shared his support, writing directly to readers of the gay rodeo program: "Welcome to Houston, and the first annual Texas Gay Rodeo. . . . I am personally pleased to extend to each of you a heartfelt welcome to the fourth largest city in the United States. . . . By your involvement, you, too show your personal commitment to the future of such organizations—a significant comment on your own sense of responsibility to our community."[41] City council member Eleanor Tinsley appreciated the statewide effort of the Texas Gay Rodeo Association to raise money for the KS/AIDS Foundation Houston and four other charities. She regretted that she was unable to attend but provided her endorsement: "I have supported all these projects on an individual basis before and am delighted to be able to do so again through my endorsement of the Texas Gay Rodeo."[42] Political support came at a time when HIV/AIDS had begun to stigmatize gay men. In western cities, not all politicians affiliated with the Democratic Party expressed support for the gay rodeo; however, in the gay rodeo programs available from the 1980s and 1990s in the IGRA archives, no Republican politician provided words of support for a successful competition. The Democratic Party sent the message to the LGBTQ rodeo community as far back as 1982 that they had representation at the local, state, and federal level.

Phil Ragsdale stressed the importance of supporting these politicians and businesses and explained this in the rodeo programs. From beer to western wear, Ragsdale wanted attendees to know that LGBTQ visitors had friendly companies in Reno. Joe Morrey, owner of the Morrey Distributing Company of Reno, had been a distributor for Budweiser for eighteen years when Ragsdale approached him to supply beer for the first Reno Gay Rodeo in 1976. Ragsdale had already been to several beer distributors in Reno and had been laughed out of all of them. In the end, Morrey's was the only company to supply beer to the first Reno rodeo, providing Budweiser and Bud Light, and Ragsdale stayed loyal to his distributor. Morrey stated, "I don't care who drinks my beer."[43] In 1980 the Morrey Distributing Company took out a full-page ad in the program claiming the title "Official N.R.G.R. Beer."[44] Over the next thirty years, Budweiser's gay rodeo advertisements evolved with pro-LGBTQ images in highly visible places in the program, like the back cover, with the message to "BE YOURSELF."[45] As the rodeo grew in attendance in the following years, other distributors attempted to gain favor with Ragsdale, but he was loyal to Morrey. Approached by the Coors and Miller corporations, he remembered that Budweiser had sponsored gay rodeo when other beer distributors refused to associate with gay and lesbian athletes and their rodeo. For nine years, Morrey supported the event. In Ragsdale's final Reno Gay Rodeo program, he thanked Morrey: "Joe Morrey has and still is an active member of the Reno Rodeo. And is always working with community services in the area. The NRGR would like to say THANKS to Joe Morrey and Morrey Distributing Company for all their years of support. So, drink up cowboys and cowgirls 'cause THIS BUD'S FOR YOU!!"[46]

The National Reno Gay Rodeo (NRGR) recognized Parker's Western Wear for seven years of support, from 1978 to 1984. Even with mixed reactions from their non-LGBTQ customers, the Parker brothers continued to support the event, and rodeo organizers acknowledged them with the following endorsement: "A finer bunch of people or store, you won't find!! Stop by and check it out for yourself. They're located at 155 North Sierra. In 1981 they were the first mainstream business to put up a banner saying, 'WELCOME RENO GAY RODEO!!'" Reno gay rodeo organizers announced their appreciation in the rodeo programs: "Friends like them are hard to come by. We, at the NRGR, say THANKS!!"[47] Visitors from out of town, whether true cowboys and cowgirls or not, certainly knew to spend their money with these allies for western attire.

Rodeo organizers stressed the importance of supporting these businesses. Programs sometimes included a special thanks, or even directly asked readers to visit their stores. At its first rodeo in San Diego, Golden State Gay Rodeo Association members admitted that none of them had experience putting together a program, or a rodeo. They followed the lead of other rodeos in creating a program and included the rules and descriptions of events—and recognized royalty and volunteers. As for the sponsors, Golden State program coordinator Rick Duffer wrote: "Please look through our program and notice the advertisers. These businesses . . . have a commitment and desire to support Lesbian and Gay rodeo. When you choose to shop or go out on the town, please go to our advertisers first. And tell them you're with the first Gay rodeo ever produced in San Diego!"[48] These announcements were often placed in the first few pages of the program.

United Airlines, American Airlines, and US Airways placed advertisements in rodeo programs. These ads featured the airlines' support for gay rodeo and the LGBTQ community long before other Fortune 500 companies took similar risks. United Airlines was the first U.S. airline to offer domestic-partner benefits for employees and retirees and the first to prohibit harassment and discrimination based on sexual orientation. Their advertisements sponsoring the Rocky Mountain Regional Rodeo stated, "We are truly united."[49] In bold font, within the outstretched arms of a man giving the impression of flying, appeared the phrase "IN-TOLERANCE JUST DOESN'T FLY" (fig. 4).[50] By 2003 American Airlines was supporting gay rodeo by purchasing ad space but cautiously did not include a supportive message. Their ads boasted about the removal of rows on aircraft to make the coach cabin more comfortable.[51] A year later, American Airlines followed United's bold lead and added the statement "American Airlines Salutes the Colorado Gay Rodeo Association."[52] The first airline to advertise in programs, and thus support the LGBTQ community, was Arrow Air, in 1984. A discount airline, the company's slogan was "Go straight for the value." They advertised round-trip flights from Denver to London, Tampa, and San Juan for $349.50, $125.00, and $225.00 respectively. Their ad in the 1984 Rocky Mountain Regional Rodeo program identified the airline as a member of the International Gay Travel Association.[53]

In addition to politicians, small-business owners, and large corporations, celebrities came out to support gay rodeo. Country singer Stella Parton performed a variety of songs that included her own hits like "I Wanna Hold You in My Dreams Tonight" and "Undercover Lovers" on an action-packed stage. Parton had a contract with Elektra Records and had earned awards and nominations from the Wembley Festival, the Music City News, and the Academy of Country Music. The governor of Texas made Parton, born in Tennessee and younger sister of Dolly Parton, an honorary Texan.[54] Also showing support was comedian, actress, and television host Joan Rivers (fig. 5). Rivers explained that she was thrilled to be grand marshal at the 1982 National Reno Gay Rodeo. Wearing a pink vest and white cowboy hat, she rode in on a flatbed truck sculpted to look like a team of Clydesdales, wielding a whip and waving multi-colored handkerchiefs at her fans.[55] Rivers said "all gays are my friends" and told the reporter for the The Advocate: "Gay audiences are the best in the world. They find you first and stick with you longer. They're brighter too. When I started in small clubs, they were the only ones who would laugh. I needed them; God bless 'em. I take the rodeo seriously because I take gay people seriously. The mainstream press wanted me to make isn't-it-a-hoot disparaging comments. I refused to talk."[56] Such a high-

Fig. 4. United Airlines gay rodeo advertisement, 2000 Rocky Mountain Regional Rodeo program, p. 8. Credit to Frank Harrell and the International Gay Rodeo Association Archives, gayrodeohistory.org.

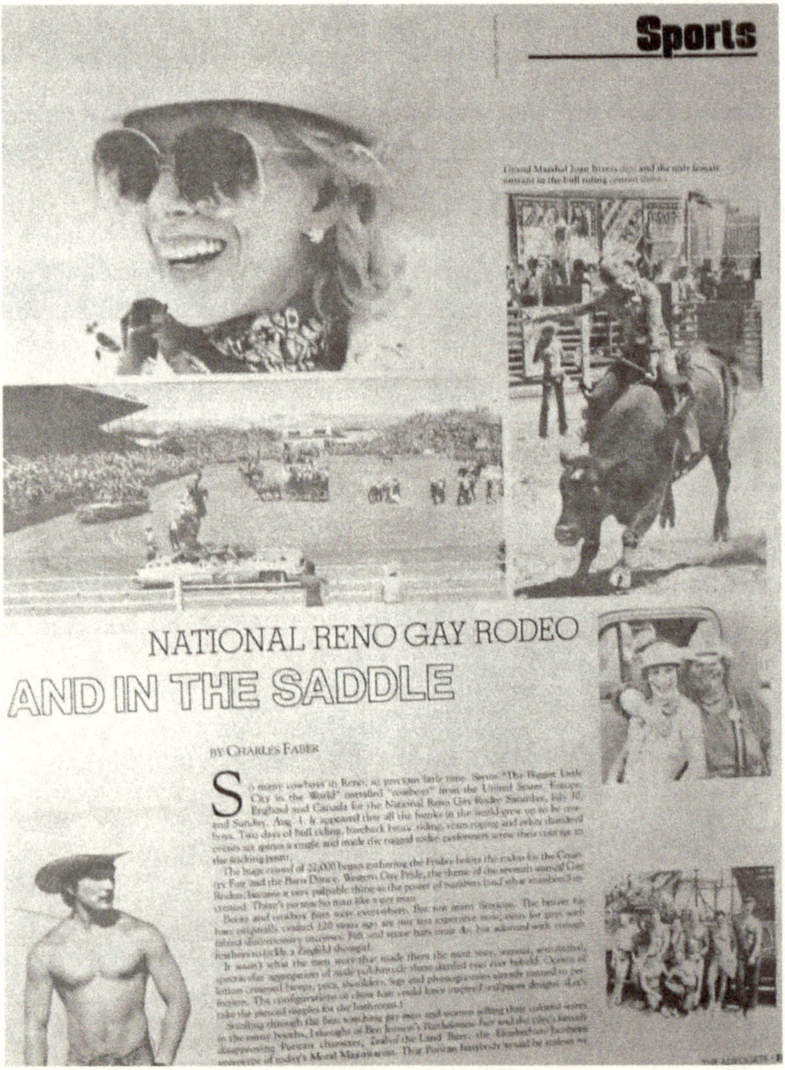

Sports

NATIONAL RENO GAY RODEO

AND IN THE SADDLE

BY CHARLES FABER

**Fig. 5.** *The Advocate* magazine featuring Joan Rivers as Grand Marshal of the 1982 National Reno Gay Rodeo program. Credit to Frank Harrell and the International Gay Rodeo Association Archives, gayrodeohistory.org.

profile celebrity, in the early 1980s, endorsing gay rodeo and, in a sense, the LGBTQ community, provided national exposure to the event. The *Boston Globe* reported: "Comedian Joan Rivers and country-western star Rose Maddox will serve as grand marshals of the 7th Annual National Gay Rodeo this summer."[57] Not only did the story gain national exposure in major cities, but smaller towns across the country mentioned Rivers and gay rodeo. The *Walla Walla* (WA) *Union-Bulletin* reported that rodeo organizers expected approximately twenty-five thousand visitors.[58] The *Port Arthur* (TX) *News* reported that events included "the crowning of Mr., Ms., and Mrs. Gay Rodeo."[59] In a June 27, 1982, edition of the *Blytheville* (AR) *Courier News*, readers learned that Phil Ragsdale planned to introduce the first gay rodeo marching band.[60] LGBTQ readers nationwide, who might have never heard of the Reno Gay Rodeo, now had over a month to plan a trip to Nevada and experience their first gay rodeo.

## CONCLUSION

Rodeo programs introduced readers to the sport of rodeo and recognized the men and women who organized the events, raised money for the organization and charities, competed in the arena, and judged the competition. More than that, these programs introduced readers to LGBTQ lifestyles, rodeo culture, and alliances. In addition to these three themes, it is important to recognize that these programs became resources for important social issues that had an impact on the LGBTQ community. During the 1980s, advertisements for services specific to the community's needs were hard to find in conservative regions of the country. Rodeo programs advertised subscriptions to magazines like *The Advocate* and made readers aware of other print resources, such as a book published by the American Civil Liberties Union, *The Rights of Gay People: A Concise, Authoritative Guide to Legal Remedies for the Injustices That Often Confront Gay Men and Women*. The organization advertised that the book was free with membership in the ACLU of Nevada. ACLU representatives attended the Reno Gay Rodeo in 1983 and invited other attendees to come to their booth in the vendor tent. The book included a list of groups in each state that could help secure legal assistance for LGBTQ people.[61]

Organizations took out ad space to announce their services. Parents and Friends of Gays (PFG) advertised that their meetings were for parents to meet others who had LGBTQ children.[62] The Gay Indians of America claimed ad space in the 1984 Reno program, inviting readers to learn about Native American art, leatherwork, and beaded jewelry. This was their second year in attendance, and they performed authentic Native American dances each day.[63] The CGRA's rodeo program in 1986 included an ad for Saint Paul's United Methodist Church, dispelling any concerns that the LGBTQ community lacked an accepting place to practice their Christian beliefs. The ad read, "We care about the gay and lesbian community. Let us show you Sundays at 11 a.m."[64] In 1987, as IGRA members were losing friends to AIDS, rodeo programs began addressing this concern. While a discussion of safe sex spread throughout the country, the Colorado AIDS Project advertised a resource that treated an underlying cause of infection: alcohol and drug abuse, which leads to risky sexual behavior. They provided their phone number for anyone who needed to reach out for help with substance abuse and unsafe sex. Their ad read, "The leading cause of unsafe sex is treatable."[65]

By the 1990s, as more members of the gay rodeo family succumbed to AIDS, rodeo programs emphasized safe sex, safe drinking behavior, and the utilization of available community resources. The Texas Gay Rodeo Association (TGRA) took out a full-page ad in the 1992 program for the Caremark Connection. This organization provided comprehensive health care services for people living with HIV/AIDS, either at their community center or in the person's home.[66] Another full-page ad in the TGRA's 1992 program addressed chemical dependence. The organization Pride in Recovery offered their services, claiming that one out of three LGBTQ people struggle with chemical dependence.[67]

Gay rodeo programs served many useful purposes for closeted and recently out LGBTQ cowboys and cowgirls. The programs were a useful tool to help the LGBTQ community in the 1980s and 1990s learn more about gay culture, before the internet became available to answer their questions. They also provided a cultural guide to western gay lifestyles and informed men and women where they could meet others like them.

Gay Rodeo Programs

At a time when the mainstream media largely ignored the mental and physical health concerns of LGBTQ people, these programs became so much more than simple lists of events and venues for entertainment. The gay rodeo program was an essential tool for the health and well-being of the LGBTQ community.

# 4 "Riding with Pride"

How the Sport of Rodeo Became
Gay Pride for LGBTQ Athletes

> Personally, I have enjoyed seeing all the different ways that each city
> shows their gay pride. So many times in the gay community we have
> divided ourselves with exclusivity. I am honored to belong to a group
> where I work with all walks of life that represent our community—
> females, butch, or fem; males from the masculine to drag; age groups
> from 21 to 65 plus. And the many supportive straight people who
> support our love for the sport of rodeo.
>
> —Tony Valdez, a.k.a Miss Chili Pepper

In 1976 rodeo athlete Phil Ragsdale initially encountered resistance to
hosting the first gay rodeo in Reno. Eventually, Reno business owners
welcomed these visitors from across the country. Gay rodeo athletes,
judges, and fans boosted the local economy with sold-out hotels and
reservation-only restaurants once the rodeo became an annual event.
Ragsdale may not have initially imagined that the gay rodeo circuit would
draw thousands of spectators from around the world and become a huge
cultural event in the LGBTQ community. He originally wanted a safe
space for gay rodeo participants and fans to enjoy the sport and avoid
the homophobia that permeated almost all facets of the sporting world.
Ragsdale said that it was crucial to him that the gay rodeo challenge stereotypes and demonstrate that in the hypermasculine sport of rodeo, gay
men could counter the assertion that they were not tough men. Ragsdale
advertised the event as a rodeo, but he believed that it was more of a
gathering for the LGBTQ community, with "carnival-type games."[1] What

he did imagine was that it would become a semiprofessional circuit that would eventually be open to the public.

In the hypermasculine, homophobic, and conservative communities of the American West, gay pride festivals were not as prevalent during the late 1970s and early 1980s as they are now. This chapter examines the political nature of the gay rodeo and the implicit message of gay pride that organizers and fans sent to residents of major western cities like Reno, Denver, and Phoenix, as well as smaller cities and towns like Santa Fe, Wichita, and Denton, Texas. In these cities, gay rodeo preceded gay pride celebrations; rodeo participants worked with community members to eventually bring the June pride festival to these western towns. This chapter maintains that gay rodeo was the pioneering gay pride of the American West, which spread to smaller towns throughout the country. It was a celebration of gay rodeo that carried out the mission of the gay liberation movement of the 1970s by rejecting the heteronormative rules of sport. In some cities, rodeo attendance outnumbered that at gay pride celebrations, and eventually gay cowboy and cowgirl culture became fashionable in the cosmopolitan nightlife of major urban cities. In small towns and large cities alike, gay rodeo became a political force that challenged the heteronormative space of the U.S. West and rural America.

When asked about the assertion that gay rodeo was the gay pride of the American West, Jack Morgan of the Colorado Gay Rodeo Association said that the question literally gave him goosebumps. Morgan has a personal archive of gay rodeo memorabilia dating back to the early 1980s. He described one of the first gay rodeo back patches from 1982. These items are stitched to the backs of contestants' shirts. On the patch was the Colorado Gay Rodeo Association logo along with the words "Riding with Pride."[2] Gay rodeo, according to Morgan, helped "normalize" the LGBTQ community because it was not as extreme as pride festivals in major cities. "I think this was a more conservative [message], 'I can still, ya know, bail hay, move manure, get in the chutes, and get on a wild animal.' So, for rural folks it was easier for them to associate with that."[3] Morgan's assertion brings a new understanding of how community members in some rural towns began to welcome the gay rodeo and provides a counternarrative of stereotypes about rural America in the process.

## GAY RODEO BEFORE GAY PRIDE

Gay rodeo, and rodeo in general, is not strictly a western sport. It might be better understood as a "country and western" or merely a "country" athletic event. Traveling outside major southern cities, a visitor will find farms, ranches, and rodeo. In larger cities in the South, country gay bars are commonly found. On April 26, 2019, the Diamond State Rodeo Association (DSRA) in Arkansas held its eighteenth IGRA-sanctioned gay rodeo. The night before the official three-day event began, a pre-rodeo welcome party took place at Chaps, a country-themed LGBTQ bar. Friday morning, the official weekend of festivities began with rodeo school in the Equestrian Center at the Arkansas State Fairgrounds. Rodeo school is an event for newcomers to learn about rodeo events and, for those who believe they have the athleticism, to try out their luck. Gay rodeo Hall of Famer Candy Pratt often hosts a rodeo school at her ranch in Texas. In addition to rodeo school, Little Rock's Rodeo in the Rock event includes trolley rides around the city, a Saturday night "HOEdown" with the tag line "dance till you can't," vendors, a silent auction, a kid zone, and, of course, rodeo events. Rodeo in the Rock 2019 proceeds benefited Out of the Woods Animal Rescue, a group of dedicated individuals who rescue and treat domestic animals and put them up for adoption, and Hearts and Hooves Therapeutic Riding. This therapeutic riding center caters to individuals with physical disabilities. In the spirit of Phil Ragsdale's philanthropic vision in 1976, the LGBTQ community in Little Rock seeks to give back to the citizens of central Arkansas.

The 2019 event was not the first gay rodeo in Arkansas. In 1994 Diamond State Rodeo Association delegates held their first official IGRA event. Democratic governor Jim Guy Tucker sent a letter of support, which rodeo organizers published in the program. He stated: "It gives me great pleasure, on behalf of the people of Arkansas, to extend a cordial welcome to the Diamond State Rodeo and to say that we hope you will enjoy your time in our capital city. . . . One of our chief assets is the spirit of friendliness. . . . Warmest regards, and best wishes."[4] The first rodeo program read more like an awards ceremony for all of the men and women who worked tirelessly to raise the money to host their first IGRA-sanctioned rodeo. The rodeo program featured pictures from early committee meetings and discussed the fatigue they experienced trying to get the first IGRA event in Arkansas. As for many other IGRA chapters, tenacity was necessary to overcome the challenges they faced in bringing gay rodeo to their city.

It took another nineteen years following the first IGRA rodeo in Little Rock for the LGBTQ community to celebrate the city's first gay pride. Little Rock CBS affiliate KTHV channel eleven (THV11) provided a segment on the evening news that featured drag performer Aurora Anna Screima, a parade participant. When interviewed, the man—wearing a pink dress, with light brown locks of hair flowing down to his hips, along with jewelry and makeup—explained: "I didn't expect there to be this many people. . . . We'll do our thing; you do yours. I'm not, I'm not expecting you to marry a man if you're a man, but I'd like to."[5] THV11 interviewed Arkansas resident Rita Jernigan and her female partner, Pam. Jernigan wore a bright orange shirt with the words "I see GAY people" across her chest, followed by "Diversity Weekend, Eureka Springs."[6] Her partner wore a sterling silver cross outside of her shirt. Jernigan shared that she was with the love of her life and would like to marry her someday. The interview concluded with a plea from Pam to LGBTQ denigrators: "People need to know that we are an important part of the community. It's not just a tiny part of the community; it's a large number of people. We give back to the community, just like everybody else."[7]

The sport of rodeo became the driving force for the emergence of gay pride celebrations in cities like Little Rock. Gay rodeo brought LGBTQ people out to celebrate their identity—rural gay cowboys and cowgirls. This chapter does not argue that gay rodeo preceded all gay pride celebrations in rural America or the West. However, it does contend that, in cities where gay rodeo preceded gay pride events, gay rodeo organizations were among pride organizers. Gay rodeo organizations were influential in helping small cities establish their gay pride events. In western Nevada, the first gay pride festival was held in 1988, more than a decade after the first Reno Gay Rodeo.[8] The Kansas City Gay Rodeo Association, founded in 1986, helped organize the first gay pride parade in Wichita in June 1990. Wichita pride committee organizers recognized the rodeo association for their support with the successful festival, in the city's streets and along the Arkansas River, and the association constructed a float for the parade. The pride celebration was considered a success despite the presence of protesters. Ceremony participants and supporters were estimated to number four hundred people, along with fifty protesters. Protesters, led by the Reverend Fred Phelps, "carried signs with messages such as 'The Sins of Sodom Doom Nations,' 'Gay—AIDS—Death,' and 'AIDS, God's Punishment for Homosexuality.'"[9] Despite these hateful messages, the event succeeded in bringing a gay pride festival to central Kansas, and the Kansas City Gay Rodeo Association played a significant role in this feat. Smaller cities and towns began organizing gay pride celebrations, and in communities where gay rodeo and gay pride both existed, rodeo attendance numbers far exceeded those of gay pride festivals in the 1980s and 1990s. Gay rodeo contestants and fans traveled from city to city, following the multicity circuit in groups. These participants and loyal fans helped regional gay rodeos achieve attendance numbers that exceeded those of local pride festivals, because, unlike the gay rodeo circuit, pride festivals mostly attracted people from within their city or region. At gay rodeos, thousands of people attended from other states and joined local LGBTQ community members.

In 1995 the Big Sky Gay Rodeo Association (BSGRA) led the organizing of both gay rodeo and gay pride, staging the largest LGBTQ event in Montana's history at that time, and the first in Billings. Rodeo director Ron Seibel welcomed participants and spectators and credited BSGRA members for the city's first pride festival. He thanked BSGRA volunteers, "who have worked tirelessly to ensure that this dream came true. You are all great people to work with, and none of this could have happened without you. . . . Montana has a long history of rodeo, and we intend to add our chapter of Gay Rodeo in that history. We thank you for joining in our goal to write that chapter."[10] The BSGRA was less successful than

"Riding with Pride"

other official IGRA member organizations: the 1995 event was the only official gay rodeo in Billings. However, it was a success for the organizers, because it celebrated that an LGBTQ presence existed in Billings, a city where LGBTQ people were widely discriminated against.

Homophobia and discrimination have prevented LGBTQ people from hosting pride events in many towns in Montana and elsewhere. Today, some cities that have hosted gay rodeos through the IGRA have no plans for a gay pride celebration. In Denton, Texas, rodeo is a part of rural life. In 2019 the Texas Gay Rodeo Association (TGRA) hosted its rodeo in this northern Texas town, and it became one of the most exciting and carnival-like events ever hosted by an IGRA chapter. TGRA president Tim Smith, along with the rodeo organizing committee, officially recognized the event as the 2019 TGRA Rodeo and Country Fair.[11] The weekend of activities included games, carnival rides, and, of course, gay rodeo.

Forty miles west of Houston, the town of Simonton, Texas, hosted the first-ever TGRA rodeo in 1984, held at the Roundup Rodeo Grounds. The indoor facility was erected in 1963, and by the 1980s the rodeo arena was in "full swing every Saturday night, drawing in people from Houston and elsewhere."[12] The arena became a favorite attraction for out-of-town visitors who wanted to experience the romanticized western rodeo and its rugged athletes. When Deng Xiaoping (Romanized as "Teng Hsiao-ping" in 1979 newspapers), China's deputy premier, traveled throughout the United States in 1979, the stop he enjoyed the most was an evening at the rodeo in Simonton. The visit humanized the man to an American public that held unfavorable beliefs about Communist China. Political leaders who saw themselves as Cold Warriors spread Sinophobic messages about the Chinese, not unlike those of Donald Trump during the COVID-19 pandemic, and encouraged anti-Chinese rhetoric and stereotypes. Deng's visit to the Simonton rodeo softened U.S. society's image of him as a Communist, after national newspapers published photos of the diplomat accepting a ten-gallon hat presented by a rodeo contestant. The crowd cheered as Deng donned the hat with a smile, "displaying a distinctively human side to the previously mysterious Chinese leader," as a *Washington Post* journalist described the moment.[13]

In 1984 the *Houston Star*, originally the *Montrose Voice*, ran a full-page story about the success of the first Texas Gay Rodeo. The event was genuinely "Texan" in character because of its hospitality and friendly atmosphere. Described as a sleepy town, Simonton welcomed more than three thousand people for the event. Houston bar owner Cliff Decker raised $9,000 for charity. In total, the Texas Gay Rodeo Association raised over $30,000.[14] The contributions served the LGBTQ community and organizations such as the KS/AIDS Foundation, the Montrose Clinic, the Montrose Counseling Center, the Montrose Guest Recovery House, and the Gay Switchboard of Houston. The *Star* reported that Terry Clark, president of the Texas Gay Rodeo Association, had worked for two years to get the event going so that Texas no longer had to "eat Reno's dust, watching Reno, Nevada, walk off with all the national publicity for its gay rodeo."[15] East Texas native Tommy Channel remembers hearing about Texas hosting a gay rodeo, and he recalls his excitement about attending. He did not meet anyone or get involved that weekend, but in an interview he said, "It was the most amazing day of my life . . . It was an amazing world that I walked into."[16] Channel was inducted into the IGRA Hall of Fame in 2017. To this day, gay rodeo is the only pride event ever hosted in Simonton, Texas.

## GAY RODEO IN THE BIG CITY

Major cities with abundant LGBTQ resources, such as Los Angeles, San Francisco, Chicago, Atlanta, and Washington, DC, have long held substantial gay pride events. The IGRA involved itself in these already-established pride festivities and introduced LGBTQ urbanites to a subculture that resonated with many city-dwelling migrants from rural areas. In 1986 the Christopher Street West/Los Angeles Gay Pride Committee teamed up with the Golden State Gay Rodeo Association (GSGRA) and announced that that year's theme would be "Forward Together." The GSGRA advertised in their rodeo program, "Gay Pride . . . It begins with the Golden State Gay Rodeo Association and Christopher Street West/Los Angeles."[17]

Chicago's LGBTQ community refers to the Lakeview area as "Boystown."[18] Sports fans prefer the moniker "Wrigleyville," in honor of

"Riding with Pride"

the Chicago Cubs' ballpark, which also lies within the neighborhood. The two communities are aligned such that two parallel streets embody their respective identities: Clark Street extends alongside Wrigley Field, the Cubby Bear (a sports tavern), and dozens of fan-favorite restaurants and bars. One city block east of the stadium, on Halsted Street, a baseball fan will find the North End, an LGBTQ sports bar. Bars, clubs, restaurants, and rainbow streetlamps line Halsted. On multiple occasions, Gay Pride Weekend has coincided with the rivalry series between the Chicago Cubs and the St. Louis Cardinals. Out-of-town visitors quickly learn they are not in a familiar sports bar when they wander into the North End, but they briefly interact with others in their common social world of sport, mostly without incident.

The Chicago rodeo attracted cowboys and cowgirls from around the country. It quickly became Chicago's third-largest LGBTQ celebration, after the annual Northalsted Market Day, the Midwest's largest LGBTQ street festival, and Chicago's annual pride festival. Each event attracts thousands of visitors. By the time the 1993–1994 rodeo circuit began, there were twenty-one regional rodeos throughout the United States. This circuit ran from November 1993 to October 1994, concluding with the IGRA Finals Rodeo (October 21–23, 1994). Nationwide, the late 1990s marked the peak of gay rodeo in attendance, number of competitors, and money raised for charity. During that time, large cities hosted these events. which brought out the inner cowboy and cowgirl of residents of the Chicago metropolitan area, East Coast cities, and Los Angeles. For one week, their cosmopolitan bars transformed into western saloons. Boots dancing in unison to "Boot Scootin' Boogie" tapped on the hard-wood floors in host-hotel banquet halls. "Cowboy drag" led some men and women to culturally appropriate a western identity they admired.

Gay rodeo spread to major metropolitan areas as U.S. pop culture interests made country music fashionable. Country music became in-creasingly trendy among pop music fans; by the 1990s noncountry bars and noncountry music stations were featuring this music more often. Pop music fans embraced the folk-sounding country music of Garth Brooks after his debut album was released in 1989. Brooks reached no. 2 on the

Billboard Top Country Albums chart and climbed to the no. 13 spot on the Billboard 200 chart. Brooks's second album reached the no. 3 spot on the Billboard 200, and in 1991 his third album, *Ropin' the Wind*, entered the Billboard 200 as the no. 1 album. No country artist before him had accomplished this feat. Country music connected with mainstream America, and gay rodeo associations rode the figurative wave and thrived throughout the decade. People could connect with the stories told in the songs and the emotions in country music, which led people to think that if they enjoyed the music, they must have some country in them.

Cowgirls broke into the Billboard charts as well. Pop and contemporary music fans joined devotees of country music in propelling the careers of LeAnn Rimes, Faith Hill, and, most notably, Shania Twain. Twain's 1995 album, *The Woman in Me*, sold more than twenty million copies worldwide, and she won a Grammy for her song "Any Man of Mine." Following the success of that album, Twain released *Come on Over* in 1997, more than doubling record sales with over forty million copies sold. The songs "You're Still the One," "From This Moment On," and "Man! I Feel Like a Woman" earned Twain more awards, eventually totaling five career Grammys. Eclipsing Brooks's success with mainstream music fans, regardless of their respective genders, Twain's *Come on Over* became the bestselling studio album of all time by a female artist in any music genre. These two country music artists excited music fans across the spectrum, and bars and dance clubs across the country featured their songs.

Enthusiasm for country music paralleled the IGRA's growth, and LGBTQ urban neighborhoods transformed into western enclaves when the rodeo arrived. Michael Vrooman remembers that there were more gay country bars than bars of any other genre within the LGBTQ community, which brought the IGRA more exposure. He explained that gay rodeo was at its peak during the late 1990s and early 2000s because "the whole western lifestyle was popular."[19] Tommy Channel remembers the Saturday night party at the host hotel for one of the rodeos in San Diego during this time had thousands of people in attendance: "They had to have two ballrooms, not one, two ballrooms to accommodate the party on Saturday night. Amazing!"[20]

"Riding with Pride"

In July 1991, at the Rocky Mountain Regional Rodeo, Phil Hastings, Phil Riggin, Mike Lentz, and Dave Hehr discussed the possibility of an Atlantic States Gay Rodeo Association (ASGRA), to be based in Washington DC, and weeks later their dream became a reality as the association came to fruition. Washington DC hosted its first gay rodeo on the weekend of October 2–4, 1992. Within three months of its founding in 1991, the ASGRA had a membership of 107. The organization launched a newsletter, *Thirteen Spurs*, and began hosting events such as rodeo seminars, "social activities, and monthly trail rides."[21] By early 1992 the contingent from the DC area had many experienced rodeo athletes and shocked the crowd in Dallas when first-time bull rider John Workman won the championship buckle for that event. The group did not set lofty goals; in their early meetings, they challenged themselves to "become an IGRA member by 1992, enlist 50 members within a year, and prepare to host a rodeo by 1994." Instead, the ASGRA "received IGRA sanctioning within ten days, swelled to over 300 members," and became the first gay rodeo east of the Mississippi River.[22] The ASGRA held its "Atlantic Stampede" each year until 2008, while country music and gay rodeo were enjoyed coast to coast in the United States.

In 1993 Washington DC held its second gay rodeo. Rodeo organizers were quick to point out, in the rodeo program, that in January 1993, "gay America celebrated as a new president [Bill Clinton] promised to bring change and a policy of inclusion to our country's view of homosexuals. . . . In March, hundreds of thousands of gays and lesbians from around America—and the world—returned to the nation's Capitol to march for our rights. A Simple Matter of Justice it was called. . . . Members of the Atlantic States Gay Rodeo Association marched alongside states' IGRA regional associations, teachers, leather groups, religious leaders, compassionate friends and family members, dykes on bikes, sports and entertainment stars, and more."[23] Gay rodeo brought a country of men and women together through a shared love for pride in the saddle, from rural regions to major metropolitan areas. During a political climate growing more conducive to social change, gay rodeo continued to grow in membership.

In September 1993 Seattle, Washington, hosted its first gay rodeo. Two years after official IGRA recognition, the Northwest Gay Rodeo Association (NWGRA) welcomed the rodeo world to the Greater Northwest International Rodeo. That same year, the North Star Regional Rodeo (NSRR) held the first gay rodeo in Minnesota. In 1994 three more cities joined in and held their first gay rodeo: Chicago, Little Rock, and Atlanta. At first glance at the Illinois Gay Rodeo Association's 1994 rodeo program, readers might think they were in Denver, Dallas, or Phoenix. Advertisements for shops and bars had country and western themes. Charlie's of Chicago was the city's most authentic country bar, with Buck's Saloon, Buddies, and Manhandler fitting in as well. The swanky video bar Side Track on North Halsted Street altered its logo for an advertisement to include boots and spurs with the slogan "lust in the dust."[24] However, Side Track was known for its many video screens showing comedy on Thursday nights and show tunes on Sunday nights; the bar did not have a western-themed night. Nevertheless, when the gay rodeo was in town, owners cashed in on the event.

Calgary, Alberta, joined the IGRA and hosted its first Canadian Rockies International Rodeo on July 1–3, 1994.[25] The location was suitable, in the Canadian Rockies, and it offered a western aesthetic. The inclusion of Canada as a host nation transformed the IGRA, demonstrating the power of gay rodeo as a transnational sensation. In 1995 the Canadian Gay Rodeo was staged by the Alberta Rockies Gay Rodeo Association (ARGRA). According to 2001 rodeo director Kevin Murray, since his involvement began in 1993, the rodeo has evolved into the "Greatest Outdoor Gay Show" in Calgary, overshadowing pride festivals. After the inclusion of the Alberta chapter, riders on horseback entered the arena during the grand entry ceremony of all IGRA-sanctioned rodeos with U.S. and Canadian flags, and the audience stood for the playing of both national anthems.

Like most rodeo programs, the first few pages of the program for the 1994 rodeo in Calgary featured letters of support from high-ranking political figures. In programs for U.S.-based rodeos, these men and women have ranged from city mayors to state governors. In the Calgary program, Canadian prime minister Jean Chrétien's office shared his regrets that he would not be able to attend but stated that he wished everyone a "success-ful event."[26] In the program for the following year (1995), Svend Robinson, the first openly gay member of the Canadian Parliament, thanked the ARGRA for their invitation; noted that he knew the previous year had been a success, with three thousand people attending; recognized the importance of "visibility and diversity"; and closed his message stating that he was "in solidarity."[27]

The North Star Gay Rodeo Association (NSGRA) originated in 1989 after five men returned from the Phoenix Finals in October of that year. They desired to bring gay rodeo to the upper Midwest. In less than one year, the NSGRA attracted seventy-five members. A year later, the IGRA recognized the organization as a member, and by 1991 the chapter had more than one hundred members. In 1992 the NSGRA hosted the IGRA annual convention, bringing seventy-five delegates to the Twin Cities. In 1993 the NSGRA hosted its first North Star Regional Rodeo.[28] The NSGRA brought rodeo culture to life and transformed the culture of Saint Paul and Minneapolis. Bars and restaurants, like Rumours & Innuendo, ad-vertised to the rodeo fans. The 1996 rodeo program features a half-page ad with a cowboy silhouette, stating, "Lasso up a good time at Rumours & Innuendo."[29]

After the gay rodeo reached cities east of the Mississippi River and urban areas like Washington DC and Chicago, thousands of urban LGBTQ people were introduced to the gay rodeo family. Rural gay cowboys and cowgirls who lived hundreds of miles outside these cities ventured into urban LGBTQ neighborhoods, some for the first time. The arrival of gay rodeo intrigued urbanites, many of whom had never been to a rodeo arena, and new rodeo fans emerged. As gay rodeo and country music became more popular in large cities, numbers of gay rodeo attendees grew. In these major cities, gay rodeo did not exceed gay pride festivals in attendance, but these new rodeo fans traveled to other gay rodeo host cities. Joining this rodeo circuit, gay rodeos in Kansas City, Colorado Springs, and Wichita had attendance numbers that surpassed those cities' pride festivals.

The IGRA continued to grow in membership and the number of annual rodeos. New rodeo fans began traveling to cities in the West. Gay rodeo historian Frank Harrell remembered his first trip to Colorado in 1967. Harrell was originally from the East Coast. Early in his two-week road trip, Harrell reached a certain elevation in Limon, Colorado, where he was able to see the Rocky Mountains for the first time. It was then that he knew he would always want to live in Colorado. In 1983 Harrell met his life partner, Lieutenant Colonel Tom Lott, and they made Clifton, Virginia, their home. As previously mentioned, Harrell subscribed to *Drummer* and *Honcho*, two gay men's magazines. In a 1995 issue, Harrell noticed an advertisement for *Roundup* magazine (fig. 6). Harrell then subscribed to *Roundup*, where he first learned about gay rodeo. With his long infatuation with the West, and an attraction to rodeo cowboys, Harrell attended his first gay rodeo the following year.[30]

Frank and Tom began attending the Atlantic Stampede Gay Rodeo in the mid-1990s, bringing Harrell closer to his desire to live in the West. Over time, they became part of the gay rodeo family, and they bought a home near Castle Rock, Colorado, in 2010. Since then, Harrell has played an essential role in the Colorado Gay Rodeo Association. In 2018 the CGRA inducted Harrell into the IGRA Hall of Fame and honored him with a Hall of Fame buckle because of his dedication to preserving gay rodeo history. These cowboys and cowgirls are a family. Friendship is essential to these men and women, and gay rodeo provided them with their chosen siblings.

Christopher J. Boyden, the Southeast Gay Rodeo Association president during the 1999 Southern Spurs Rodeo in Atlanta, stated: "There is a familiar rope that runs through all the rodeos I have attended. It seems that with each passing rodeo, my circle of chosen family grows. I understand the meaning of the Spirit Stick, and I truly believe we all carry it with us.[31] In the rough non-rodeo world, we can always carry forth the comfort, camaraderie, love, and support that we learn and have from our rodeo world. And that, believe it or not, does make the world a better place."[32]

The migration of the IGRA east of the Mississippi River brought gay rodeo athletes and fans to cities like Pittsburgh, and the philanthropic goals of gay rodeo came with them as well. In 1992, in response to the growing interest in gay rodeo in Pittsburgh, the social club Horse of a

"Riding with Pride"

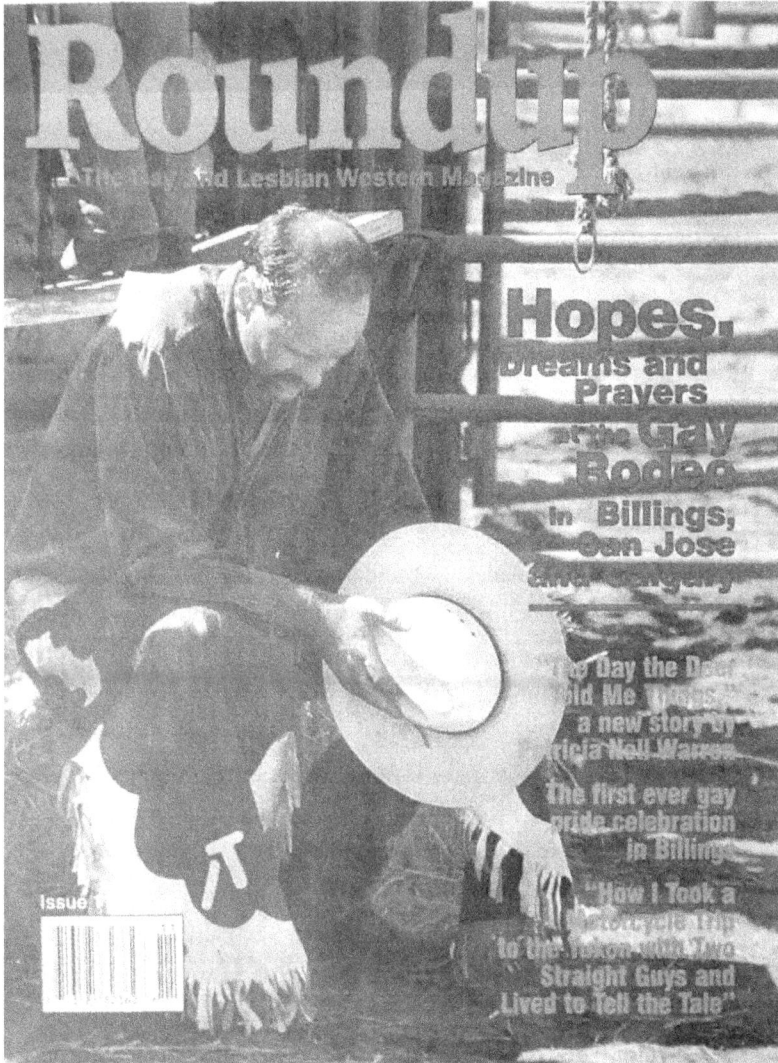

Fig. 6. *Roundup: The Gay and Lesbian Western Magazine.* A feature story about gay rodeo in Billings, Montana, and the first gay pride festival in Billings. Credit to Frank Harrell and the International Gay Rodeo Association Archives, gayrodeohistory.org.

Different Color was established with a membership of more than one hundred.[33] The organization, as its mission, sought to give back to its community. Members organized a fundraising event they called "East Meets West," which raised over $5,300 over a three-day period in April 1994. More than three hundred cowboys and cowgirls attended the Friday night dance party, which featured live country music and became "the largest dance floor in the city of Pittsburgh" that evening.[34] The money went to the Shepherd Wellness Community, a multifaceted organization that provided resources for people affected by HIV and AIDS in Pittsburgh.[35] By the end of the weekend, there were more than a few country converts. Entertainment, dancing, and country music filled the weekend, "yet no one forgot its purpose—helping our community!"[36]

## POLITICS OF PRIDE AND GAY RODEO

Large stretches of rural America, including much of the Mountain West and Great Plains, is in conservative states with Republican-controlled state legislatures. In these regions, gay rodeo cowboys and cowgirls have experienced tremendous backlash when organizing gay rodeos and gay pride celebrations. In some places, the LGBTQ community has witnessed the enactment of laws that have limited their civil rights. For instance, some local authorities threatened to enforce outdated sodomy laws to scare off gay rodeo organizers from hosting an event. In pre–Stonewall riots fashion, it is no longer only law enforcement personnel who have attacked the LGBTQ community; lawmakers have also assailed LGBTQ rights. It was politically dangerous in the 1980s to support the LGBTQ community, and conservative politicians in the twenty-first century remain cautious of advocating for this marginalized group. Vice President Mike Pence stated that "Congress should oppose any effort to recognize homosexuals as a 'discrete and insular minority' entitled to the protection of anti-discrimination laws similar to those extended to women and ethnic minorities."[37] In 2000, when running for Congress, Pence argued for funding stipulations for HIV-positive individuals from the LGBTQ community when referring to the Ryan White Comprehensive AIDS Resources Emergency Act (CARE). The 1990 law provided HIV/

AIDS patients with funding for treatment if they lacked the income or insurance coverage to pay for their care. Pence believed that conversion therapy was a better use of taxpayer money.[38] In many smaller cities nationwide, support by local politicians for LGBTQ causes can be scarce at times. In 2019 the Republican mayor of Carbon Hill, Alabama, expressed his displeasure with the 2019 gay pride celebration. In a now-deleted Facebook post, he called for the killing of the LGBTQ community: "The only way to change it would be to kill the problem out. I know it's bad to say, but without killing them out, there's no way to fix it."[39]

In contrast, the success of gay rodeo led many liberal politicians to support the endeavor in the 1980s and 1990s, even though it was politically unsafe. By the early 1980s, Democratic politicians were joining the likes of Reno mayor Barbara Bennett, mentioned in chapter one, by writing letters of support for gay rodeo. In Denver, Pat Schroeder, the first woman from Colorado elected to the U.S. House of Representatives, sent a greeting and welcome letter to the CGRA. Published on page 8 of *Guide Magazine*, the official program for the second annual Rocky Mountain Regional Rodeo, Schroeder stated: "Greetings to all who will be participating in and supporting the Second Annual Rocky Mountain Regional Rodeo. Welcome to the Denver area! May you experience western hospitality with a special Colorado spirit and warmth."[40]

Schroeder had a history in Congress of fighting discrimination, especially in public policy. An outspoken opponent of the Defense of Marriage Act, a federal law that defined marriage as a union between one man and one woman for federal legal purposes, Schroeder argued: "You can't amend the Constitution with a statute. Everybody knows that. This is just stirring the political waters and seeing what hate you can unleash."[41] Other politicians came out in support of LGBTQ rights, their community, and gay rodeo when it was not politically safe to do so. In 1988 Democratic mayor of Denver Federico Peña welcomed visitors to Colorado for that year's gay rodeo, calling it the "premier gay and lesbian rodeo."[42] Peña stated: "I also salute Pridefest '88 to be held in conjunction with the rodeo. As the theme states, the gay and lesbian community can be 'rightfully proud' of the progress toward civil rights."[43] Democratic governor Roy Romer supported the Rocky Mountain Regional Rodeo and Pridefest in a letter as well. That same year, the Democratic mayor of Austin, Texas, extended his support to the Texas Gay Rodeo Association: "The city of Austin is pleased that you have chosen our city for the Fifth Annual Rodeo. . . . I am sure you will enjoy much fellowship during your gathering and wish you much success."[44] Public support like this showed that political gains were being made through the IGRA's efforts and the growing number of gay rodeos, all while Republican president Ronald Reagan avoided demonstrating any support for the LGBTQ community.

Reagan dismissed the LGBTQ community. Historians have theorized that his rise to the office of the presidency was partly due to his being likened to his friend John Wayne. At a time when masculinity was "in crisis," the Republican Party doubled down on everything masculine, everything that extolled traditional familyhood. Historian Susan Jeffords explains that Reagan's predecessor, Jimmy Carter, was seen as weak and defeated in foreign policy, and that Reagan's win over the incumbent revealed voters' desire for an administration that would be seen as successful and "distinctly masculine, not merely as men but as decisive, tough, aggressive, strong, domineering men," unlike Carter.[45]

Even though homophobia was more prevalent in the 1980s than it is now, western towns hosted gay rodeos, and these events often surpassed the attendance at gay pride celebrations in larger cities. The gay rodeo brought men and women to IGRA events around the country. Rather than the LGBTQ community celebrating their identity with pride once every June, the IGRA provided a space for a nearly year-round celebration of pride, resulting in rodeo events far exceeding attendance expectations. Part of the reason that turnout at the rodeo was higher than at pride festivals was the family that the IGRA had created and the competitive nature of these athletes. And in order to qualify for the finals, a competitor had to place high in their event in a regional competition. As the IGRA grew in membership, political activism became part of the rodeo tradition as well.

Politics permeated the family environment of the IGRA. The question of gender identity in sport at the turn of the millennium became a

"Riding with Pride"

growing issue. "Gay pride" as used within the LGBTQ community encompasses all identities of sexuality and gender identity, including gender-nonconforming people. However, as with the nickname of the Lakeview neighborhood in Chicago, "Boystown," it can appear that the phrase "gay pride" or "gay rodeo" does not represent the entire LGBTQ community. Transgender individuals are part of an already marginalized group who are, at times, marginalized within this larger community. Gay rodeo made history as the first international sporting organization to address transgender athlete participation and permit an athlete to compete in the gender category with which they identify, rather than strictly enforcing participation based on gender assigned at birth. In tennis, Renée Richards became the first transgender woman to compete in the U.S. Open, in 1977. However, as an international organization, the World Tennis Association examined sex chromosomes rather than gender identity in the 1970s. The International Olympic Committee (IOC) addressed transgender participation in 2003 and allowed transgender athletes to compete in the 2004 Olympic Games in Athens. The IGRA preceded the IOC with a gender identity policy drafted by Roger Bergmann at the IGRA convention in Las Vegas in 2000.[46] Bergmann explained the difficulty with creating a policy that had no precedent, and thus no model, in any other sport. There were rumors that the ASGRA would propose a rule change for transgender athlete participation. Bergmann recalls sitting down with a man from the ASGRA and discussing all the transgender issues that needed to be addressed with a change in the rules. "I learned a lot in a short time," he said. "We went our ways, and I got ready to go dancing. I went outside and tried to flag down a taxi, but they would not stop. I went inside and tried to phone for a taxi and was disconnected two times. I went back to my room, sat down on the bed, and wrote the proposal to present on the main convention floor on Saturday."[47]

Bergmann presented the proposal to ASGRA members, who responded to him with recommendations. On Saturday, during one of the session breaks, Bergmann called for the rules committee to reconvene and approve the proposal. It passed on the committee floor with little discussion. The new rules went into effect during the next rodeo season. "There have been a few changes since, but I believe we were possibly the first sports organization to allow individuals to select their competition gender."[48] One male contestant objected to the new rule and attempted to mock the decision. He entered events as a woman, thinking he would prove he had an advantage. Bergmann explained that a larger physical frame should have provided the man an advantage, "but some of the women could beat him in chute dogging and steer riding."[49]

Gay rodeo provided an inclusive atmosphere, and it included men and women from all over the United States and several other countries. IGRA members followed the rodeo circuit and supported neighboring chapters. Not all IGRA members attend every rodeo, but it was common to find cowboys and cowgirls from Little Rock, Arkansas, rooming with friends from Santa Fe, New Mexico, or camping together near their horse trailer in Denver. Whether at the host hotel or a local campsite, when IGRA members gather, it resembles a family reunion. It is also a way for some members to reconnect with a potential life partner or have a casual encounter. And as these rodeo contestants, judges, and volunteers traveled from city to city to support each other, so did their fans with their financial resources, and their political message of acceptance. The rodeo programs included social activities for the overwhelming number of out-of-town visitors. Additionally, IGRA regional associations advertised their upcoming rodeos and provided a roadmap and timeline, which usually included the entire list of regional rodeos on a calendar. It is not surprising that by the mid-1990s, as gay rodeo became a substantial financial boost for local businesses, national and international corporations wanted to cash in on the events, and politicians wanted to be seen as allies.

## CONCLUSION

In 1982 Reno Gay Rodeo founder Phil Ragsdale was already bragging about the growth of the gay rodeo and how it had become an international success. "THE NATIONAL RENO RODEO has become an 'international event,' with visitors from over 14 foreign countries joining us, here in Reno. This year we welcome some of our guests from Switzerland, England, Germany, France, Sweden, and Italy. Each year, the rodeo grows bigger, and we try to keep up with it, by adding MORE and MORE to it. Next year's Rodeo/Country Fair will be expanded to at least four days!!"[50] Whether these cities and towns were successful or not with eventually hosting official gay pride celebrations, Phil Ragsdale was on to something in 1980 when he referred to the Reno event as "Western Gay Day."[51] Two years later he declared: "The Theme for the 1982 National Reno Gay Rodeo is 'Western Gay Pride' and we encourage YOU to JOIN US in projecting this theme."[52] Ragsdale repeated this in the 1983 program (fig. 7), telling readers that western gay pride would educate people in local communities: "We hope that you will share with us, once again, in this year's theme, WESTERN GAY PRIDE!! As it can be nothing but productive for all of us! As I stated previously, WESTERN GAY PRIDE by each of us can help to overcome much of the Gay Ignorance some people still have" (fig. 8).[53]

The IGRA provided the LGBTQ community with a space to call their own in sports. The family that came together over a period of months and years provided IGRA members with a support system. Gay rodeos provided fundraising and support for cowboys and cowgirls when they needed medical bills paid or assistance traveling from state to state to compete in gay rodeos, and even for impromptu drag queen performances at a rodeo to raise money for an injured contestant. Gay rodeo reached out beyond the arena, welcoming new members, and provided role models for LGBTQ youth. Wade Earp, the descendant of Wyatt Earp mentioned in the introduction, told an inspirational story. Earp is described as a paradox on the IGRA Hall of Fame web page because he "is one of the toughest competitors you will never want to face, and he is one of the nicest guys you will ever meet."[54]

In an interview a few years after the filming of *Queens and Cowboys*, a documentary film about gay rodeo, Earp shared a proud story. He explained that the documentary had had a lasting impact on his life— not because of the attention he received, but because of the impact it had on a mother and her child. The woman wanted her son to see gay role models in sport. As a youth in Texas, he mostly heard negative stories about the LGBTQ community. Together, mother and son watched this

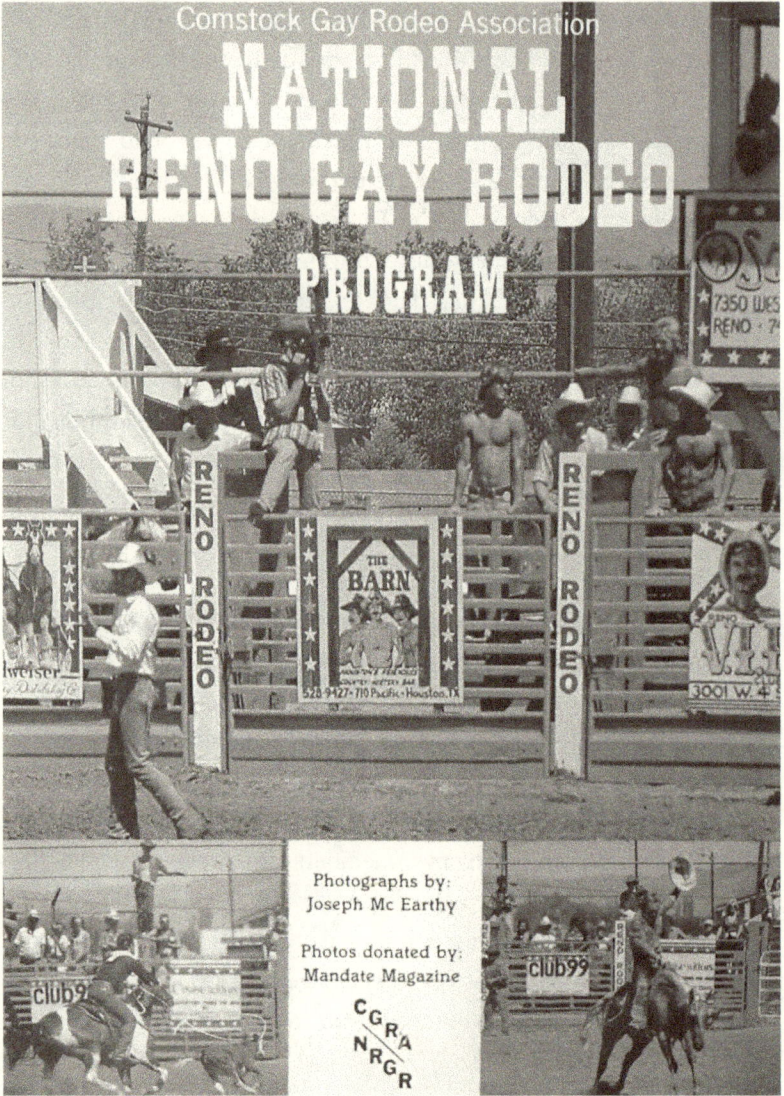

Fig. 7. 1992 and 1993 National Reno Gay Rodeo program cover. Credit to Frank Harrell and the International Gay Rodeo Archives, gayrodeohistory.org.

Comstock Gay Rodeo Association
NATIONAL RENO GAY RODEO
Post Office Box 2372
Reno, Nevada 89505
[702] 677-0742

C
G N
R R
A G
R

Phil Ragsdale                                    Joseph Sedlack
President/Founder                                Vice President

••••••••••••••••••••••• The "ORIGINAL", Founded 1976 •••••••••••••••••••••••

WELCOME, COWBOYS AND COWGIRLS!!
TO THE EIGHTH ANNUAL
NATIONAL RENO GAY RODEO & COUNTRY FAIR

As President and Founder of the COMSTOCK GAY RODEO ASSOCIATION / NATIONAL RENO GAY RODEO & COUNTRY FAIR, I'm pleased to welcome you to this years Eighth Annual NATIONAL RENO GAY RODEO & COUNTRY FAIR. If this is your first visit with us, we hope that you will visit us once again next year. And, if this is your second or more visit, we just want to say Thanks, to you and we always look forward to your return.

The majority of this years rodeo proceeds have been designated to go to the A.I.D.S. Foundation, for research of this disease. As well, as to other "worthwhile" local charities.

We hope that you will share with us, once again, in this years theme, WESTERN GAY PRIDE!! As it can be nothing but productive for all of us! As I stated previously, WESTERN GAY PRIDE by each of us can help to overcome much of the Gay Ignorance some people still have.

The Rodeo and Fair are events where Gay Men, Lesbian Women and Anyone, wanting to get along side of us can come, for a good time. And, possibly, walk away with a greater understanding for each other.

A COUPLE OF WORTHWHILE NOTES; Even though drinking is TOLERATED on the streets, in the downtown area, IT IS AGAINST THE LAW and we advise you to heed any direction you are given, regarding it.
THE LEGAL AGE for drinking and gambling is TWENTY-ONE (21) years of age.
Nevada HAS STRICT LAWS REGARDING ALL DRUGS, so we urge you to take heed.

Due to a "conflict" of dates, next year, with the "OLYMPIC GAMES, to be held in the Los Angeles area, WE are MOVING OUR USUAL DATES, the First Weekend in August, BACK TO MID-JULY. Next years Rodeo dates are JULY 19th, - 22nd, 1984!! (Please, note this on your calendar!)

We hope that your visit to the NATIONAL RENO GAY RODEO & COUNTRY FAIR and RENO, will be most enjoyable. Be sure to stop by the NRGR Souvenir Booth and pick up a souvenir for yourself or/and a friend!

REMEMBER, NEXT YEAR ONLY, JULY 19th, - 22nd, 1984!!

In Western Gay Pride,

*Phil Ragsdale*

Phil Ragsdale
President/ Founder

Fig. 8. "In Western Pride," letter by Phil Ragsdale in the 1993 National Reno Gay Rodeo program. Credit to Frank Harrell and the International Gay Rodeo Archives, gayrodeohistory.org.

documentary. When the Texas Gay Rodeo brought gay cowboys and cowgirls to a nearby Texas town, the family attended the event and met up with Earp. The boy was excited to meet a real-life rodeo cowboy he had seen only on TV; Earp was a sport celebrity to the boy. The boy thanked Earp for being his real-life hero. Overcome with emotion, and tearing up as he told the story, Earp explained, "Never in my life did I think someone would call me their hero."[55]

By 1995, three years after Phil Ragsdale succumbed to AIDS, there were thirty-six gay rodeo chapters representing twenty-seven states, the District of Columbia, and two Canadian provinces. The first gay rodeo in Reno brought pride to the American West and smaller cities throughout the country, as Ragsdale had suggested. As late as 1981, Reno did not have a gay pride parade, "so the Gay Rodeo functioned as their collective letting off of steam."[56] Gay rodeo continues to support the LGBTQ community and provides a family-friendly environment for sports enthusiasts. The IGRA continues to be an organization that helps many LGBTQ people celebrate their identity and their pride in the saddle.

# 5 Riding, Roughstock, and Camp Events

A Rodeo to Call Their Own

> Nick, you take a bag of marbles and each time you 'cover' in steer
> riding, you toss out one marble. Once you've lost all your marbles,
> you're ready to ride a bull.
>
> —John Beck (repeating a joke that many bull riders tell)

When John Beck arrived in Denver in late fall 1981, he only had fourteen dollars, but he found a new family of men and women at a bar named Charlie's, which had a country and western theme. Today, Charlie's Bar continues to provide this rugged aesthetic and appeal to rodeo participants. While it has changed over the years and doubles as a dance club later at night, the bar's iconic disco boot continues to twirl above the center of the dance floor. It was at Charlie's where Beck's rodeo knowledge played a significant role. By the end of the year, the Colorado Gay Rodeo Association (CGRA) had formed, and it became the first gay rodeo association outside of Reno to host a gay rodeo. In November 1981 Beck wrote down all the events, fifteen at that time, that would be part of the first Rocky Mountain Gay Rodeo in 1983.

Gay rodeos award a buckle to the winner of each event for cowboys and each event for cowgirls. Participants compete in the gender with which they identify, and at the end of the competition, the organizers award a buckle to the all-around cowboy and all-around cowgirl. Local businesses, corporations, and individuals sponsor these buckles. When gay rodeo started, it reinforced the mission of the gay liberation movement. Gay rodeo did not follow all the same rules as mainstream rodeo, denying heteronormativity in their sport and creating something of its own. This chapter examines how gay rodeo organizers took the foundation of rodeo competition and created their unique version. The authenticity of gay rodeo and its liberation from the heteronormative social world of sport is demonstrated through the distinctiveness of the events one needs to complete in order to earn the all-around cowboy or all-around cowgirl honor.

Today, to compete in the all-around competition, an athlete must participate in one or more events from at least three of four categories and finish first through eighth in at least two of the categories. Roughstock events include bull riding, steer riding, and chute dogging. Next, there are camp events: steer decorating, the wild drag race, and goat dressing. These events are truly distinctive because of their campiness, and at most gay rodeos these are crowd favorites. Some of these events have a long history with rodeo. In 1929 the Rodeo Association of America (RAA) was formed and listed steer decorating and wild cow milking, events that were listed as camp events in gay rodeo, as official RAA events.[1] John Beck designed and introduced a new event, the wild drag race, based on a dream he had. Participation in a camp event is a requirement for the all-around competition as well. Finally, an athlete contending for the all-around title must compete in at least one of the next two categories—speed events or roping events. Speed events include the barrel race, pole bending, and the flag race. In many mainstream rodeos, the barrel race follows a gender ideology that separates men and women into events "more suited" to each of them and marginalizes women. Barrel racing in mainstream rodeo has traditionally been viewed as a women's speed event. At gay rodeo, men and women compete in the same events, and barrel racing is open to all. Roping events include calf roping on foot, mounted breakaway roping, and team roping (fig. 9).

This chapter considers the following questions: What heteronormative rules did gay rodeo break? How did gay rodeo reinforce the gay liberation movement? What social or political concerns did gay rodeo address? Gay rodeo organizers ignored gendered stereotypes that have long been associated with rodeo events and replaced some events with a category of camp events that allowed the International Gay Rodeo Association (IGRA) to liberate itself from traditional rodeo. Through these changes,

Fig. 9. Women's Pole Bending competitor and IGRA ally Lori Casados at the Rocky Mountain Regional Rodeo, Golden, Colorado, July 2019. Photograph courtesy of Ryan Villanueva.

gay rodeo truly aligned itself with the gay liberation movement of the 1970s. Today, the sporting world in the United States has become political, with heterosexual-identifying Christian men continuing to write the unofficial social rules of sport. Gay rodeo events and rules liberated LGBTQ athletes from the dysfunction of the social world of sport by celebrating inclusion, compassion, courage, and pride. This is not to say that all mainstream rodeos excluded women historically or continue to do this today. Gay rodeo, however, has been inclusive throughout its duration.

## SPEED AND ROPING EVENTS

Many IGRA-sanctioned rodeos hold a rodeo school on the Friday morning before a Saturday and Sunday competition begins. Rodeo school is led by experienced competitors to allow newcomers to learn about beginner events and to give suggestions on how to improve. For the newcomer, rodeo school is the place to go. The cost ranges from twenty to thirty dollars and usually includes an introduction to roping on foot, chute dogging, and camp events. It is a great way to meet new people and try a new sport.

To begin, speed and roping events show off the skills many cowboys and cowgirls have developed through years on the ranch, but even a novice has an opportunity to compete in these categories. These events also reveal the uniqueness of gay rodeo regarding the rules of competition. The IGRA provides full transparency with respect to the decision-making process at its annual convention, and the association has eliminated events for safety reasons, and has altered events for animal welfare. There are currently three roping events: calf roping on foot, mounted breakaway roping, and team roping. Calf roping on foot is an excellent start for gay rodeo beginners. The newcomer can find their way into the gay rodeo family by participating in this introductory-level event without the added expense of having to own a competitive horse, which can cost more than $10,000. All these events begin with a contestant in the roping box. An imaginary start line runs across the front of the roping box and the chute where the calf or steer is held. Should the contestant cross this line, called the barrier, before the calf or steer clears the chute, a 10-second penalty shall be assessed and added to the time.[2]

*The Advocate*, a magazine founded in 1967, addresses critical social issues impacting the LGBTQ community. First published in Los Angeles by the activist group Personal Rights in Defense and Education (PRIDE), the magazine was a response to police raids on gay bars and police brutality toward gay men. In 1974, under the ownership of David Goodstein, *The Advocate* came to fruition and was the first nationally sold LGBTQ magazine.[3] Ads for *The Advocate* appeared in rodeo programs across the country. Liz Galst published an article about gay rodeo in the July 27, 1993, issue titled "Sacred Cows," focused on animal rights at the rodeo. Galst interviewed IGRA officials as well as animal rights activists. Tracy Reiman, head of the Gay and Lesbian Animal Rights Caucus of People for the Ethical Treatment of Animals (PETA), likened gay rodeo promoters to the forces which were responsible for the oppression of gay men and lesbians. Reiman went on to say, "It glorifies a time when violence against women, ethnic minorities, and gays was accepted. The way I think about it, human domination over animals is the same as human domination over other people. It's appalling."[4] Readers had to critically think about Reiman's assertion about gay rodeo and the social history of marginalization and abuse, forcing them to reevaluate their conception of rodeo.

"Sacred Cows" addressed these claims with IGRA organizers, and what Galst found was that the IGRA and professional rodeo diverged on some of the concerns raised by PETA. Jonny Van Orman, chairperson of the IGRA's chute coordinators committee, was quick to respond: "A good portion of the people who are against gay rodeos don't even know what they're protesting."[5] Orman explained that gay rodeo organizers have either altered or eliminated some events because of concern for the safety of the animals:

Tie-down calf roping, in which a calf is lassoed by a contestant on horseback, yanked off its feet, thrown to the ground, and tied up, had been replaced by breakaway calf roping. In breakaway roping, the lasso is loosely tethered by a string to the contestant's saddle horn, and when the calf pulls against the rope, the tether comes undone. Also, instead of bulldogging—chasing a steer on horseback, jumping off, and wrestling it to the ground by twisting its head and neck until the steer flips over—IGRA contestants participate in chute dogging. In this event, the contestant begins the event standing beside the steer and then wrestles it to the ground.[6]

Readers learned about the IGRA's effort to make the rodeo safe for humans and animals, but there is little that can be done to avoid a six-hundred-pound steer falling on top of a rodeo contestant in chute dogging.

From the range to the arena, calf roping is the oldest rodeo event, arising from the need for cowboys to do "doctoring" on the range and handle roping duties during branding. A timed mounted breakaway roping is a contest between a quick, agile calf and a skilled roper mounted on a lightning-fast, highly trained horse. The calf leaving the chute will trip the barrier line, signaling the roper and horse to leave the box in rapid pursuit. Should rider and horse "break" early and cross the barrier line before it is tripped, a ten-second penalty is added to the contestant's time. The cowboy or cowgirl then ropes the calf, which usually falls to the ground when hitting the end of the twenty-five-foot lariat. In gay rodeo, contestants use a breakaway rope, and the athletes do not follow the traditional rules that require them to dismount from their horse, then tie three of the calf's legs together with a "piggin string," simultaneously throwing their arms up to signal for time. For a beginner competing in the calf roping on foot event, riding is not required. The contestant stands in the roping box, waiting for the release of the calf, and then attempts the maneuver mentioned earlier, but on foot.

As an event, team roping had its origins on the ranch when it became necessary to "doctor" stock on the open range. In this event, two contestants work as a team to rope and stretch a steer jointly in the fastest possible time. The "header" leaves the box first, after the barrier line has been broken, and drops their loop over the steer's horns while turning the steer away from their partner, the "heeler." The heeler then throws their rope to catch both back legs, and then each rider pulls their line taut, and time is called. With hours of practicing to perfect their timing, competitive team ropers are exciting to watch as they and their skilled mounts compete for these catches in a matter of a few seconds. The barrier-break time penalty of ten seconds is in effect should the header break out of the box before the breaker line is broken. The heeler can also incur a five-second penalty for the team should they catch only one rear leg in their loop. A successful team rope ends with both ropers on horseback facing the steer, pulling their ropes taut. Team roping is only for skilled ropers and horses because the risk of injury is high, and hazards include "collisions, entanglements, and worst of all, possible loss of fingers."[7]

Along with calf roping, saddle bronc riding rates as one of rodeo's oldest events. The ability of a cowboy to "stay with" a stout, unbroken range colt is a point of pride with any "real hand" in an outfit. Today's rodeo cowboy or cowgirl climbs aboard a regulation bucking saddle, grabs a six-foot halter rope, and takes an eight-second ride on a horse bred specifically for his ability to buck. Fifty points are awarded for both

Riding, Roughstock, and Camp Events

the horse and the rider. However, for the rider, the judges are looking more for style, balance, and cadence than in other roughstock events. In a top ride, the contestant's spurring action should be in full time with the bucking motion of the horse. Once again, disqualifications for this event are a "buck off" before the eight-second whistle, or the cowboy or cowgirl touching the horse, the equipment, or themselves with their free hand.

Over the past forty-plus years of gay rodeo, events have been added, eliminated, and altered for the safety of all involved. Animal safety is just as crucial to IGRA members as the safety of the contestants. Statements about animal welfare are included in many of the IGRA regional and finals programs. The earliest published statement on this topic in a rodeo program was in the 1994 IGRA Finals program.

The International Gay Rodeo Association imposes specific rules, which are strictly enforced, and penalizes any contestant found to be guilty of inhumane treatment of animals, the least of which is their immediate disqualification from further competition. Gay rodeos operate under greatly modified rules of straight rodeo while still preserving this American tradition. . . . IGRA bylaws are public record and include numerous rules which strongly protect animals from abuse, including passages that prohibit the use of lame, sore, sick, or undersized stock; mandate the availability for veterinary care; prohibit the beating or cruel prodding of animals; direct the release of any animal from competition that appears in danger of injuring itself; and forbid the use of metal or fiberglass rigging, any equipment judged to be too tight, or the concealed use of caustic ointments or burrs.[8]

Regional chapters posted similar messages in the following years.

Gay rodeo historian Frank Harrell explained that each year at the IGRA convention, all IGRA members are welcome to express concerns and address the rules and rule changes. Professional mainstream rodeo is not as inviting or transparent. IGRA rodeo programs address concerns people have about animal safety and welfare. IGRA includes strict guidelines in their contracts about the use of healthy animals and has penalized stock organizations for violating any of the rules. Harrell recalled inviting rodeo protestors into the arena to see exactly what they were calling abuse, because he believed they were calling to shut down something they had never witnessed. Harrell even explained how humanely IGRA members treated those who had protested their rodeo. One blazing hot summer day in Florida, the American Veterans Association protested an IGRA rodeo in Fort Lauderdale, and Harrell's husband, Tom, approached the group with bottles of cold water, concerned for their well-being, further illustrating the group's concern for safety.[9] IGRA bylaws are public record, and any person or organization can access this information.

Safety of the men and women in rough stock events was a major concern in both mainstream rodeo and gay rodeo. High impact, high intensity sports inevitably have a higher occurrence of head injuries that result in concussions. Rodeo is a sport with a high incidence of injuries, yet this is underrepresented in the literature on concussions. Scholars Alissa Wicklund, Shayla Foster, and Ashley Roy contend several factors explain why concussions in rodeo are underreported and education for these athletes is lacking. They argue that elements include: "the solo nature of the sport, a lack of consistent access to or follow-up with health care professionals, and a culture that encourages a swift return to competition," and, "the compensatory structure of rodeo encourages participation despite injury and contributes to the underreporting of symptoms, given that missing an event means forfeiting entry fees as well as potential earnings."[10] Clinical evidence provided by these scholars helps explain why research on concussions and rodeo athletes is limited, and mainstream rodeo and the Professional Bull Riding Association need to catch up with organizations like the National Football League (NFL) to keep athletes safe.

Bull rider Ty Pozzobon remembered little from one day in November 2014, when he was unconscious for twenty-seven minutes following a "ride-gone-wrong," as bull riders call it. The eight-second ride, now immortalized in a YouTube video, ended with Pozzobon on the ground seconds before a two-ton bull landed on and split open his protective helmet. With the helmet now off, a second hoof came crashing down on his skull. His wife, Jayd, explained that he continued to ride after his initial recovery. In 2016 he finished fourth in the world and was named the Bull Riding Canadian Champion, but after additional head injuries and over a dozen concussions, Pozzobon went "down the path to depression, rage, separation from family, and eventually suicide."[11] In a February 2019 article for News Four San Antonio, a representative for the PBR answered a reporter's safety questions regarding head injuries. When asked whether the PBR was taking steps to help mitigate head injuries, like the NFL, the representative gave vague responses. They mentioned working with the new Western Sports Foundations, and that they had "[access to] general safety awareness and education for PBR athletes."[12] Finally, when asked about what they were doing to educate future bull riders, the representative responded: "PBR has held such clinics in the past in which seasoned veterans and current riders teach youngsters and athletes who wish to become bull riders, the basics of riding. There are none planned for the immediate future but hope to have several by year's end." This response demonstrates that the PBR does not recognize Chronic Traumatic Encephalopathy (CTE) with the same urgency as the NFL.

IGRA athletes encounter similar dangers of injuries and long-term effects that CTE can bring. In 2000 the IGRA Health and Safety Committee convened and published its first rodeo health and safety newsletter. It was titled "Horse Sense," and the first topic addressed was head injuries.[13] "Head Injury Study Gives Sound Guidance," by Brian Helander, explained that recent studies indicated that an athlete who suffered two consecutive concussions within forty-eight hours would "run a great risk of sudden death."[14] Helander, a health care provider, was abreast of the trauma football players had experienced in recent years in the NCAA. His article provided athletes with guidelines to help them decide about participating on the second day after a severe head injury on day one. Once again, the IGRA was ahead of many other national and international sporting organizations regarding topics largely unaddressed by mainstream sports until the 2010s. Chapter four revealed that the IGRA recognized and permitted transgender athletes to compete as the gender with which they identify, and the IGRA urged injured rodeo athletes to consider their grade of concussion and recommended treatment and contemplate when it is safe to return to competition after a severe head injury. This visible concern about head injuries did not become commonplace in the NFL until after 4,500 former players brought on a lawsuit that claimed league executives knew for decades that concussions could lead to long-term neurological problems and death but did little to prevent players from returning after the appearance of a major head injury. The NFL settled with the players, in 2013, for $765 million. Shortly thereafter, the NCAA took on a highly visible concern for players' cognitive safety as well.[15]

"Speed and agility are two highly prized qualities in these contestants' horses. The three Speed Events pit the horse, under the skillful hand of its rider, against the clock."[16] A running start is permitted, as the rider and horse demonstrate the rider's skill and the horse's speed and agility. First, there is barrel racing, in which contestants and horses run a three-point cloverleaf pattern around three barrels and vie for the fastest time. Time starts and ends on crossing a visible line, and a five-second penalty is assessed for knocking over a barrel. Disqualification takes place if the team goes off course. The pattern can be started to the right or the left. Pole bending is another event on horseback in which contestants vie for the fastest time while traversing a linear set of poles spaced twenty-one feet apart. Finally, flag racing is an event in which rider and horse run a modified triangular pattern around three spaced barrels; the rider picks up a flag at the first barrel and deposits it at the third barrel. Rolling a barrel results in a five-second penalty, and a rider is disqualified if the flag is not picked up at the first barrel or misses the bucket on the third barrel. In the speed events, horse and rider compete as a team.

## ROUGHSTOCK

"Mounted on top or standing beside an animal many times their size and weight, it's contestant against beast."[17] Roughstock events are designed to test an athlete's ability to outbalance or outmaneuver an animal's instinct to escape a situation or rid itself of an unusual weight or object. These events further prove that gay rodeo is unique in the social world of sport and is all-inclusive. Once again, men and women compete in all the same events, challenging a gender ideology that exists in other sports. In mainstream rodeo, historically, some events were designated for women and others for men. During the early twentieth century, women began competing in rodeo, and by the 1920s it was not unusual to see women competing in roughstock. During the Great Depression, however, women's participation declined as women became increasingly marginalized. In addition to the Depression leading to the demise in participation, "the death of a famous rodeo queen" had rodeo organizers share a "common concern for the proper role for women."[18] Throughout the existence of gay rodeo, and specifically the IGRA, women have not had to fight marginalization to participate. Moreover, during financial setbacks, member associations have canceled entire rodeos, rather than eliminate women's events, which was the case during World War II, when sporting organizations promoted women's events.[19]

As women's participation in sport increased during the latter half of the twentieth century, so too did the backlash by men in the male-dominated social world of sport. Sport has long followed a gender ideology that has marginalized women and reinforced male positions of power when challenged. Sport sociologist Jay Coakley argues that gender ideology in sport incorporates the systemic belief that women are inferior to men and that "heterosexuality is nature's foundation. . . . Other expressions of sexual feelings, thoughts, and actions are abnormal, deviant, or immoral," thus marginalizing women and gay men in sport and society.[20] The marginalization of women in sport continues today and has created a disparity in economic opportunities.

Sport in the latter half of the twentieth century functioned in a heteronormative space. Gay athletes, coaches, and officials lived in a "don't ask, don't tell" social world, and coming out of the closet happened after their playing careers. Phrases like "man up" and "you throw like a girl" were, and in some regions of the country still are, commonly heard. Such expressions are dangerous in sport and society because they reinforce a gender ideology that places men and masculinity as superior and women as lesser subjects. Heterosexual-identifying women and girls in sports understand that there is a balancing act between being tough in competition, "like one of the guys," and being appropriately feminine, avoiding being too "butch."

Bareback bronc riding is an "arena-bred" event that pits a cowboy or cowgirl against 1,100 pounds or more of muscle and anger for an eight-second ride. The bucking horse carries a "rigging" with a single handhold, and the rider bears down without the benefit of reins, saddle, or stirrups. As in all roughstock events, judges evaluate the rider and the horse. Up to 50 points each can be awarded to the horse and the rider, for a total of 100 points. The bucking horse is given points for his power and bucking pattern, while the rider receives points for their strength, form, and spurring action. Disqualifications for this event are a "buck off" before the eight-second whistle, or if the cowboy or cowgirl touches the horse, equipment, or themselves with their free hand. Beginning in 2017, ranch saddle bronc riding, also known as ranch bronc riding, was introduced as an alternative, optional event to bareback bronc riding, which was eliminated for safety reasons.

Chute dogging, or steer wrestling, is another "arena-born" event, in which the contestant wrestles a five-hundred-pound-plus horned steer to the ground against a clock—the fastest time takes the money. As the steer leaves the chute, he trips a barrier line, which tells the contestant to leave the box.[21] Described by Frank Harrell as an event for the roughstock novice, chute dogging provides a gay rodeo beginner with an event that tests their strength. The steer and contestant start in the chute. Once the contestant leaves the box, they have sixty seconds to drag the steer to a line ten feet from the chute and attempt to wrestle the animal to the ground. Harrell explained, "In this event either the contestant 'dogs' or gets 'dogged.'"[22]

Newcomer Bruce Casey entered his first roughstock event on a dare. Casey competed in chute dogging and finished third with zero practice, although he does not recommend this approach. On day one, Casey broke five bones, including a fracture in his leg, and tore his bicep, "and of course, I sought no medical attention and continued to compete with my injuries."[23] Never having broken a bone in his life, Casey said that he was stubborn and competed both days for the chute dogging buckle.

It would be three months later, when visiting his doctor for something unrelated, that X-rays confirmed the injuries.

One of rodeo's most dangerous events, bull riding, is also the most exciting, and one of spectators' favorite events. Bull riding has the added factor of danger, because the competitor is swinging their leg over an unpredictable bull that may decide to come looking for them after they complete their ride. Erratic and violent in their twists and leaps, these bulls require the stoutest of cowboys and cowgirls to stay with them until the seven-second whistle is blown (eight seconds in professional bull riding). If the athlete meets or exceeds the time limit, they have officially "covered." As in all roughstock events, the rider holds on with only one hand, and if they touch the bull or themself with their free hand, or if they "buck off," they are disqualified. In this event, the rider maintains their position by hanging on, with a leather-gloved hand, to a heavy rope that encircles the bull. The points system is like that of other roughstock riding events: 50 points awarded for the bull's power and his bucking pattern, and 50 points to the rider for their form, control, and spurring action. The final score, from 100 available points, is determined by two judges. Unlike some mainstream rodeos in the United States, bull riding is open to women. Sherry Puls leads the women with three IGRA finals championship buckles in her bull riding career (1993, 1994, 2004), followed by Candy Bell (1992, 1999) and Vanessa Hodgson (2007, 2008), who are tied with two each.

Gay rodeo is not without its tragedies, and the deaths of two bull riders led to rule changes to ensure rider safety. Steer riding and bull riding are two of the more dangerous events in the sport of rodeo. On October 2, 1999, Dean John Berkan, age thirty-six, of Sacramento, was fatally injured at the Atlantic Stampede Rodeo in Gaithersburg, Maryland. Berkan was in the chute, preparing to make his first steer ride in an IGRA rodeo. Wes Givens of the Diamond State Rodeo Association remembered the day and had this to say in a Facebook post twenty years later, with a photo of Berkan (fig. 10): "Twenty years' yesterday, October 2, 1999, I watched this man die before my eyes, his brown eyes looking into mine for help. Dean was getting ready to ride a steer. A freak accident and a

Fig. 10. IGRA statement in memoriam Dean John Berkan. Credit to Frank Harrell and the International Gay Rodeo Association Archives, gayrodeohistory.org.

tip horn with a spur, and he was gone. I remember Brian Helander doing everything to save him. Chuck Browning was helping too. Chuck was in the next chute, and Brian was helping him get ready. . . . We can't bring Dean back, but we can make sure people remember him, and he isn't forgotten."[24] Givens explained that many chute rules and safety rules were changed or newly implemented because of Berkan's death. Gay rodeo and gay pride festivals provided a safe place for the LGBTQ community to celebrate their identity, but there is the reality that the rodeo presents many dangers other than homophobia and transphobia.

An alternative to bull riding is steer riding. The rules are similar; the main difference is that the rider mounts a steer—a castrated bull. Riders are advised to attempt steer riding before working their way to bull riding. However, the event can be just as dangerous. I attended rodeos, both gay and mainstream, in the late 1990s and throughout the first decade of the twenty-first century. However, it was while researching this book that I had the opportunity to be close to athletes and animals, and even stand over the chute before a ride. In Santa Fe, I witnessed a cowboy being stepped on by a bull. I asked a cowboy sitting near me a question: "How does a rider know he is ready to move from steer riding to bull riding?" He looked at me and must have noticed that I needed a light-hearted response after what I had just witnessed, and he said: "Nick, you take a bag of marbles and each time you 'cover' in steer riding, you toss out one marble. Once you've lost all of your marbles, you're ready to ride a bull."[25] After a short pause, we both broke out laughing. I was looking for something much more systematic and sophisticated, but this is a rodeo family. At that moment, the man knew that I needed some rodeo humor.

The International Gay Rodeo Association hosts rodeo competitions around the world and is open to any gender identity or sexual orientation. Men and women have the opportunity to compete in all the same events. Some mainstream rodeos have prohibited women from competing in events that have traditionally been reserved for men. The IGRA has attempted to break stereotypes of the LGBTQ community as well as gendered rules in sports by adhering to four main principles:

- Both men and women, regardless of orientation, ride the same roughstock livestock under the same rules and requirements. Unlike most other rodeo organizations, in IGRA, both men and women alike fully compete in bull riding and bronc riding.
- In IGRA team events . . . men and women can create teams of any combination of gender that they desire.
- In the Wild Drag Race, we celebrate the contributions of 'drag' by incorporating fundamentals of female impersonation into a dangerous rough and tumble event that brings together a woman, a man, and person of either gender in drag.
- IGRA has a diverse leadership group . . . rodeo directors, arena crews, scorekeepers, judges, trustees, chute crew, announcers, and support.[26]

Gay rodeo is about inclusion, and the IGRA celebrates the diversity of not only the LGBTQ community but race, age, country of origin, and ability.

## CAMP

From Tim Curry's performance in women's lingerie in *The Rocky Horror Picture Show* (1975) to Faye Dunaway's performance as Joan Crawford in *Mommie Dearest* (1981), camp developed into a significant artistic genre in the 1970s and 1980s. Many of these films are now cult classics, with each subsequent generation indoctrinated with their midnight viewing of *The Rocky Horror Picture Show* in cities around the world. Some camp movies have been nominated for Golden Raspberry awards, the Oscar-alternative prize for the worst film of the year. In 1981 two films earned this recognition: *Xanadu* and *Can't Stop the Music*. The latter, marketed to a gay audience, is "loosely based on the story of the Village People, a disco band created to wink hard at the dance genre's built-in gay audience . . . with gay 'Macho Man' fantasy stereotypes."[27] As Susan Sontag wrote in her 1964 essay "Notes on 'Camp,'" "The essence of Camp is its love of the unnatural: of artifice and exaggeration. And camp is esoteric—something of a private code, a badge of identity even, among small urban cliques."[28] Literary critics argue, however, that queerness is missing from her essay. Sontag made a bold claim that someone else would have invented camp "if homosexuals hadn't more or less" done it already.[29] However, linguist Chi Luu responded in 2018, "Would they have? I wonder. What other subculture would have the drive and the expressive urgency to develop something as frivolously influential as Camp?"[30] Camp is alive and well at gay rodeo; you can't have gay rodeo without camp.

Gay rodeo is unique for many reasons, but camp events are audience favorites and welcome newcomers into the sport of rodeo. Mainstream rodeo includes camp for spectator enjoyment, but camp events are required for the All-Around Cowboy and Cowgirl awards. Another uniqueness about gay rodeo and camp is that newcomers who would like to learn rodeo events begin with camp events. The IGRA claims that 60 percent of gay rodeo contestants enter gay rodeo as competitors this way, and for some their only championship buckle is from Wild Drag Race, Goat Dressing, or Steer Deco. How did these become sporting events? Anything can happen when you get a group of cowhands together for a good time. "Cowhands generally have their own definition of fun and challenge. After a few beers and some serious ego pumping, it is amazing what a group of hands can come up with! Prerequisites for participation are a willingness to eat dirt and the ability to hold your own with an ornery steer or goat."[31] Gay rodeo organizers urge anyone interested in trying out rodeo to come to gay rodeo and sign up for rodeo school.

Goat dressing is a two-person event in which the team races to a goat and dresses the animal in men's white briefs. The team member without the underwear picks up the goat's rear hooves, grabs the underwear from around the other member's arms, and pulls it up the legs of the goat. Both team members must then race back to the start/finish line and cross the finish line to stop the time. In the event one athlete falls, the timer continues until both contestants cross the line.

Another event, this one with a bit more potential for injury, is steer deco (steer decorating). Deco is a two-person team event. One team member holds one end of a twenty-five-foot rope tied to a steer's horns. The other team member waits forty feet away from the chute holding a ribbon. When the chute gate opens, the athlete holding the rope attempts to pull the steer out of the chute and across a white line ten feet from the chute gate. Once that happens, the member holding the ribbon tries to tie the ribbon around the steer's tail while the other member works to remove the ropes from the animal's horns. After tying the ribbon, that contestant must tag the timer near the chute, but only after the steer's horns are successfully untied.

Finally, there is another fan-favorite event known as wild drag, truly the campiest of all the events. Dreamed up by John Beck, wild drag has become popular at all IGRA rodeos. Wild drag is not only a departure from mainstream rodeo in its campiness, but it is special in that the team includes both men and women. A team is required to have one man, one woman, and one drag, either a man or a woman. The woman holds a twenty-five-foot rope attached to the horns of a steer waiting in a chute. The man and the drag stand forty feet from the chute. When the gate opens, the team works at pulling or harassing the steer across a white line seventy feet from the chute. The drag then mounts the steer and attempts to ride the animal until all four of its feet cross the finish line. "The drag costumes come from Goodwill stores, from second-hand stores, and many from raiding mom's closet."[32]

The wild drag race does have its risks, yet it is an opportunity for a beginner to test their skill, no matter what their age. At the Show-Me State Rodeo in Kansas City, Missouri, sixty-two-year-old Momma Linda stole the show in the wild drag race event. Momma Linda is the mother of a gay rodeo contestant who was not in attendance that day. She said that she had always wanted to try a rodeo event like the wild drag race. She attended rodeos to watch her son compete, and sometimes she went on her own because she enjoyed the atmosphere and the rodeo family, which had embraced her. Unknown to her son, Momma Linda entered the wild drag on Saturday, September 2, 2017. Her partners in the event were concerned about her safety, as well as their own safety from her son if anything bad happened to her. Wes Givens, Chad Kaiser, and about twenty other people helped Momma Linda prepare for the event, sharing equipment such as a helmet and providing advice about technique. As the trio's turn approached, Givens remembered that someone said, "Damn! It's too bad we don't have a mouth guard to use [to protect her teeth]."[33] Immediately, Momma Linda reached into her mouth, pulled out both sets of dentures, and handed them to one of the cowboys. Momma Linda became a rodeo cowgirl that day and proved that one is never too old to try gay rodeo.[34]

Some rural communities dismissed gay rodeo as not being authentic. Celeste McGovern wrote a story for the *Alberta Report* that focused specifically on the camp aspects of gay rodeo. However, McGovern ended up writing a story based on her own preconceived notions. Interviewees had hoped that she would produce a story that would allow "society at large to see us as a normal group of people."[35] However, she focused more on men kissing men and contestant Tim Haskin's Miss Firecracker persona, while omitting female bull riders from her story. LGBTQ interviewees were quoted as saying: "We're all a bunch of freaks, anyway."[36] Moreover, McGovern interviewed a well-known "straight" professional rodeo cowboy, Craig Butterfield. When asked for his opinion about gay rodeo, Butterfield replied: "Probably what I got to say you wouldn't want to print in your magazine. I think it's a pile of bullshit."[37]

Shelagh Anderson wrote a response to McGovern's article for *Roundup* in which she interrogates Butterfield's opposition to gay rodeo because he claimed that it mocked professional rodeo with its campiness. Anderson argues that rural Canadians held traditional rodeos that featured their own unique events such as "chariot races, bed races, [and] women's tractor rodeos," and questions whether such nonserious events were not also mocking Butterfield's professional rodeo.[38] She goes on to argue that gay rodeo is necessary for the LGBTQ community, that it helps them alleviate the daily pressures of being LGBTQ, and that it is a place to have fun without fear that some disapproving local might hit them in the head with a horseshoe. The article also points out that a variation of steer decorating can be traced back to the early days of traditional rodeo. Anderson concludes: "Why should there even be an issue when we wish to dress our goats in jockey shorts? Maybe it's because . . . they would rather be in boxers."[39]

Camp at gay rodeo is fun, but it also celebrates individuality and the rejection of heteronormative social rules in the sport of rodeo. It embodies gay liberation, which was a powerful message for the community in the late 1970s and 1980s. Camp encouraged a gay liberation ideology "that called for open, prideful display of . . . sexual identity."[40] Gay rodeo participants were no longer willing to compete in the male hegemonic sport of rodeo following heterosexual rules. Here, at gay rodeo, the marches and protests of the early gay liberation movement survive through the performance of and participation in camp events. Camp is a protest against normative rules in society. Applying Bruce's argument about pride festivals, one could say that camp is an expression that defies these rules "by turning up the volume" as well.[41] At IGRA rodeos, queer identity is celebrated as part of its heritage, and camp events are liberating activities. Camp events increase inclusion and, for newcomers, do not require exceptional skills to participate.

## CONCLUSION

At the end of a two-day rodeo, judges tally up the scores and award ribbons and prize money to finalists, as well as the championship buckle for each event. The buckles are designed by the rodeo chapter holding the event, and it is the coveted prize that each cowboy and cowgirl strives for. At each event, contestants who compete in at least three of four categories—speed, riding, roughstock, and camp—are eligible to receive the weekend's highest honor of All-Around Cowboy and Cowgirl. Two of the longest-running continuous competitors, Candy Pratt and John Beck, have combined for countless buckles. Throughout the rodeo season, contestants accumulate points for their successful cover of each event. These points help determine who qualifies for the IGRA finals. And, just as with the regional rodeos, there is an All-Around Cowboy and Cowgirl named each year at finals.

In addition to All-Around Cowboy and Cowgirl, the IGRA awards a rookie of the year buckle to the top-performing newcomer. But be careful if you are interested in gay rodeo; if you compete in just one event, no matter when during the year, that year counts as your rookie season. Bruce Casey learned that the hard way, stating that his biggest regret was that he tried his luck at the final regional rodeo the year before he took up competing on a regular basis: "I competed in one rodeo (the last one) my first year, which disqualified me from the rookie buckle the next year, which I would have won in spades."[42] Casey might not have officially won the title, but he was warmly welcomed into the gay rodeo family nevertheless.

Gay rodeo events are different from those of other rodeos. The inclusive atmosphere brings in contestants who do not identify as LGBTQ as well. Matt Story can attest to this. Story, who identifies as a cisgender, heterosexual man, competes in the gay rodeo circuit. Story appreciates the concerns for animal and participant safety. He described a dangerous situation that arose during a traditional amateur rodeo in which he was competing. The bull selected for him was a "ranked" bull, meaning that the animal participated in the professional circuit and, thus, was unsafe for riders in the amateur division. Story appreciates the strict adherence to the rules and the comradery at the gay rodeo.[43] The bonding that occurs at the gay rodeo is far greater than at its mainstream counterpart. At the latter, men and women don't often share horses or protective gear, but at the Rocky Mountain Regional Rodeo, observers will find athletes like Story helping a novice steer rider with his grips and balance before he

Riding, Roughstock, and Camp Events

Fig. 11. Final words of advice, Pawel Orlinski (left) and Matt Story (right), before the bull riding event at the Rocky Mountain Regional Rodeo, Golden, Colorado, July 2019. Photograph courtesy of Ryan Villanueva.

enters the chute (fig. 11). The new competitor had learned about gay rodeo from friends of his in Rapid City, South Dakota. He arrived at his first gay rodeo with roping experience, and, with help from Story, he entered bull riding for the first time. He appreciated the support and attention he received and commented that people did not pass judgment at gay rodeo—they seemed to love one another. The new rider explained, "All of these people gave me advice before I sat on the bull. The guys calmed me down. Guys don't even talk to each other in mainstream team roping."[44] This has held true throughout the forty-four-year history of gay rodeo. In a 1978 article in *In Touch for Men*, Bill Arsenaux reported: "It is standard procedure on the circuit to pick your best events and, if you don't have a mount with you, to arrange to borrow one, splitting any prize money won in the event. You never borrow another's rope."[45]

Gay rodeo altered some events and eliminated others for the safety of animals and participants alike. Gay rodeo athletes, organizers, judges, and fans have made the rodeo undeniably their own by rejecting sporting practices and gendered ideologies that are not in the best interest of all athletes. Because they have dismissed the heteronormative practices of mainstream rodeo, a gay rodeo is an inclusive place for men, women, and gender-nonconforming athletes to compete in their genuine skin— how they identify. Finally, through camp events, IGRA athletes exercise their freedom from the heteronormative rules associated with the sport and demonstrate that sport can be pure. The message projected by gay rodeo is that this sport is a celebration of inclusion, compassion, courage, and pride.

# 6 Masculine Capital

## Gay Rodeo Cowboy Identity

What is most beautiful in men is something feminine; what is most beautiful in feminine women is something masculine. . . . Allied to the Camp taste for the androgynous is something that seems quite different but isn't: a relish for the exaggeration of sexual characteristics and personality mannerism.

—Susan Sontag

Sociologist D'Lane R. Compton has explained that "the gay rodeo is an example of how an excluded population is able to dismantle social constructs—or social fictions—by deconstructing the event's association with hegemonic systems of discourses and symbols as they appear in mainstream rodeos. . . . When non-heterosexual individuals rodeo, they create a new space that is challenging and disruptive to the system; an action becomes a form of performance politics whether intended or not."[1] The previous chapters have articulated how the LGBTQ community created a space that disrupted the hegemony that existed in rodeo, and that much of the performance politics was intended. This chapter examines what Compton refers to as "social fictions" of rodeo, specifically the construction, or fiction, of masculinity. The concurrence of gay rodeo's popularity with the progress of the gay liberation movement has brought gay men out of the closet and into society as men who love other men and the rodeo.

This chapter considers that the construction of masculinity requires a cultural capital known as masculine capital. These men do not disavow gay liberation with the appearance of conformity to heteronormativity and the rodeo cowboy image. Some of these men have arrived at gay rodeo with a wealth of masculine capital, demonstrating that they have already established their identities without the need of heterosexual male approval. Society does not define what is masculine for gay cowboys; gay rodeo men construct this on their own. Sociologist Martin Levine writes that gay men in the 1970s claimed masculinity by dressing in working-class attire. He explains: "Traditional masculine themes were heartily embraced—in part as a new kind of camp . . . and in part as a vigorous assertion of a newfound, and passionately embraced successful masculinity."[2] This "Marlboro Man" became a gay clone in gay male enclaves of major cities across the United States. Michael Kimmel explains that the gay liberation movement made a counterclaim about heteronormative masculinity, "that gay men were as much 'real' men as straight men . . . the clone looked more like a 'real man' than most straight men," because of their hypermasculine appearance, dressed in blue jeans and leather with a mustache and short hair.[3] The gay clone often identifies with a look or mannerism found in pop culture. This was not the case with gay rodeo men. They created gay rodeo so that they could be their true selves. If they ventured into the city to meet other gay men, they ended up in bars with disco music and consequently felt like strangers in a strange land. At the gay rodeo, they were strictly cowboys.

During the early 1980s, the term "straight-acting" emerged to describe gay men who appeared "straight," the word "acting" suggesting gender performativity. If that were true, and masculine capital might be obtained through roughstock events like bull riding, then gay rodeo men were performing for "straight" male approval. This could not be further from the truth. These men did not risk their health and safety on a two-ton animal for "straight" male approbation. This chapter considers the proposition that these cowboys were not seeking approval from society by emulating what appeared to be masculine, such as playing a sport, having a rugged physique, and living a country life. They had developed their own masculine identities from their environments long before many of them knew or accepted that they were gay. I contend that gay rodeo cowboys at this time typified masculine identity. They did not have to learn how to two-step to follow the urban cowboy trend of the 1980s; they had two-stepped as adolescents. "Cowboy" became synonymous with "masculine" through early twentieth-century novels, midcentury Western films, and late-century popular music. If society equated "cowboy" with "masculine" in the 1980s, gay rodeo cowboys were truly authentic.

This chapter examines the complexity of masculinity and men of gay rodeo. I draw upon theories by sociologist Eric Anderson regarding masculine capital, in which cultural capital such as an All-Around Cowboy buckle or a championship buckle for bull riding increases one's masculine worth. Sociologist Jay Coakey, researching gender ideology, argues that "heterosexuality" is widely perceived as the most authentic form of relationships. And D'Lane R. Compton recognizes that language provides legitimacy or, indeed, delegitimizes identity through marking, such as the use of a term like "gay" rodeo. Such a qualification serves to render an activity less authentic, like gender marking in other sports—the Women's National Basketball Association versus the National Basketball Association, for instance. Compton asserts: "Heteronormative America associates cowboys with heterosexuality and this would make a 'gay cowboy' seem 'unnatural' and less real."[4]

The cowboys discussed in this chapter are mostly founding members of gay rodeos, and I focus on the late 1970s through the 1980s. By the 1990s gay rodeo had spread across the country and to major cities. That is not to say that these rodeos failed to produce genuine cowboys, but the popularity of country music and the intrigue surrounding gay rodeo brought many newcomers from urban America. Thus, the men and women discussed in chapter three, who wanted to dress the part while the rodeo was in town, are not the focus of this chapter. As stated previously, gay rodeo provided the LGBTQ community with a safe place to openly compete without the fear of encountering homophobia. This chapter maintains that gay rodeo gave these men an opportunity to break down social stereotypes about gay men by performing as their authentic selves—as cowboys.

The most successful way to demonstrate masculinity is to accumulate masculine capital. "Capital" is a term used to explain degrees of wealth or net worth. The more capital one has, such as property, luxury goods, or financial investments, the wealthier one might be. According to Eric Anderson, similar principles can be found in sport. The cultural characteristics of masculine capital are items or identifying features that increase one's masculine wealth.[5] Who has more masculine wealth on an American football team, a kicker or an offensive lineman? If you answered offensive lineman, you understand masculine capital. Identities that develop over time are socially constructed. A kicker might weigh 100–150 pounds less than an offensive lineman; thus, size matters. These linemen are part of a group of players tasked with protecting the quarterback; thus, being an active group member is important. Additionally, the word "offensive" indicates that the person is aggressive, possibly dominant. An offensive player can earn more masculine capital with each scoring play, reinforced by replays on the jumbotron and highlighted on ESPN's top-ten plays list, with the player celebrating by flexing his muscles. Rarely does a kicker receive similar adulation for a field goal or extra point. When attempting an extra point or field goal, play is stopped as the kicker tees up the ball, takes calculated steps to back away from the ball, and signals to the team that he (or sometimes she) is ready. Once the ball is hiked and in place, the kicker swings a stretched leg forward and launches the ball toward the goal, toe pointed and nearly at head level. If an opposing athlete contacts the kicker's extended leg and not the ball, a penalty is assessed for "running into the kicker." If the planted leg is contacted, the more severe "roughing the kicker" penalty is charged. Moreover, most of the women who have competed in men's college football to date have played the kicker position, thus, in the social world of sport, feminizing the position. After returning from a gold-medal-winning World Cup, Carli Lloyd showed up at a Philadelphia Eagles' practice and kicked a football fifty-five yards and through the uprights.[6] Examples like Lloyd might be seen as a threat to men and the dominant gender ideology in sport.

This is how masculine capital functions in sport and society. Sexual encounters add to the accumulation of masculine capital. The more sex these male athletes have and the more stories they tell each other, the greater their masculine worth. It is a toxic environment that perpetuates physical abuse and sexual assault. Casual sex, or hooking up, can be thought of as more about a man's relationship with other men than with women. Michael Kimmel interviewed boys and men for his book *Guyland: The Perilous World Where Boys Become Men* and reported similar findings. "Hooking up is a way that guys communicate with other guys—it's about homosociality. It's a way that guys compete with each other, establish a pecking order of cool studliness, and attempt to move up in their ranking."[7] Closeted gay male athletes are immediately at a disadvantage because they cannot talk about their own sexual encounters in the locker room.

Today, more and more allies are coming forward in sport, such as Chris Long, who criticized the press for asking about openly gay NFL player Michael Sam's shower habits. Long, an outspoken two-time Super Bowl champion defensive lineman, tweeted to ESPN: "Dear ESPN, Everyone but you is over it."[8] The discussion of LGBTQ allies in the world of sport is becoming more frequent, and some athletes are expressing their support for gay teammates. Yet, the institution of sport makes it an uphill battle for LGBTQ athletes and has created a "don't ask, don't tell" environment: a social world where coaches and teammates ask few questions when they are curious about someone's sexuality, and where in hypermasculine sports like football, hockey, and rodeo, gay men tend to remain in the closet. But social change in sport is on the horizon. The NFL released a video in October 2020 acknowledging National Coming Out Day. During the video, athletes stated: "When you are ready [to come out], we are ready." Athletes expressed their support: the Minnesota Vikings' Anthony Harris said, "I got you"; his teammate Anthony Barr said, "I got you"; the Denver Broncos' Dalton Risner announced, "We got you"; and high-profile Rob Gronkowski, the Gronk, stated: "It takes all of us."[9] The significance of these statements, and the publication of this book, is a testament to the courage of LGBTQ athletes in gay rodeo as forerunners of future LGBTQ athletes long before their acceptability by mainstream sports participants improved.

The power in sport is not only held by the dominant group in positions of authority but includes the fan base. Washington State University (WSU) alumni complained to the university administration that their beloved mascot, Butch the Cougar, should not have marched alongside the LGBTQ community at the 1996 Seattle Gay Pride parade. Butch the Cougar's costume was worn by a lesbian alumna and photographed for the school newspaper, the *Summer Evergreen*. Director of the Gay, Lesbian, Bisexual, and Allies Program at WSU Bobbi Bonace dismissed complaints that Butch was being used to make a political statement; she argued that Butch's appearance was in line with WSU pride and school spirit. Associate athletic director Harold Gibson defended the appearance as in "keeping with the practice of lending out cougar costumes for events involving official school groups."[10] Enraged WSU alumni grew concerned about how other fan bases might use the incident to discredit their beloved mascot. By marching in the Seattle Gay Pride parade, Butch lost some of his masculine capital. Even though the use of Butch the Cougar had Gibson's support, many alumni threatened to withhold future donations. The following year, Butch stayed home and returned to the closet.[11]

Roughstock events provided athletes with opportunities to earn that masculine cowboy image. Even gay bars attempted to appeal to men who wanted to embody that rough and tumble persona. The Wrangler in Denver welcomed rodeo fans and contestants with an advertisement depicting a cowboy wrestling a steer. The bar sponsored sixteen chute dogging buckles across the country that year; the ad read: "When you're done wrestling your steer, come wrangle some men at our place!"[12] Events like chute dogging, in which the contestant wrestles down a steer, joined bull riding and steer riding as some of the most dangerous events in gay rodeo. The violent ride, which places an athlete at risk in the arena, created a perceived hierarchy of events that were considered masculine. However, longtime gay rodeo cowboy John Beck said that more injuries occurred during the wild drag race, a camp event, than during any other event. Yet, through violence, roughstock events were socially constructed as the most masculine.

During the early years of gay rodeo, roughstock and speed events were the events most highly respected by rodeo cowboys who competed nationally outside of the LGBTQ-friendly circuit. Often, these cowboys remarked negatively about the camp events, lowering their masculine credibility. In 1978, at the Reno Gay Rodeo, a participant named Sony (who wished to remain anonymous because of his participation in mainstream rodeo) was concerned about the weekend event. He told reporter Bill Arsenaux that a week earlier he had phoned the organizers and had been told that his registration required that he enter five events each day. Upon arrival there seemed to be some confusion: registration might require only five events all weekend. Sony's only interest was in stock events. He opposed competing in barrel racing, because in mainstream rodeo it is often reserved for women, and greased pig catching was beneath his dignity. When he learned about the wild cow milking contest, Sony paused "with a blank stare," seemingly offended that his sport did not follow the masculine script he had always known.[13] Cowboys like Sony believed that they defined cowboy masculinity, claiming that participants in camp events failed to maintain the masculine capital they believed the sport of rodeo afforded them.

Not only were some of the gay cowboys frustrated with camp, they did not want to share the arena with women and drag queens either. What is important to understand about gay rodeo is that organizers rejected sexism and heteronormative judgment, and organizers such as Ragsdale stayed true to his commitment to inclusivity. In 1980 Ragsdale explained that he had received many complaints from the "Macho Cowboys" that they would participate in gay rodeo only if Ragsdale "would eliminate the Lesbians and Drags."[14] In sticking to his convictions, upholding the principles of gay liberation and gay pride, Ragsdale responded, "I refused and told them to stay home and miss a fun weekend. After repeated calls of this type, I tried to think of an event whereby I could use ALL THREE TOGETHER. And Yes, you guessed it, it was the Wild Cow Milking Contest."[15] In response to the "macho cowboys," he included an event that requires a cowgirl to hold onto a cow with a rope. A person dressed in drag then grabs the animal by its head and neck, while a cowboy attempts to squeeze out at least two drops of milk.

One's assigned role in an event is important for capital as well. For instance, in Wild Drag Race, the most strenuous role is that of the person pulling the rope attached to the large animal. And while the drag may have a more dangerous role, having to lead the steer across the finish line, they do so comically while wearing dresses and wigs. The contestants on foot and the drag riding the steer compete for the same prize—the event buckle. The shiny trophy, strapped to leather and worn just below the navel, is a jewel admired by cowboys and cowgirls from any distance. A champion wearing their prize obtains that elusive respect even if, from a distance, the event is unknown. And the participants on foot earn a degree of capital after a drag race. As they exit the arena, they have a higher degree of masculine capital by default—they were not the one in a dress.

One of the most obvious ways to earn masculine capital is through competition in speed and roughstock events. Speed events test a combination of speed, agility, and skill. In some events there is an added component involving lassos and flags. Riders have fallen from their horses and suffered life-threatening injuries. It's the thrill of danger that excites these men. West Texas historian Alex Hunt praised bronco rider Robert Etbauer for his bloody injury in the arena. Hunt remembers watching Etbauer search the dirt floor of the arena for his severed thumb following his ride at the 1995 Denver Stock Show and Rodeo, which will forever summon an image of toughness for him.[16] At the ZIA Gay Rodeo in Santa Fe, New Mexico, bull rider Matt Story felt the weight of a two-thousand-pound bull land on his thigh. At the awards ceremony later that evening, I approached Story to see how he was doing. The man limped over and pulled up his shorts to show me the purple and green bruise on his leg. I apologized for almost taking a picture, and he interrupted, saying, "Oh, Nick, take as many pictures as you want, and text them to me." With a smile on his face, he was proud of the injury. He did cover the event, and walking away that afternoon and drinking a Bud Light at the evening festivity earned him the respect of his peers.[17]

Masculine capital is not limited to men. Rodeo is unlike any other sport regarding the treatment of men versus women when an injury occurs. Historian Mary Lou LeCompte argues that the media tends to glorify injuries that occur to rodeo women, whereas in most other sports the event receives an outcry of criticism. LeCompte recalls a trick riding competition that took place in San Antonio during which Florence Randolph was knocked unconscious, but she continued her competition once she awoke: "To the amazement of all present, Randolph awoke, waved off the stretcher, and resumed her ride, completing the trick that had caused her fall. She finished to thunderous applause, and in an interview afterward said simply, 'It's all in the game.'"[18]

## THREATENING WOMEN? AND A MASCULINE PARADOX

In the social world of sport, heterosexual men hold most of the power. This is true regarding administrative positions, team ownership, and the definition of sport, which establishes what I call the "rules of the game." These rules have two components: who can play and how to play. Psychologist Robert Brannon lists these four rudimentary rules of masculinity and manhood: "(1) 'No Sissy Stuff!' Being a man means not being a sissy, not being perceived as weak, effeminate, or gay. Masculinity is the relentless repudiation of the feminine. (2) 'Be a Big Wheel.' This rule refers to the centrality of success and power in the definition of masculinity. Masculinity is measured more by wealth, power, and status than by any body part. (3) 'Be a Sturdy Oak.' What makes a man is that he is reliable in a crisis. And what makes him so reliable in a crisis is not that he is able to respond fully and appropriately to the situation at hand, but rather that he resembles an inanimate object. A rock, a pillar, a species of tree. (4) 'Give 'em hell.' Exude an aura of daring and aggression. Live life out on the edge. Take risks. Go for it. Pay no attention to what others think."[19] Eric Anderson summarizes: "In order to achieve the most socially valued form of masculinity, men had to repress fear, weakness, intimidation, or pain."[20] Psychologist James Garbarino writes: "It's better to be mad than sad."[21]

Sociologist Jay Coakley defines who can play with his explanation of gender ideology. This belief system, prevalent in the sporting world, not only considers women inferior to men but also identifies "heterosexuality" as the only accepted union within this social world.[22] These beliefs have long been challenged, as lesbian athletes emerged in professional sports decades ago. However, gay men, who violate this gender ideology because of their same-sex relationships, are held to a standard of hegemonic masculinity. A gay male athlete was most likely wrapped in a light blue towel shortly after birth and sent home from the hospital with a light blue stocking hat and booties; his parents likely gave no thought to considering the pink alternative. As Brannon's first rule states: "No Sissy Stuff." Sport requires athletes to follow these gendered tenets of play. Women must be competitive and strong on the field but adhere to appropriate femininity off the field. Masculinity requires violence on the field in contact sports and the taking of risks, following Brannon's fourth requirement. Finally, an athlete must play through pain and never show emotions other than anger, excitement, and joy—"Be a Sturdy Oak." These socially constricted rules must be followed both on and off the field.

When the group that holds the most power within an institution feels threatened, the reaction can be discriminatory or violent toward the marginalized group. The power dynamic that exists in sport places men in the position of power. That power structure has slowly been restructured with Title IX, a U.S. federal law that passed in 1972 as part of the Education Amendments: "No person in the United States shall, on the basis of sex, be excluded from participation in, be denied the benefits of, or be subjected to discrimination in any education program or activity receiving Federal financial assistance."[23] These words changed the gendered world of sport forever. Women at universities and in high schools began participating in sports in unprecedented numbers. These federally funded institutions now had to provide equal extracurricular opportunities, such as sports, to everyone.

In high schools throughout the United States, girls' participation in sports increased from 294,000 in 1971 to 3.4 million in 2011.[24] However, the dominant world of sport is controlled by men, and Brannon's second rule of masculinity explains the frustration with and rejection of Title IX by some men. Gender equity is not required in the hiring process, however, and does not apply to employees of an athletic department. As sporting programs for women in colleges increased, so did the need for head coaches for these programs, and the male-dominated athletic departments hired men for women's teams' head coach positions: "As opportunities for female athletes opened up and high school and college sports programs expanded, positions in coaching and athletic administration formerly held by women were sought and filled by men."[25] In fact, women filled only a little over 40 percent of coaching positions on college women's teams in 2014, versus 90 percent in 1972.[26] Moreover, inequities remain in financial support for equipment, transportation, and physical facilities, as such support is largely provided for men's sports over women's sports. The male dominant group in the social world of sport has prevailed. Men have held most of the power in sport as athletic department administrators, head coaches, and owners of professional teams.

Following the implementation of Title IX, universities began to cut men's National Collegiate Athletic Association (NCAA) programs like gymnastics, wrestling, and swimming because scholarship programs and other funding sources had to be equitable between men's and women's sports. The dominant (male) group in sport, among both fans and administrators, blamed Title IX for the loss of these programs, but this simplistic cause-and-effect answer is false. Title IX did not eliminate these men's programs—football did. Following the passage of Title IX, the NCAA addressed the scholarship question and called for an equitable distribution between men's and women's sports. This appeared to be an equitable solution. If men's and women's sports are each given one hundred scholarships to hand out, for example, then they can distribute them as they choose. There is no team in women's sports that has as many scholarship athletes as men's football. Women can divide these one hundred scholarships among many sports and provide twenty-four scholarships to track and field, twelve to basketball, twelve to soccer, and twelve to lacrosse, and still have forty remaining for sports like swimming, softball, and tennis. Currently, the NCAA allows Division I men's teams to offer eighty-five scholarships to football and another twelve to basketball, leaving only three scholarships, in this hypothetical example, for the remaining men's team sports. To put this example into perspective, most Division I baseball teams have a twenty-seven-player roster, so they would only be able to offer a scholarship to two pitchers and a catcher. Even though the one-hundred-scholarship number is a hypothetical example, it is arguably football that has forced athletic departments to eliminate other men's sports because of the number of scholarships it receives.

If college athletic departments are so concerned with the loss of these men's programs, why haven't they redistributed scholarships from football? An argument can be made that they are simply cutting non–revenue producing sports, but athletic administrators also know that having a successful football program is important for their institution, and homecoming games provide alumni donors a reason to return each year. The dominant group in sports controls the media, and most sports writers are drowning out the reality about Title IX with their cries about men being wronged by women. These arguments led President Ronald Reagan to decry Title IX. In March 1988 the Civil Rights Restoration Act of 1987 was enacted into law, reversing the Grove City v. Bell court decision and requiring that when "any program or activity in an educational institution receives federal funds, all of the institution's programs and activities must comply with Title IX."[27] Reagan, a proponent of "masculinity" in men, vetoed the bill, but he was overridden by Congress.

As men fought to maintain control over women in mainstream sport, gay rodeo celebrated unity. Possibly, these gay men were more secure in their masculinity and were not threatened by women competing as equals in gay rodeos. Masculinity is fluid at gay rodeo. While the denim jeans, Stetson hats, and cowboy boots give the impression that the gay cowboy is attempting to appear hypermasculine, the opposite is true. They are celebrating their identity as rodeo cowboys first and gay men

Masculine Capital

second. Confident in their cowboy masculinity, they have become comfortable with dressing as cowboys. In the 1980s it was fashionable among gay rodeo cowboys to wear anklets on their boots. Usually, an anklet is a linked silver or gold chain, which sometimes includes charms, that women wear around their ankles as summer fashion. At the gay rodeo, these metal charms were silver ankle straps that go under your heel and around the outside of your boot, and contestants were proud to show off their accessories.

## THE HETERONORMATIVE COWBOY COMPLICATES GAY LIBERATION

The founders of gay rodeo in Reno in 1976, and many other regional associations that followed during the 1980s, used the rodeo venue to break down the stereotypes mainstream society held about gay men. Those involved, from rodeo organizers to participants, argued that the term "gay cowboy" was not a paradox. Gay cowboys and gay rodeo organizers consciously adopted heteronormative ideals about masculinity and rejected feminine aspects. By examining statements made by early gay rodeo participants, considering the hypermasculine images found in every rodeo program from 1976 to 2021, and interrogating cowboy aesthetic and identifying it as drag, we can see how masculinity is fluid and socially constructed in cowboy culture and rodeo. For this identity one does not have to live on a ranch or a farm, because it includes other characteristics of the identity such as moral beliefs, a persona, and a western lifestyle. Gay rodeo is not a paradox. It is more complex than that because of the masculine and feminine tensions that exist—literally with personal feelings and figuratively when examining cowboy performance as enacted by all, including heterosexual men.

The emergence of gay rodeo and participants' desire to prove their masculine identities through sport paralleled broader changes in U.S. society. The Stonewall riots in 1969 boosted the gay liberation movement during the decade that followed. As mentioned in chapter one, however, the media focused on extraordinary images of drag queens and effeminate men. Rebecca Scofield argues that U.S. society embraced the western cowboy image of John Wayne in their political leaders. After the "emasculating" years of the 1960s and the "whining protesters of the counterculture, Black Power, feminists and civil rights movements, [Ronald] Reagan's supporters heralded the return of the 'hard line.'"[28] Scofield explains that the pressure of "Reaganite masculinity" befell gay men in the early 1980s, and books about masculinity became popular among them.[29] A cultural shift occurred in the early 1980s that continues to the present day. Scofield explains that in early 1982 gay men began using the phrase "straight-acting," which distinguished them from the effeminate stereotype.[30] Christian conservatives had become a powerful voice within the Republican Party—an almost Theodore Rooseveltian theme could be detected, sprinkled with Manifest Destiny, both of which argued for manly strife, domination, and colonialism— and so, among gay men, an effeminate demeanor was seen as disadvantageous.

Men in gay rodeo do not all typify the social and political views of the broader LGBTQ community, and a significant number identify as Christian and politically conservative. Many gay cowboys during the early 1980s admired Reagan and his John Wayne appearance. These men had grown up in Christian conservative America. When politicians went on the offensive regarding LGBTQ political issues, these men did not abandon the Republican Party for the Democratic Party. Doing so would have made them appear weak and reinforced the effeminate stereotypes they fought to dismantle. Thus, a narrative about gay liberationists being politically liberal is an oversimplification; gay rodeo cowboys and cowgirls are more interesting than that. The IGRA became a powerful organization in LGBTQ rights over the years, but no one can say with certainty what happened at the voting box. Similarly, not all rural Americans were homophobic. There was homophobia and violence, as discussed in chapter two, but there was acceptance of gay cowboys, at times, for the same reason these cowboys maintained their conservative roots—a desire for masculine identity. This was not necessarily a contradiction with the liberation movement. It only complicates, in a good way, what liberation meant to some of these forgotten pioneers of the movement.

Masculine Capital

Gay rodeo, and specifically gay cowboys, were a threat to male masculinity. If a gay cowboy was "straight-acting," he could be on any ranch, in any saloon, or in any family. The reality that masculinity was socially constructed and that heterosexual-identifying males could no longer stake sole claim to this attribute challenged contemporary thought about gay men. The "crisis of male masculinity" in the early 1980s paralleled the rise of conservatism. Family values, traditional households, and "making men become men" again dominated the rhetoric of the day. Christopher Le Coney and Zoe Trodd argue that Hollywood attempted to rehabilitate the "lost myth of frontier-masculinity" with films like *Uncommon Valor* (1983), *Missing in Action* (1984), and *Rambo: First Blood Part II* (1985), all retelling the history of U.S. military failures with a new script.[31] Moreover, satiric books about male masculinity, like Bruce Feirstein's *Real Men Don't Eat Quiche* and Clark Henley's *The Butch Manual*, mocked heterosexual males and offered gay men advice on how to be markedly masculine.

In gay rodeo, masculinity is important among those who compete in the sport. From the earliest rodeos to today, these men say that gay rodeo has been a way to dispel stereotypes and notions that gay men are not as strong or masculine as heterosexual men. In dozens of interviews, gay rodeo cowboys tell similar stories about their hard work, their injuries, and the other masculine men they meet while competing. Masculinity, however, is fluid, and how it is defined depends on one's internal feeling about oneself. The image of masculinity has been fabricated by society, but for gay rodeo men what is deemed "masculine" is inherently part of their western or rural identity.

In the social world of gay rodeo, masculine capital plays a role like its role in the mainstream sports discussed earlier. Athletes, mascots, and organizations depend on this capital to uphold their masculine worth. Athletes, obviously, can earn such capital through competition. Mascots are subject to different criteria. Butch the Cougar, Washington State's mascot, mentioned earlier, is performed by a student or alumnus inside the costume and is featured on posters and game-day programs. Gay rodeo does not have a mascot, but each year regional rodeos publish programs that greatly emphasize hypermasculinity, using an abundance of exaggerated imagery (fig. 12).

In 1981 an image of gay rodeo cowboy Ron Jesser circulated rapidly—"went viral"—in the national press. The photograph was taken at the Reno Gay Rodeo. Mick Hicks, a syndicated photographer, snapped the picture of Jesser, remembered today as one of the fathers of gay rodeo for his participation in the early Reno events. "Hot, sweaty, dirty and trudging back to the chutes after bombing out in calf roping, Ron was decked out with his ropes and thinking about his next event. . . . Suddenly someone yelled 'Hold it!' and Mick Hicks snapped a picture of a gay cowboy that eventually was reprinted by newspapers across the country."[32] Thus, the image of this gay rodeo cowboy went viral. Later, Jesser received international attention as a gay rodeo cowboy, and he posed for photographers from England, France, the Netherlands, and Germany. Real People, a weekly news and entertainment show that was televised on NBC, featured Jesser in one episode. Nationally, his photo appeared in The Advocate, This Week Texas, and the gay pornography magazines Honcho, Mandate, and Blueboy, the latter bringing even more attention from his new fans. When asked about his fame, Jesser replied, "Shucks, I didn't even pose for that one." (fig. 13).[33] As for Jesser's masculine capital, this was surely given a boost, because Jesser was an authentic Colorado cowboy, born in Fort Collins and living on a ranch in Adams County when the photograph was taken. In sports, Jesser was the captain of the Denver Athletic Union volleyball team. He had served in the U.S. Air Force, and he had worked on a ranch as well as in a warehouse. Jesser was a founding member of the Colorado Gay Rodeo Association and had served as the events chairman for the association's first three years. Proud of his affiliation, Jesser carried the Colorado flag for the CGRA's mounted drill team, "riding a registered chestnut quarter horse mare named Ginny Bar Quick."[34] He succumbed to AIDS-related complications in October 1986, and he is remembered by his co-contestants for embodying "the true cowboy spirit—he helped and trained other contestants and kept his infectious smile in good times and bad."[35] Jesser was every bit the quintessential image of the Marlboro Man, and the media loved sharing his image during the summer of 1981.

Fig. 12. "Howdy," Floyds, a Los Angeles bar, advertisement in the 1985 Texas Gay Rodeo Association program. Credit to Frank Harrell and the International Gay Rodeo Association Archives, gayrodeohistory.org.

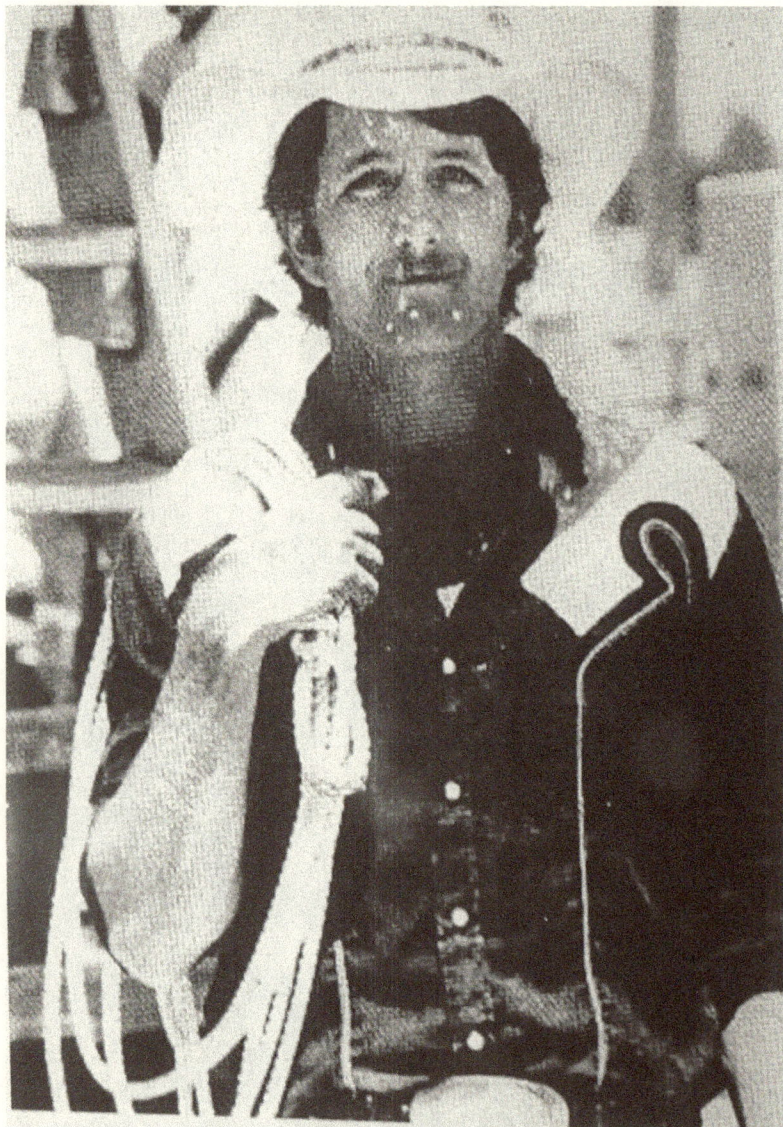

Fig. 13. Ron Jesser, 1982 Reno Gay Rodeo, Reno, Nevada. "IGRA Hall of Fame: Ron Jesser." Credit to Frank Harrell and the International Gay Rodeo Association Archives, gayrodeohistory.org.

If a genuine masculine cowboy was not enough to break down stereotypes about gay men, IGRA sponsors provided images of what it meant to be masculine and a cowboy. Their advertisements featured shirtless men, often with hairy chests, positioned in such a way as to attract the reader's interest. The oldest rodeo program in the IGRA archives is from 1979, and an advertisement for Artie's Trapp Lounge, in Reno, features a drawing of a shirtless cowboy with a chiseled, muscular chest sporting six-pack abs. The 1983 Reno Gay Rodeo program was among the first to include full-color photographs of men, not just simple drawings as in previous programs. Featured on page 29 is a man in chaps with his shirt unbuttoned, exposing his chest. When hand-drawn art of typified cowboys appeared in rodeo programs, it often exaggerated the male physique, drawing attention to their arms, chest, or crotch. *Guide Magazine* served as the program for the second annual Rocky Mountain Regional Rodeo, and it featured the hand-drawn advertisement for Floyds in Long Beach County, California, once again. This masculine cowboy image, featuring a model with a hairy chest, mustache, and beard, became a commonly used figure in such advertisements.

Decades later, muscles, a beard, and a hairy chest remain the standard look if one aspires to be a gay rodeo cowboy. In 2012 an ad appeared in the Palm Springs (California) Gay Rodeo program. Featured were two cowboys appearing to remove their clothes. The advertisement—"Model Search: Takin' It Off for Charity!"—aimed to recruit men to be featured in the pages of an annual fundraising calendar: 2013 Men of HomoRodeo .com (fig. 14) These two anonymous cowboys were not alone: eleven other shirtless men were featured throughout the thirty-four-page program.[36] As for the resulting calendar, it pictures twelve men exposing either full frontal or backside nudity.

If anyone needs more instructions on how to obtain masculine capital in the gay rodeo world, their best source is the magazine *Roundup: The Gay and Lesbian Western Magazine*. *Roundup* informs readers, in their marketing campaigns, that they provide complete coverage of IGRA rodeos. The magazine includes articles written by experts, as well as

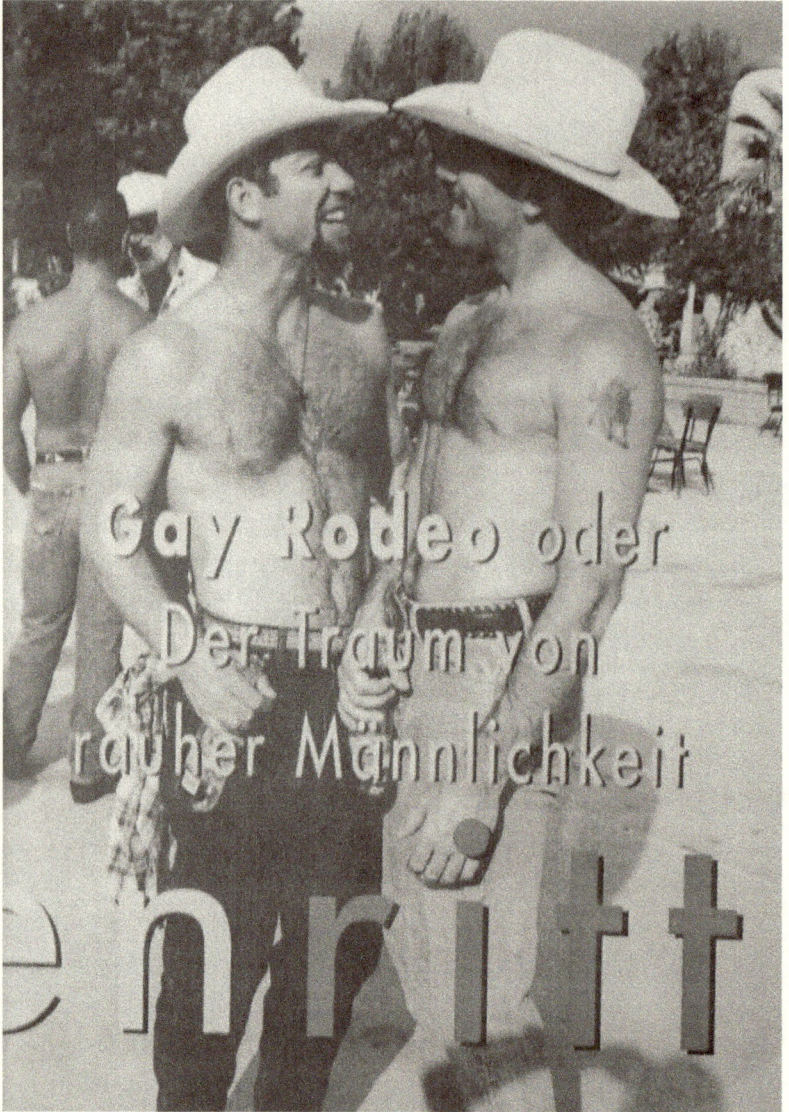

**Fig. 14.** Gay rodeo article in *MÄNNERaktuell* magazine. Credit to Frank Harrell and the International Gay Rodeo Association Archives, gayrodeohistory.org.

Fig. 15. *Roundup: The Gay Western and Rodeo Magazine*, Fall 1993. Credit to Frank Harrell and the International Gay Rodeo Archives, gayrodeohistory.org.

behind-the-scenes coverage of today's gay western lifestyles; readers are told that they need to subscribe to be fully equipped and informed. The magazine provides information about cowboys and rodeos from coast to coast and always features images of cowboys similar to the sketches and photographs previously described. Even international magazines feature this quintessential cowboy image. German soft-porn magazine MAN-NER*aktuell* published a story about gay rodeo with an image of cowboys hitchhiking to America's country music capital—Nashville, Tennessee (fig. 15). Such international media exposure brought men from Europe to the American West to experience cowboy culture.

## MEN ONLY

In addition to facing the dangers associated with rodeo and having to appear in the guise of masculine cowboys, gay rodeo participants solidified their masculine identities by having sex with other men. As discussed in chapter one, "sexual relations between men were viewed as an experience that intensified masculinity because it left women out of the equation."[37] Gay rodeo programs used homoerotic imagery to entice readers to shop at a certain store or use a specific travel agency that had nothing to do with sex. Yet an exaggerated narrative of gay liberation was used to attract the curious eyes of consumers. These documents were filled with sexually suggestive images. The 1984 Reno Gay Rodeo program provided addresses for bathhouses in six major U.S. cities.[38] Nine pages later, a reader found an ad for *In Touch for Men*: "Our hats are off to the many men and women who make this such a special event. Our models, on the other hand, prefer to take their pants off, and we're not going to stop them. Best wishes for continuing success. We love you all. Now ride 'em, cowboys."[39] The ad featured a male model wearing only a cowboy hat and chaps. Sex between men became a key component of advertisements in the programs.

Journalist Bill Arsenaux attended the third annual Reno Gay Rodeo on the weekend of August 4, 1978, and chronicled the experience in *In Touch for Men*. Shortly after his United Airlines flight landed in Reno, Arsenaux and a group of other men met with Phil Ragsdale, director of the rodeo, outside the airport. Ragsdale, dressed in an "easy 'nothing special' western shirt and Levi's," lined the bed of his red pickup truck with bales of hay.[40] As the men climbed in for their short ride to their lodgings at the River Inn, Ragsdale shouted, "Hold on to your hats!"[41] Arsenaux looked around the group and spotted two men, who were strangers before their curbside encounter at the airport, who had quickly taken to each other. "Two guys across from me are busy discovering each other by using verbal as well as braille anatomy. They will stay together all this weekend."[42] Conversely, Arsenaux spent his first evening interviewing rodeo participant Sony, mentioned earlier, in his hotel room drinking Budweiser. Sony's evening ended after the interview. In Phoenix, he worked at a bathhouse surrounded by hypersexual men, but this was rodeo, and he paid little attention to the after-hours activities. Sony returned to his hotel room, while Arsenaux went outside to observe the late-night festivities: "Until dawn on Saturday, there were more events around the outside tennis courts which could be called 'wild cowboy milking,' 'room racing,' not to mention a large number of 'greased pork' events, than could ever have been held in the rodeo arena."[43]

Masculine Capital

In 1981 another writer for *In Touch for Men*, John Calendo, traveled from Los Angeles to Reno for the gay rodeo. Magazines like *In Touch for Men* and *Roundup* often published stories about gay rodeo and included images of hypersexualized and hypermasculinized gay rodeo men. On this occasion, the reporter traveled with forty-one other men, dressed in western wear and all in their late thirties. Assisted by an agency, Gala Tours, the group maneuvered through LAX together. Some of these men traveled for the rodeo and others for the late-night escapades previously mentioned. One of the cowboys triggered the metal detector because of a metal ring he wore around his genitals, a device for prolonging a sexual encounter. Calendo reported, "I hadn't even gotten on the plane yet and already I saw the weekend shaping up. It was going to be *Where the Boys Are* with everyone wanting to [play] Yvette Mimieux's role. I wondered how many sexed-out rodeo boys would be found, come Sunday, staggering down the middle of the Nevada State Highway."[44] Once on the plane, when the flight crew learned that the men were on their way to the gay rodeo, flirting with the flight attendants became a masculine capital competition. The travelers spotted a male flight attendant, who spotted them as well and then vanished. "Oh!" A loud gasp was heard. The attendant reappeared, excited and nervous: "Hunks to the left of him, hunks to the right of him, furred arms throwing bags into overhead compartments. . . . The drinking doubles began almost before we left the ground."[45] Throughout the short flight, the attendant made several playful announcements, concluding: "We regret that this was such a short hop and that we couldn't show you how friendly the friendly skies can be."[46] The cowboys erupted with laughter and applause.

Social activities and the subculture itself influenced the degree of masculine capital expected as well. The 1990s IGRA Finals program included an ad for the Ranch, a bar in Albuquerque. Featured in the ad is a cowboy with his shirt unbuttoned and wide open, once again exposing the ever-important muscular chest. Additionally, his pants are unbuttoned, and his hand appears to be reaching downward as he casually looks to his left. The ad describes the Ranch as "a Man's Bar," which includes a back bar, separate from the main bar, called Cuffs, "A Bar for Men in Leather."[47] Other rodeo programs advertised shops and bars that catered to the leather subculture of sadomasochism. Initially, S&M was seen by some as taboo or perverse, but its repeated imagery on rodeo programs throughout the IGRA circuit normalized the practice as a subculture, and as a rejection of heteronormativity. Heterosexual couples engage in S&M as well; however, the openness in advertising and discussions about S&M practices in the LGBTQ community were truly unique and liberating. Involvement in the leather scene of the S&M world provided gay men with the semblance of something to fear—the hint of something dangerous.

Taking another angle, Rebecca Scofield discusses a risky behavior of some gay men: the practice of barebacking—referring not to riding a bronc but to unsafe sex. Scofield contends that men who engage in this risky behavior do so with a similar attitude to that with which they participate in roughstock events at the rodeo, quoting sexuality scholar Thomas Linneman: "Making sex safer, by definition, reduces the risk involved in the sexual activity, thus demasculinizing it. Some gay men engaging in unsafe sex even refer to the act as 'barebacking,' making an allusion to the days of the risk-taking, masculine frontier."[48] Using Scofield's theory, sex between men can be seen as risky and, thus, is one more way in which masculine capital is earned.

## CONCLUSION

Masculine capital was largely constructed in sport by straight men imposing heteronormative rules on their games. Gay cowboy couple Jeffrey McCasland and Philip Lister explain that, to them, whether a gay cowboy is masculine or feminine is not a concern. While they both identify as masculine, they are comfortable just being gay men. Regarding heteronormative rules in sports like rodeo, they explain that gay rodeo breaks the heteronormative stereotypes imposed on these athletes. "In the same vein that heteronormativity focuses on heterosexuality being the norm for relationships, marriage, etc., there is clearly a bias that rodeo is for masculine heterosexual men that are rough and tough. Similarly, women are only meant to barrel race. Gay rodeo breaks these stereotypical barriers, showing that gay men and women can have just as much of a love of the western lifestyle, horses, livestock, and rodeo as their heterosexual counterparts. . . . Gay rodeos put a spotlight on how narrow-minded the heteronormative view of rodeo and rough physical sports can be."[49]

Some sports tend to be seen as "more masculine" or "somewhat feminine." These are socially constructed ideas that are not instinctive; they are taught and learned. Think of it as like the social construction of race. Racism is not something that people are born believing; they are taught stereotypes about people of color. Through selective perception, stereotypes are reinforced. Selective perception is a process whereby a person witnesses a single action or behavior by another person that reinforces a stereotype, thus making the witness believe that the behavior must be true about the entire group. However, the "selective" aspect of this process is that the witness ignores the hundreds or even thousands of examples that contradict this belief. Applying this concept to sport and masculinity, consider a male athlete who can lift twice his body weight and is internationally known for this ability. If the athlete happens to be an artistic gymnast, his "masculinity" is suspect; if he is a football offensive lineman, he is seen in more masculine terms. Using the word "artistic" in the context of sport limits the amount of masculine capital available, because of societal preconceptions about sports that are artistic. What defines masculinity in sport is a greater level of violence, not only muscle and hard work. Similarly, considering a cowboy on a ranch, it might seem paradoxical to family and friends if that man comes out of the closet, because of their preconceptions about gay men.

Paul Vigil, a cowboy from New Mexico mentioned in chapter one, explained that his middle brother, Mike, found it hard to believe because Paul did not fit any of the gay stereotypes. Vigil described a conversation he had with Mike shortly after he came out, and only a few hours after they had finished branding some two hundred head of cattle.

**Him:** Nah!
**Me:** Nah what?
**Him:** No, you're not gay.

**Me**: Mike, yes I'm gay.

**Him**: You can't be, look at what we've done this weekend. We fixed
fences, branded a bunch of cattle, and fixed waters. We did manly
stuff, you can't be gay.

**Me**: What the hell do you want me to do, run around here prancing
in a tutu?

**Him**: Well, yeah, or something like that . . . something that shows me
you're gay.[50]

Mike had lived his life up to this point believing that a gay man could
not engage in the hard work of ranching. Mike denied that gay men
could be successful ranchers and rodeo athletes, or maybe he had never
known a gay man who ranched or competed in rodeo until he found out
about his brother.

The accumulation of masculine capital by men of gay rodeo provides
them with social wealth in the LGBTQ community and recognition by
heterosexual men. Such capital is obtained through their physical appearance, the events in which they compete, and their sexual encounters. Through this examination, we see that the phrase "gay cowboy" is
not a paradox, nor is the mainstream rodeo cowboy the embodiment of
masculinity; society deemed him the most authentic. In a scene in the
1996 comedy *The Birdcage*, Armand (played by Robin Williams) tries to
teach his flamboyant partner, Albert (played by Nathan Lane), to walk
like a "real man." For inspiration, Armand advises Albert to walk through
a restaurant patio like John Wayne. Albert struts past tables with his hips
swinging from side to side, loose wrists reaching out in front of him, and
carefully pointed feet crossing one in front of the other. A perplexed
Armand tilts his head. Albert asks with a frown, "No good?" Armand
responds, "Actually, it's perfect. I just never realized John Wayne walked
like that."[51] Cowboy culture in general might not be as masculine as once
believed; as a society, we can socially reconstruct masculinity and sport.
If, in our estimation, gay rodeo cowboys are not the most authentic,
masculine cowboys, then we might need to reevaluate everything that
we think we know about masculinity and sport.

# 7 Our Chosen Family

Cowboys, Cowgirls, and Coupling at the Gay Rodeo

I want to live that romantic cowboy way of life. It's not realistic for me to rodeo for a living but I will work to support my rodeo habit. And the romantic side of that is, yes, I'm in love with a cowboy, and he loves rodeo, too. I went a lot of my youth coming out and living in cities, gay ghettos, as it were. And I would prefer that my neighbors all know that I'm gay and don't care. They're more concerned with how I ride my horse . . . They're more concerned about did I catch my steer.

—Ken Pool

"Not long after arriving in Arizona in 1986, a young Midwestern farmer named Greg Olson walked into Charlie's, a gay bar in Phoenix, and looked around. The International Gay Rodeo Association's (IGRA) future top cowboy knew he had found a home. Charlie's provided an atmosphere that felt comfortable to members of the LGBTQ community who were raised in rural areas, and never seemed to fit in at their 'straight,' hometown pubs."[1] "Starting off as a cocktail waiter, the slim, muscular, blond was teased by the other employees because of the way he darted around the bar, attempting to avoid various pinches and gropes of the bar's most forward patrons. 'You look like Sheena of the Jungle,' one of the bartenders laughingly told him, because of the way he ran through the 'jungle' of men 'with his tray up in his hair.'"[2] And the nickname stuck. Sheena became a popular bartender at Charlie's and even invented a cocktail that is still served at the bar today. The Sheena is a shot glass filled to three-quarters with root beer schnapps and topped off with a "healthy splash" of Southern Comfort. For Olson, the Arizona Gay Rodeo

Association (AGRA) became his new family, and he is remembered for his fun-loving personality.

The gay rodeo brought people together. The circuit of rodeos, month after month, created annual gatherings in states coast to coast. Cowboys and cowgirls with similar interests reunited at rodeos and connected with their true natures. The rodeo also became a wedge for some. Patrick Terry recalls attending "20 to 25 rodeos a year," and, at times, they were "back-to-back."[3] The commitment strained his relationship with his partner. In an interview with historian Rebecca Scofield, Terry stated, "No. Oh, no. I tried to get him interested once and boy, was that the wrong thing to do. He just didn't care for that. But in the beginning he supported me completely but then, I just got too involved. I didn't realize until it was too late, you know, how involved I was."[4] Even though the relationship might have ended, one thing that almost all of the IGRA members interviewed have said is that the IGRA is a family, albeit not always cohesive. This chapter examines the IGRA family and the relationships that form because the gay rodeo brings LGBTQ people together and provides a social world where the LGBTQ rodeo community shares a love of rural life, western culture, and rodeo.

Beginning around 1990, the technology revolution transformed all aspects of society. Meeting another cowboy or cowgirl took on new forms. Dating, and cruising, in the twenty-first century has drastically evolved as well. Some of the pickup lines might remain intact, but the method of delivery has unquestionably become digitally enhanced. For a person seeking love, online dating services are available for almost all segments of society. Dating apps exist for gay men, people of color, Christian conservatives, and baby boomers (Grindr, Soul Swipe, Christian Mingle, and SilverSingles, respectively), to name just a few examples. For a person seeking temporary companionship, a "one-night stand," well, there is an app for that too. Today, in much of the United States, however, an LGBTQ person is less restricted when seeking companionship than they were forty years ago. Thus, in the 1980s gay rodeo provided a place for people to enjoy the sport of rodeo and possibly meet a partner for the weekend, or much longer.

Our Chosen Family

LGBTQ rodeo participants found friends, family, lovers, hookups, and life partners; the judgment-free zone accepted all who attended. At the 1981 Reno Gay Rodeo, there were special moments that could not have occurred in mainstream rodeo at that time, or possibly even now, "like two cowpokes who successfully roped their calf, then danced around the arena together while the crowd roared its support. Or the two other cowboys dancing to Sharon McNight's 'Stand By Your Man,' their hats tipped back, tears running down their faces with love for one another."[5] LGBTQ rodeo athletes were drawn to gay rodeo because they did not have to hide their identities; gay rodeo allowed them to fall in love in plain sight.

This chapter explores coupling at the gay rodeo. Gay rodeo has provided an alternative venue for like-minded cowboys and cowgirls to meet for rodeo and, at times, fall in love. Looking through archived gay rodeo programs, a reader will find advertisements for gay bars throughout the country as well as more uninhibited establishments such as bathhouses and video arcades. The gay rodeo has provided an alternative to these options with a carnival-like event that celebrates western culture and the sport of rodeo. That is not to say that promiscuity and polyamorous relationships have not existed otherwise; however, I wish to illustrate that the bonds that were created through gay rodeo might have never developed without it. Moreover, these bonds became increasingly important and necessary in the mid-1980s and 1990s as the HIV/AIDS pandemic disrupted this family and broke the hearts of many. The IGRA became a leading organization in promoting safe sex practices and philanthropy for those impacted by the virus, later discussed in chapters 8 and 9. And, for some, gay rodeo helped couples meet to begin writing their lifelong love story.

## A SAFE SOCIAL SPACE

In mainstream sport throughout the twentieth and twenty-first centuries, a semblance of the military's "Don't ask, don't tell" policy prevailed, as discussed in previous chapters. In return, LGBTQ men and women avoided demonstrating any obvious signs of their true sexual identity. This social rule made it difficult for gay rodeo cowboys and cowgirls to find each other at mainstream events. Sociologist Eric Anderson argues that "combined with Christian dogma, sport became a vessel for male youth to prove they were heterosexual."[6] I would take this assertion further and argue that sport became a vessel for closeted male youth to hide their gay identity. Heteronormative rules dictated that LGBTQ athletes were not welcome in sports during the twentieth century.

Whether in beach volleyball or college football, heterosexual-identifying athletes are celebrated in sport. For example, the media published more articles online about Kerri Walsh Jennings being pregnant while winning the 2012 Olympic gold medal in beach volleyball than they did about her gold-medal-winning performance itself. Coverage of her fertility and her husband, watching from the stands and eager to be a father, is what sociologist Jay Coakley calls an example of compulsory heterosexuality.[7] Similarly, media broadcasts of college football games often provide details about the quarterbacks' personal relationships. During one University of Georgia game in 2014, the announcers became enamored with quarterback Aaron Murray's girlfriend at the time, Kacie McDonnell, sitting in the stands with Murray's parents. The announcers appeared to be more interested in his relationship with a beautiful woman than the game that viewers had tuned in to watch.

Sport has long been a social world where men are dominant, and those who emphasize their heterosexual identities are seen as the most authentic. Athletes who came out after their playing careers ended often explain how they hid their secret lives, concealing their homosexual romances or encounters with false stories about where they were going after games. After athletes come out of the closet to their friends and former teammates and coaches, they sometimes learn that their lives were not as secret as they had believed. Former college football player, and now member of the Pennsylvania House of Representatives, Brian Sims learned this truth about his teammates. Sims explained that when he was the senior captain of the Bloomsburg University football team he came out to his team, and few of his teammates seemed surprised. Sims influenced his teammates to become allies for LGBTQ adults and youth;

he explained that one teammate, who is currently the head coach at a Catholic high school in Pennsylvania, is "the biggest ally" in that school.[8] Sims, like many other athletes who came out to teammates or former teammates, has helped correct misconceptions and stereotypes about LGBTQ athletes in sports. The more visible the LGBTQ community is, the more social improvement can occur, and gay rodeos accomplished that. In a 2001 interview published in the IGRA Finals Rodeo program, Andy Goeler, a Bud Light marketing director, noted that Bud Light's sponsorship of gay rodeo "represents a merging of two important demographics."[9] Through these sponsorships, gay rodeo organizers helped bridge that gap.

Yet, "don't ask, don't tell" continues to exist in many sports teams today as an unofficial policy. Coaches like Rene Portland of Penn State University's women's basketball team violated the "don't ask" rule and actively sought out lesbians on her team to remove them. Players described the experience as a witch hunt. One player tried to transfer out, and Portland sabotaged the athlete's transfer eligibility by having team physicians state in her medical records that she had a chronic condition that required monitoring. Thus, that athlete's playing career was over; no division-one team had any interest in her. Transfer universities declined to offer the once high-profile high school player a scholarship. For athletes who had not come out to their families, the recruitment process pushed them further into the closet. Portland engaged in what the NCAA defines as "negative recruiting," mentioning to potential players and their parents that she had heard rumors that the other schools the recruit was considering had lesbians on the team.[10]

Gay rodeo is not only a place for LGBTQ athletes, but also a welcoming place for all those who are struggling to accept their sexual or gender identities. LGBTQ people who are interested in gay rodeo do not have to compete; they can volunteer at an event or sit in the stands as fans. Many rodeo programs include addresses and phone numbers of LGBTQ services such as youth counseling, safe sex information, and help lines for people who might feel they can no longer cope. Many interviewees have commented that gay rodeo saved their lives. It is impossible to quantify how many lives have been saved because of this organization and its efforts to reach out and help others muddle through bigotry and homophobia. The liberating environment of gay rodeo is a place in the American West where an LGBTQ person can openly express their feelings for someone who has caught their attention, and who also enjoys rural life.

In the late 1970s and early 1980s, there were few places in the West for LGBTQ people to openly express themselves in such a way, outside of urban gay bars and social clubs. Open displays of same-sex fondness were taboo, and public displays of affection were reserved for couples believed to be of different sexes. Even by the late 1990s, gay rodeo was one of the few spaces where LGBTQ couples could openly express affection safely, outside of gay bars. Arguably, it is the only sport today where this holds true, although professional baseball, for one night, has an LGBTQ appreciation event, and other sports sometimes hold similar events. Gay rodeo has always provided a continuously safe environment. And while mainstream sports may artificially produce love with the "kiss cam," gay rodeo has always been authentic in such expressions. Where else but the Jefferson County Fairgrounds in Golden, Colorado, could you have seen Justin Meadows propose marriage to Devon Garcia in the center of the arena? These two men met and fell in love at an IGRA rodeo.[11]

## CRUISING FOR COWBOYS

Gay rodeo has brought people together who have similar interests in country culture, as well as a sexual attraction to a country cowboy or cowgirl look. Country bars like Charlie's have provided a space where men dance with men and women with other women. It is common for two strangers to meet and dance one dance, or all evening long. As Michael Vrooman explained about gay rodeo and coupling: "Just like any organization or any large group where there are attractive people, you have no problem finding immediate romance."[12] These country bars were often connected to gay rodeo via advertisements in rodeo programs, and advertisements for the rodeo in local bars.

Bars and dance clubs became important places for social gatherings for the LGBTQ community. One of the most important and influential bar owners is John King, who owns the popular bar Charlie's, located in several cities. Charlie's advertises in gay rodeo programs throughout the country, with the cover displaying a "disco boot," resembling a disco ball. At every Charlie's in the country one will find the disco boot hanging above the center of the dance floor. This advertisement in rodeo programs transformed that shiny boot into a beacon of hope for lonely LGBTQ westerners (fig. 16). Country music has always been important to cowboy and cowgirl culture, and *Roundup* magazine featured stories about the Country Music Awards and articles about artists like Garth Brooks. However, country dancing appears to have been the most important factor in popularizing cowboy culture among gay men. Almost every gay rodeo included a dance party, and LGBTQ-friendly bars that advertised in rodeo programs featured two-stepping or line dancing. The Tornado Club, a bar in Fort Collins, Colorado, featured country dance lessons at 8:30 p.m., so newcomers could be ready for the 9:00 p.m.-to-closing country dance night.[13] Nightclubs in cities like Los Angeles and Minneapolis transformed into country dance halls when the rodeo was in town and advertised in gay rodeo programs. In various regions of the West, country gay bars had dance floors for two-stepping and the intimate shadow dancing discussed in chapter three. The Spurs Saloon in Cathedral City, California, with its slogan "The Romance of the West," advertised that patrons could dance to country music seven nights a week.[14]

Whether it was dancing or cruising, the music was roaring, the venue was packed, and LGBTQ attendees had an opportunity to meet the person of their preference. Yet, many of the advertisements targeted the largest demographic of gay rodeo participants and attendees—men. An advertisement in the 1992 Texas Gay Rodeo program by the Brick Bar in Dallas read: "Cruise/Dance Bar; Open 7 Days a Week; Western Wednesdays; $.25 Draft All Day/All Night; Shirtless Sunday T-Dance; Levi/Leather after 9 PM."[15] The ad featured the silhouette of a cowboy with his hat, denim jeans, and boots. This bar did not shy away from announcing the two main reasons to visit: either dance with men or "cruise" for something more. In the thousands of pages within hundreds

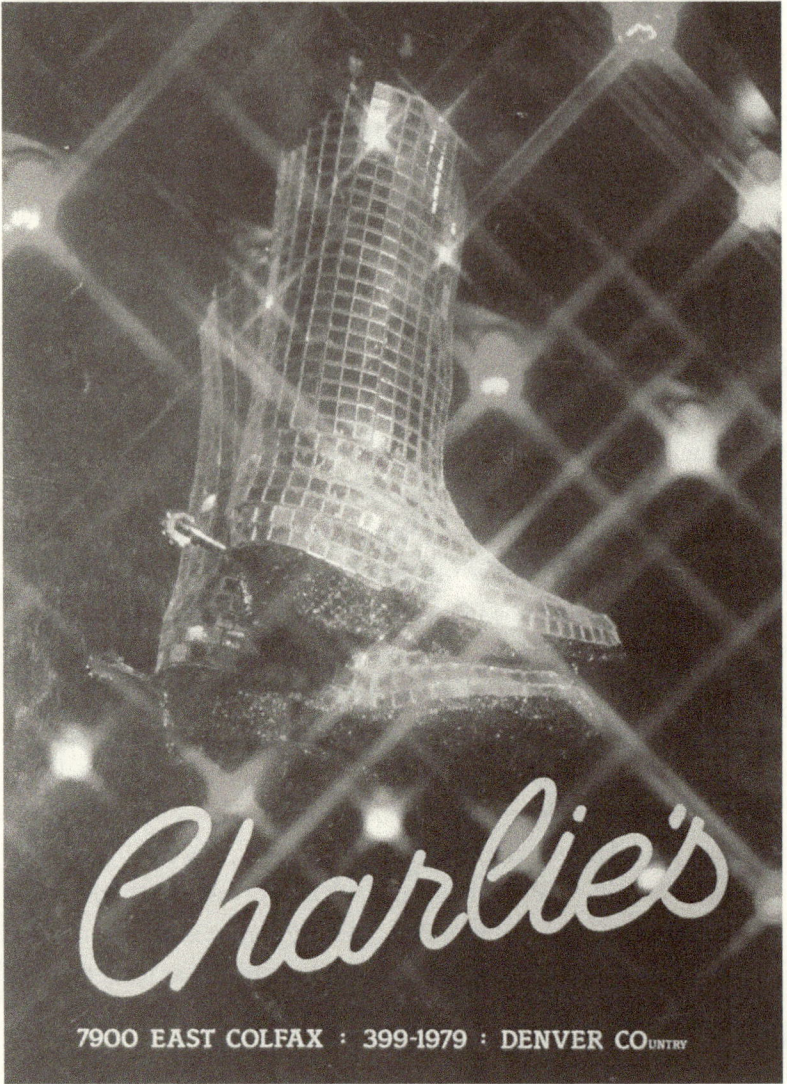

**Fig. 16.** Charlie's Disco Boot. Advertisement for Charlie's country and western gay bar in Denver. Credit to Frank Harrell and the International Gay Rodeo Association Archives, gayrodeohistory.org.

of archived rodeo programs from 1979 to November 2019, two of the most prevalent themes represented in advertisements for gay bars were that they were dancing establishments or places to cruise and meet men.

## ARCADES, BATHS, AND PUBLIC SPACES

For some gay men who are closeted, going to a gay bar is too risky. Depending on where you are in the world, identifying as gay, lesbian, bisexual, transgender, or queer can be dangerous. Society in the United States has progressed in the fifty years since the Stonewall riots, but people have not always been as accepting of the LGBTQ community. Examining the past reveals how resourceful LGBTQ people were in creating a community, establishing LGBTQ-friendly neighborhoods, and developing secret codes for men and women to find suitable partners. The colloquial term used to describe an intuitive ability to identify a queer person is "gaydar," a blend of "gay" and "radar." It is often used by gay men to spot other gay men, and some cisgender men and women who identify as heterosexual claim that they, too, have this ability. LGBTQ people in the United States, in earlier decades, lived in a secret world, often trying to remain hidden from friends and family. As society progressed, certain elements of gay male culture remained taboo or hidden, and gay men created a "hanky code" to signify subcultural preferences.

The hanky code is based on two variables: the location and color of one's handkerchief. A man would tuck a handkerchief in the back pocket of his blue jeans. If he placed it in his right back pocket, the person preferred submission; placed in the left back pocket, he preferred domination. This indicated the sexual role he would typically play. Armband tattoos were also often used to signify a preference for an active or passive role in sex. Likewise, the color of a handkerchief indicated the activity the bearer enjoyed. For example, a dark blue handkerchief represents anal sex, light blue indicates oral sex, gray signifies an interest in bondage, and orange lets potential partners know that "anything goes."[16] Thus, an orange handkerchief in the left jeans pocket means that the bearer is dominant in just about anything a potential partner is looking for.

Cruising in public spaces might seem dark, uninhibited, and seedy, but it is like the use of an app on a smartphone today to locate a person in proximity. Dating during the new millennium transformed in unprecedented ways. During the early twenty-first century, face-to-face encounters with pickup lines, and personal ads in newspapers and magazines, were replaced by smartphone apps that allow the user to virtually break the ice with an instant message. Rather than risk face-to-face rejection following a well-planned pickup line, smartphone apps such as Grindr or Scruff provide as much information in an open forum as a user is willing to reveal, and they allow for private images one can send once a romantic connection is confirmed. For example, on Scruff, a profile details how a user identifies, their ideal partner, their preferred sexual practices, and any additional information they wish to include. These apps sort men by distance; thus, the first ad is usually a person in proximity. Testing this app in the 2019 IGRA Finals arena on the afternoon of Saturday, October 26, revealed there were fifty-two logged-in cowboys, all within two hundred feet of the smartphone. Profiles ranged from men looking for men interested in sexual encounters to men looking for romance or possibly just new friends. One profile was of a thirty-nine-year-old white male, five feet nine inches tall, weighing two hundred pounds, and in an "open relationship," meaning that he and his partner allowed each other to have sexual experiences with others. He identified as a muscular guy and a "bear" looking for muscular guys, bears, jocks, or leather-inclined men, and he revealed his HIV status. The word "bear" in gay male culture usually indicates a man who is hairy, large in frame, often projecting an image of over-the-top masculinity. Another profile was of a thirty-three-year-old man who identified as a muscular jock, looking to meet "military, jocks, muscle, geeks" or discreet men for friendships, "random play/NSA [no strings attached]" or chat only. The broad variety in his preferences is a way of, as they say, casting a wide net, but it enhanced the possibility of a chance meeting. Before these apps became popular, internet dating websites, such as gay.com and manhunt.com, and internet chat rooms on providers like AOL had already supplanted the personal ads found in print media. However, then and now, the randomness of these encounters puts these men at risk of contracting HIV.

By the early 1990s testing for HIV had become common among gay men, and testing sites provided the service often at low cost or free of charge. However, disclosing an HIV-positive status was difficult for some because of its social stigma. Society stereotyped gay men as almost certainly having AIDS and believed this to be true because of lifestyles of promiscuity. And, even within the LGBTQ community, HIV-positive men were stigmatized because it was assumed that they had been careless or "got it because they were a slut."[17] An HIV-positive status also limited that person's dating pool. Herndon L. Davis argues that HIV-positive men had two options. The first was to voluntarily disclose their status to a sexual partner. The second was to be honest about their status only if the sexual partner asked. Davis states: "Many HIV-negative individuals believe that if HIV-positive people engage in sex (whether protected or not) without having fully disclosing [sic] their HIV status, they've committed attempted murder. However, many HIV-positive people say that 'you should ask, and don't just assume.'"[18] The stigma of an HIV-positive status has made dating a challenge for some men. Today, many dating apps have an option whereby a person can reveal their HIV status.

Certain locations are conducive to men meeting other men who are either less concerned about contracting HIV or confident that they are practicing safe sex. Gay rodeo programs contain advertisements for these venues, primarily video arcades and bathhouses. Almost all gay rodeo programs, from the earliest archived program to those during the early 2000s, contain ads for bathhouses, video arcades, and bars known to have private dark rooms. These places provide space for the uninhibited to tempt their sexual desires. Advertisers filled their ads with sexual overtones. In addition to depicting mostly naked, attractive men in their ads, they entice readers with daily specials, discounts for those with rodeo tickets, or free entrance at the baths for rodeo contestants. The clever promotion attracted rodeo attendees because entrance was free, but it also led rodeo men to believe they might meet other rodeo men, which was not easy to do in some of their rural hometowns. These promotional ads are also printed in local LGBTQ magazines. Anyone who might have an attraction to cowboys can assume that, during rodeo weekend, they'll have an opportunity to meet some. While bathhouses in the early days of AIDS were suspected of being places where the disease was easily spread, eventually they became the first places to advocate for safe sex and provide free condoms and HIV testing. Gay rodeo by the 2010s became more family-friendly, and it is less common to see advertisements for baths and arcades today than the 1980s and 1990s.

## GAY RODEO LOVE STORIES

Love, for a gay cowboy on the ranch, is not easy to find even today and was especially risky in the 1980s. A Montana cowboy found an advertisement for a country and western gay correspondence club known as the Mavericks. This was the snail-mail version of Facebook and other social media platforms today. The man wrote in:

> I saw your ad for a national club for gay cowboys and admirers. I really think what you're doing is great! I have a few head of cattle, have almost always lived in the country, and one way or another worked with cattle since I was eleven years old. A very major drawback, one of the few from my perspective, is trying to meet other gay men with similar interests, especially in very small towns where you never know if you dare say something to someone when they seem to be cruising—or are they just friendly? It would be nice to actually meet others who are into ranching and rural life. The few men I do know are already involved in committed relationships, but with a little luck, your club may be the answer to the frustrations of being a cattleman and being gay. Well, Bud . . . looking forward to receiving more information about Mavericks.[19]

Same-sex coupling is more accepted in society today, thanks to decades of advocacy for marriage equality, partner benefits, and specific policies that protect people from discrimination because of their sexual orientation or gender identity. This was hardly the case in the early 1980s, unless you were at a gay rodeo event. Thus, when rural gay cowboys and cowgirls learned about gay rodeo, they were eager to attend, especially when local newspapers reported on the event and its participants. In a May 1981 *Lawrence* (KS) *Journal-World* article, gay rodeo cowboy Patrick Kelly's story was printed on page six: "He can rope a calf, sport a Stetson and bust a bronc with the best of them. But when the rodeo is over, he wants to feel free to enjoy a congratulatory hug and kiss in public from his male companion."[20] For an LGBTQ person living in a conservative region of the country, learning about gay rodeo was exhilarating.

Kelly talked about his enthusiasm for hugging and kissing his male companion in public: "Someday, we'd like to get to the point where we wouldn't have to do this. . . . None of us like to be separated from the rest of the population, but that's the reality we're facing. Someday we hope people understand that we're human beings and no different from anybody else." One thing is certain: social progress and acceptance of LGBTQ people in society and in sport has increased because of Kelly and the rodeo cowboys and cowgirls who have shared their stories for these chapters.[21]

Cowboys Jeffrey McCasland and Philip (Phil) Lister, also known as "the Velcro Cowboys," remember holding hands on their first date. Their "Velcro" identity comes from the fact that twelve years after coupling, they admit, their public hand holding has never abated, even though they endure a bit of teasing with the nickname.[22] Lister and McCasland met in Denver at the November 2004 IGRA Convention: "We both remember that day vividly when we first saw each other in the lobby of the Marriott Hotel and walked into each other's lives. We knew there was a special connection between us from that first day, but Jeffrey was in a relationship at the time."[23] Phil remembers thinking, "Another good cowboy taken," and the two enjoyed talking and getting to know each other as friends.[24]

Thanks to the website Homorodeo.com, Phil and Jeffrey reconnected three years after they first met. Mainstream sites such as Match.com, designed for heterosexual coupling, quickly evolved to include search options for women looking for women and men looking for men. Within the LGBTQ community, sites such as Gay.com broke into the cyberdating market as well. Encouraged by his friend Harley Deuce, Phil added a dating profile on the Homorodeo.com website, and, when scanning through the eligible cowboys, he found Jeffrey's profile page—he was now a single man. Phil lived in Omaha and Jeffrey lived in Albuquerque, but that didn't stop Phil from thinking fondly of the Land of Enchantment, and he sent Jeffrey a message. Unknowingly, the two were online at the same time, and Phil received an immediate response. The two men later explained:

> For us, our love story truly started the spring of 2007 as we reacquainted through email, phone calls, and nightly video chats. Although we lived 1,000 miles apart, we picked up right where we left off in Denver three years earlier. We each drove back to Denver on Easter weekend of 2007 to have our first official date in the place where we first met. We both remember fondly that first weekend date together, the connection we had, the fun we had and being lost in our excitement for each other that we wouldn't realize we were walking down Colfax Avenue or in shopping malls holding hands. When a stranger's head would snap around after realizing there were two cowboys walking by holding hands, it would make us laugh. . . . We have endured years of teasing with the name "the Velcro Cowboys." We don't mind the teasing, as we wear that descriptive name with pride![25]

They admitted that as their relationship grew strong over the following four years, the long distance was tough. In 2011 Phil found a new job and a new chapter in his life and career, moving to Albuquerque to be with Jeffrey, and in December 2014 they "were blessed with a wonderful wedding day surrounded by friends and family" at their home in the East Mountains of Albuquerque (fig. 17).[26]

Gay rodeo brought two cowgirls together. When Candy Pratt first saw a flyer for gay rodeo, she thought, "gay rodeo, are you kidding?" and she entered a couple of rodeos in 1988. Pratt had heard about rodeo for Black athletes and Native Americans, but this was new to her. A year later she

Our Chosen Family

Fig. 17. Engagement photograph. Philip Lister and Jeffrey McCasland. Photo courtesy of Armando DeAguero.

entered a few more competitions, and by 1990 she was hooked on it.[27] She competed in speed events at first, then she took on camp events, followed by roughstock; eventually, she won numerous All-Around Cowgirl titles. In 1992, at the IGRA convention in Minneapolis/Saint Paul, Pratt noticed a woman she thought was beautiful. Later that year, the same woman was at the Atlantic Stampede Rodeo awards, where Pratt took home numerous honors, which led her to walk past this woman's table several times. The following year, at the North Star Gay Rodeo in Minnesota, her mother and her friend David Renier were standing with the beautiful woman whom Pratt admired. Her name was Dorine, and the two were introduced. Pratt explained: "So it was kind of, it was kind of meant to be."[28] They would eventually get married in Maui, one year before same-sex marriage became legal in the state of Texas, a development that surprised Pratt. She had thought that Texas would be the last state to legalize same-sex marriage, "and it shocked me that the very next year it was legalized."[29]

Not all the cowboys and cowgirls interviewed came from rural backgrounds. Cowboy Paul Vigil grew up ranching and branding cattle, and he even believes that he was on horseback before he could walk. However, Vigil refers to his life partner as a "city kid." Anticipating that his interview about his relationship was intended to bring forth intimate details about his personal life, Vigil said:

> I don't have anything juicy to share, but I can tell you that my current partner and I have grown as a couple because of gay rodeo. My partner is a city kid, doesn't like the outdoors, is allergic to most animal dander, and will not work outside for any reason. However, he had been to "straight rodeo," but never a gay rodeo, and the first rodeo that I took him to was the IGRA Finals Rodeo in 2017, here in Albuquerque, New Mexico. He loved it, but most of all it's been the people that he's met in our rodeo family that have brought us closer together. The support that we all have for each other and the way we will do whatever is needed to help and lift each other up has made him a lifelong fan. He's even considering competing now in 2020. He's my biggest success . . . I'm turning this city kid into a country kid.[30]

Vigil's relationship signifies what gay rodeo can do by uniting people from completely different social worlds and exemplifies the love that can develop through gay rodeo.

As a final example, the company Male America often advertised in gay rodeo programs. Those gay cowboys who did not find love at the rodeo could subscribe and receive an assortment of six cards by mail order. These cards included nonpornographic photographs of men. Images like the one of two sailors sitting on a dock (fig. 18) leave it up to the recipient's imagination to create the story: "The pictures are linked to tell a story and do all the talking. No printed message is included, allowing each viewer to create his own."[31]

# MALE AMERICA
# CARDS FOR MEN

MALE AMERICA's new 2-photo sequence cards are specifically designed to appeal to gay men.

MALE AMERICA cards contain 2 full-size 4-color photographs. The pictures are linked to tell a story, and do all the talking. No printed message is included, allowing you to create your own.

To receive an assortment of 6 sequence cards by first-class mail, send us your check or money order for $10. Offer valid in USA only to persons 21 or over. Make checks payable to MALE AMERICA.

MALE AMERICA, 141 West 26th Street, New York NY 10001

Name _____

Address _____

City _____ State _____ ZIP _____

Signature _____
I am 21 or over

**Fig. 18.** "Male America Cards for Men." Credit to Frank Harrell and the International Gay Rodeo Association Archives, gayrodeohistory.org.

## CONCLUSION

For the LGBTQ community, the rodeo is a safe place for coupling with common ground. Forty years after the first gay rodeo, gay cowboys and cowgirls can share hundreds of love stories. However, not all the coupling led to happily-ever-after love stories like that of the Velcro Cowboys. As gay men met each other during the 1970s and early 1980s, they were not aware of a silent killer. A sexually transmitted virus was unknowingly being spread throughout the LGBTQ community. This virus indiscriminately attacked the immune system and, over a course of several years, weakened immune responses, allowing opportunistic infections to ravage the bodies of young and healthy people. The media initially referred to it as Gay Related Immune Deficiency (GRID), Gay Cancer, and the Gay Plague. "The gay-specific nomenclature of the early 1980s not only reflected the presumption of epidemiological prevalence of disease in gay and bisexual male populations but also forged an early social and cultural link between homosexuality and AIDS."[32] A perfect storm was on the horizon. As gay men celebrated their individuality and took advantage of new opportunities to break from the heteronormative social rules of coupling during an era of sexual liberation, the virus later known as HIV spread from lover to lover. In rodeo, the term "covering" describes when a rider manages to stay on a bronc or a bull long enough to qualify for a score and potentially win that event. Metaphorically speaking, as the early 1980s progressed, gay rodeo cowboys were going to have to fight and hold on and cover. However, for thousands of gay rodeo participants and fans, HIV/AIDS would take their lives, leaving their names and tributes on the pages of rodeo programs in the months and years that followed.

Gay rodeo is a rarity in sports because it is a place where men and women compete together, enter all the same events, and form a family that is self-supporting. Michael Vrooman explained that his first gay rodeo felt like home, that it provided something in his life that had been missing. To him, this rodeo family provided a shared sense of love. Vrooman explained that the gay rodeo "is a comfortable environment, with people that I can trust, that I can relate to, and feel safe. . . . All the things I'm

Our Chosen Family

sure everyone else says . . . Kiss and hold hands with the one that you love. And that environment, are you crazy? That was a miracle to me."[33] Amy Griffin explained that, unlike in almost any other sport, goodwill transcends competition, and competitors help each other before and after competing against each other. Griffin remembered competing in chute dogging at a rodeo in San Diego in which, on the second day of the rodeo, it was between her and her friend Angie for the championship buckle. Griffin competed and was less successful than she had been on the first day. After her attempt, she went back behind the chute and encouraged Angie as she was preparing for her own go at it. Angie went out and dogged quickly, winning the championship buckle. Shortly thereafter, a woman who was a new contestant approached Griffin and asked why she had helped her biggest competitor that day, and Griffin responded: "Because she's, my friend. . . . That's how we do things here. Ya know. The first person likely to give you suggestions, give you advice, point out what you did right, what you might be able to do differently in the future to make your run better, is gonna be your best competition. That's how we roll at IGRA."[34] These are the relationships formed at IGRA rodeos. In these arenas are countless stories about friendship, family, and love.

# 8 The Riderless Horse

HIV/AIDS in America and the Gay Rodeo Community

> The disease, like a vampire, could manifest itself in many forms; and, like a vampire, it seemed impossible to track down. It was out at night, stalking the backrooms of bars and lonely docks, its power lying in its attraction, its seductiveness, in the prey's willingness to surrender. Most of its victims were relatively young; it seemed to draw strength from the strong, leaving them drained.
>
> —David Black

The Ceremony of the Riderless Horse is a tribute to those who have passed and symbolizes the end of the relationship between a horse and a rider. It is symbolized by a single horse, without a rider, and cowboy boots positioned in reverse in the stirrups. The ceremony and tradition began with the U.S. cavalry to remember fallen soldiers. The Golden State Gay Rodeo Association (GSGRA) permanently retired the number "1" as a contestant number at gay rodeo events in California in the mid-1980s. In the association's 1992 rodeo program, an organizer announced: "It is now the number for those who have been taken, that they may always have their place at our rodeos, still loved, still missed. We know they ride with us today."[1] This chapter examines how the HIV/AIDS pandemic affected the LGBTQ community in the 1980s and the response of International Gay Rodeo Association (IGRA) members and gay rodeo fans. Like much of the world, IGRA members felt the impact of AIDS. Many of these young and strong men, who fearlessly rode 1,200-pound beasts in the center of a packed arena, would succumb to a microscopic virus. And, as many died alone, the gay rodeo family came together in support.

People unknowingly infected with HIV in the 1970s began to be diagnosed in the early 1980s, when doctors and scientists still knew little about treatment, transmission, or a possible cure. At that time, life expectancy was an estimated eighteen months postdiagnosis.[2] Many of those diagnosed in the 1980s worked to bring HIV/AIDS awareness to the general population, in the face of hostile religious and political conservatives. Most of all, they fought for their lives against a virus that indiscriminately infected men, women, and children. In the mid-1990s new drugs called protease inhibitors provided new hope for a longer life expectancy. In 1996 a twenty-year-old person with HIV had a life expectancy of thirty-nine years. "In 2011, the total life expectancy bumped up to about seventy years."[3]

From the start of the gay rodeo, philanthropy was a vital part of its culture. Giving back to the local community was a way to defuse the widespread homophobia that stigmatized, even endangered, LGBTQ people. By the early 1980s gay rodeos were raising thousands of dollars for charities such as the Muscular Dystrophy Association. In 1983 the Colorado Gay Rodeo Association took a new path. Proceeds from the Rocky Mountain Regional Rodeo would support the National Gay Health Education Foundation. Over the next few years, other regional gay rodeos followed this lead. During the 1980s, President Ronald Reagan and the federal government were slow to respond to the virus, as the first victims were mostly gay men. Christian conservatives argued this was "God's wrath" on the LGBTQ community. Since 1976 the gay rodeo had been an event of inclusion that worked toward combating homophobia and bringing people together. The AIDS crisis, marked by increased homophobia and misinformation about the disease, transformed gay rodeo into an inward-looking philanthropic organization providing support for the LGBTQ community, when few mainstream charities were helping HIV-positive people. The IGRA broke the silence about HIV/AIDS in communities that did not speak of the virus, provided information that helped educate the LGBTQ community about how to keep themselves safe, and, in the process, saved the lives of people who, without a social network like the IGRA, might not have had the resources to learn about prevention or cope with a positive diagnosis. The IGRA became one of the first charitable organizations for those infected with HIV/AIDS, as well as a political platform advocating for more research toward a cure. While the IGRA continued to raise money for many of the same charities as in the past, taking care of their own led to an even stronger sense of community.

## THE EARLY YEARS OF AIDS

As reported in *Newsweek* in 1983, "for Gay America, a decade of care-free sexual adventure, a headlong gambol on the far side of the human libido, has all but come to a close."[4] During the 1970s and early 1980s, LGBTQ Americans celebrated pride in their identity more than ever before. Rejecting heteronormative social rules, LGBTQ people embraced their difference. For gay men, as discussed in the previous chapter, sexual expression became a critical way to defy dominant social rules about sex and the growing conservatism in politics. Christian conservatives saw the gay male lifestyle as sinful, condemned LGBTQ openness in society, and called for laws to curtail their civil rights. For some gay men, sexual expression and a rejection of monogamy were ways to reject heteronormative social pressure. As historian Katherine McFarland Bruce explains, gay and lesbian Americans were "no longer willing to put on a mask of heterosexuality."[5] Gay liberation meant that a cultural lifestyle that required meeting in the shadows of secret social clubs and underground bars was no longer necessary. Unwilling to submit to heteronormative standards in society, Bruce continues, "gays and lesbians now demanded that society change to accommodate them, making room in the culture for sexual and gender difference."[6]

During this early period of liberation, an unidentified virus was already present in the United States, spreading through the sharing of needles by heroin users, through hospital blood transfusions, and during unprotected sex. By 1980 data collected by the Centers for Disease Control and Prevention (CDC) had identified gay men as the demographic with the highest rates of sexually transmitted infections. The CDC reported that over half of all syphilis infections occurred in gay men, and that gonorrhea, hepatitis A, and hepatitis B were more common in men who had sex with other men than those who had sex with women.[7] Although scientists have traced HIV back to 1910 and Léopoldville, the capital city of the Belgian Congo (now Kinshasa in the Democratic Republic of the Congo), it began to spread exponentially during the 1970s.[8] In the early months of the pandemic, some people living with the virus reported that they had had many different sexual partners. Some gay men believed that sex was about social freedom. New Yorker Michael Callen explained in a *Newsweek* article: "The belief that was handed to me was that sex was liberating and more sex was more liberating."[9] This idea of sexual freedom, apparently linked to high rates of sexually transmitted infections, suggests why gay men appeared to be the most vulnerable to this deadly virus.

During the summer of 1981, five cases of a mysterious disease were reported to the CDC. All these patients were either gay men or intravenous heroin users. Historian Victoria A. Harden identifies June 5, 1981, as "the moment when medically trained individuals had become sufficiently aware that a new disease existed."[10] Harden references Randy Shilts and his book *And the Band Played On: Politics, People, and the AIDS Epidemic*, which identified the early 1980s as a moment of triumph for the LGBTQ community in large cities like San Francisco, where "gay life had become open after such a long period of oppression."[11] After achieving so much progress in the previous decade, it was difficult for many gay men to believe that they now had a new and deadlier opponent.

As discussed in chapter three, gay rodeo programs shared information about LGBTQ-friendly businesses, and bathhouses often paid for ad space. The back cover of the 1979 Reno Gay Rodeo program was a full-page advertisement for Club CB Reno Baths, a men's bathhouse.[12] Open since 1962 and now co-owned, this bathhouse still exists, under the name Steve's Bathhouse, and claims to be the oldest operating bathhouse in the country (except for a temporary closure due to the 2020 COVID-19 pandemic).[13] In the 1979 Reno rodeo program, in addition to the advertisement for Club CB Baths, several pages included sexually suggestive images. As Reno organizers prepared for their fourth rodeo, the virus was surreptitiously spreading, and these men's social clubs fostered further transmission.

In the early 1980s rumors began to spread of a "gay cancer" in New York City. In August 1981 the *New York Times* reported that two rare diseases, Kaposi's sarcoma and pneumocystis, had been diagnosed in more than one hundred gay men since the start of that year, with twenty-six cases in June and July alone. The *Times* reported:

> Kaposi's sarcoma is a rare disease that characteristically strikes elderly men and is seldom fatal. But many homosexual patients were young men, and seventeen percent of those who were stricken have died so far. The disease agency [the Center for Disease Control (CDC)] says that of every three million Americans, two persons could be expected to get that form of cancer. . . . Nobody knows why homosexual men get the disease, Dr. [Harold] Jaffe said. There may be a link to some previous infection, or the victims may have a problem with their immune systems. The diseases may be linked to their sexual lifestyle, drug or some other environmental cause, although no evidence of those connections has been found.[14]

Researchers eventually learned that the men had developed Kaposi's sarcoma because their immune systems had been compromised as a result of contracting HIV. Environmental factors such as bathhouses and a culture of sexual liberation may have left these men vulnerable to infection, but a counterargument was made by the mid-1980s that bathhouses were a place to educate men about AIDS.

The deaths of these men because of opportunistic infections were physically and emotionally painful. In the advanced stage of Kaposi's sarcoma, the rare and fatal skin cancer attacks the brain, making speech difficult and causing unyielding headaches. These young men "would die of their dementias the way eighty-year-olds do, where they curl up in bed and die. . . . Combined with the stigma and isolation that a lot of patients had to endure, made it not just a terrible death physically, but a terrible death in every other way as well."[15] The CDC identified that the first one hundred cases had struck men who had been openly gay for at least ten years. And the agency recognized that these men "had a complicated social lifestyle involving a number of recreational drugs, as well as a large number of sexual partners. So it wasn't surprising that if a new infection were to come along it could be focused on the gay community."[16]

In June 1981 the CDC published the first reported cases of AIDS in the *Morbidity and Mortality Weekly Report* (MMWR). This report, read by physicians around the world, detailed what many now believed was a new disease that infected gay men. Dr. Margaret Fischl of the University of Miami School of Medicine found the MMWR report interesting, because she had started to see patients with similar rare opportunistic infections. However, Dr. Fischl's patients were men and women of Haitian descent. By November 1981 heterosexual intravenous drug users had begun showing up in hospitals in the Bronx with the same signs and symptoms discussed in the MMWR, identifying a new infected demographic. These men and women visited "shooting galleries," where they rented a needle to inject heroin and returned it for the next visitor. The sharing of needles in large groups contributed to the rapid spread of the disease.[17] In 1982 the media referred to AIDS as the 4-H disease, or as GRIDS. The term "4-H" referred to hemophiliacs, heroin users, homosexuals, and Haitians.[18] As for the acronym GRIDS (gay-related immune deficiency), the media used it to name the illness and created a panic about gay men.

By 1985 New York State was urging New York City health officials to shut down bathhouses and other places known for public sexual activity. Bathhouses began providing free condoms and posted warnings about unprotected sex. These were some of the first public places where men talked about AIDS and, moreover, where volunteers offered anonymous free testing for HIV and other sexually transmitted infections. There was ambivalence among gay men about closing the baths down. Some gay liberationists saw this as a step backward, but the baths were also a place where this deadly virus could be sexually transmitted to many others. On October 25, 1985, thirteen members of the state's Public Health Council voted 12–0 in favor of closing bathhouses. One member, Dr. Victor Sidel, an Albert Einstein College of Medicine professor, abstained because he believed that the closures were unnecessarily hasty. The decision gave city health officials the power to padlock bathhouse doors for two months as "public nuisances." Jack Stoddard, manager of New St. Marks Baths, one of the largest bathhouses in the city, said that he would fight the decision in court. New York City's health commissioner, Dr. David J. Sencer, criticized the decision, expressing his belief that education was necessary. Sencer argued: "The issue is human behavior, not where the behavior takes place."[19] He provided evidence that sexual contact in bathhouses had declined in recent years because of greater awareness about HIV/AIDS. Sencer believed that city health officials should consider public warnings focused on HIV/AIDS and sexual activity. In San Francisco, a similar ban was struck down in 1984. Eventually all bathhouses shut down because of their reputation as breeding grounds for infection, which scared off customers.[20]

Rodeo Hall of Fame inductee Jack Morgan said that he struggled as a young man in the 1980s. He had just been introduced to gay rodeo as a traveling member of Charlie's Clogging Team when safe sex was first openly discussed within the LGBTQ community. Morgan struggled with being attracted to men, who were admiring him as well, while fearing the virus that was tearing through the community. Morgan witnessed the pain and suffering around him, and he learned to use this fear to keep himself safe. Pausing to wipe tears from his eyes during an interview, he continued: "When you see someone that, that was always very attractive to you, and sweet and enthusiastic and smiling and stuff like that, and you see him on a fairly regular basis and you see a significant deterioration quickly, and you see, ya know, the lesions, and then you see him when they are nothing, and you are attending their funeral. You know as a twenty-something-year-old kid . . ." Morgan paused, attempting to collect himself. Like many gay men who came of age during the AIDS pandemic, he realized that knowledge of the virus was power. One generation removed from the men who were unaware that a deadly virus was circulating throughout their social networks, many of these young men say it is a miracle that they are alive thirty to forty years later. Morgan continued and spoke of his friend Amy. "Amy . . . back in the nineties you know . . . she had a couple of black dresses, and I had a couple of black suits, and one of them was always at the cleaners because it was memorial after memorial."[21] Because of AIDS, gay rodeo brought Morgan and the rodeo family together to talk about those friends who had passed. That was the purpose of the riderless horse. It became a symbol of remembrance, so rodeo family members would not be forgotten. Morgan went on to say that the ceremony is not just about the LGBTQ community, but is a moment for people to remember their mothers, fathers, and community leaders, yet he confessed to having mixed feelings about such a somber memorial during a weekend of fun and celebrations.

In the early years of the virus, false rumors spread that gay men typically had thousands of sexual partners. Morgan likened AIDS to the 2020 COVID-19 pandemic. He argued: "There are some people who are very fearful, and there are some people who are not. There are some people who are taking precautions and wearing masks and social distancing, and there are some who are not, that are risk takers. . . . For me, I see a lot of those similarities. It's more from a nonsexual position as opposed to a sexual position like HIV was, ya know, more risky versus less risky . . . it's that same risk-fear tradeoff."[22] While a subculture of promiscuity existed, the reality was that these statistics stigmatized monogamous gay men. As people became more aware of the virus and its modes of transmission, both men and women began to talk about HIV/AIDS, discuss their sexual histories with their partners, and practice safer sex. While the media published information that demonized gay men as hypersexual, spreading a false narrative throughout society that this was a "gay disease," the people who ultimately became the most at risk—heterosexual-identifying men who lived secret lives that included same-sex encounters—remained too uncomfortable to openly discuss their sexual histories. Closeted Christian conservative white men and men of color soon also became infected, and eventually heterosexual-identifying women who trusted that their sexual partners were monogamous tested positive for the virus as well.

HIV/AIDS did not discriminate, but society did by taking resources away from the vulnerable people who needed them the most. Many who were diagnosed with HIV lost their jobs; family and friends abandoned them if the diagnosis revealed that they were gay; and landlords evicted gay men because of the AIDS panic, leaving them homeless. Abandoned, scared, and without the resources to care for themselves, AIDS patients in their final days were often alone and in pain. However, the first Americans to openly talk about AIDS were from the LGBTQ community, and IGRA members did not turn their backs on infected members of their rodeo family.

## THE POLITICS OF AIDS

In a packed courthouse, a legal battle raged to shut down the Reno Gay Rodeo. "Why—those big, bad gay cowboys was a-comin' to have a rodeo right here! And they was gonna bring in AIDS and give it to all of them fine, upstanding rednecks!"[23] Statements like this were common during the first decade of the AIDS pandemic. Restaurant workers lost their jobs, people were worried that they could get it from toilet seats, families were afraid to send their children to school if a fellow student was infected, and even Catholic churches stopped using a single communion cup out of fear of spreading AIDS. However, the myth that AIDS was a "gay disease" lost some traction when Americans learned about thirteen-year-old Ryan White and his battle with the virus. In December 1984 White received HIV-infected blood during a transfusion in a hospital. White was diagnosed a year later, and doctors gave him six months to live. He surpassed that and lived five more years, much of which he spent educating the American public about the virus. During his five-year battle with HIV/AIDS, Ryan and his mother, Jeanne White-Ginder, fought AIDS-related discrimination in their Kokomo, Indiana, community. The local school board prohibited Ryan from returning to classes once they learned of his diagnosis. Ryan and his mother then helped focus national attention on HIV/AIDS and public education. They won their legal battle and White returned to school, attending until his death in April 1990, one month before his high school graduation.[24]

Civil and human rights were ignored within the criminal justice system. Discussed earlier, in chapter two, law enforcement denied the "equal protection" clause of the Fourteenth Amendment to the United States Constitution by ignoring the personal safety of LGBTQ community members. In Sacramento, California, a gay man was arrested for an outstanding traffic warrant. Deputies at the Rio Cossumnes Correctional Center booked the man, who was dressed to be easily identified as a gay man by other prisoners. Officials provided him with a black shirt rather than a standard prison uniform with identifiable numbers, forced him to wear a pink ID bracelet, and "issued trousers which were quickly replaced with a very tight pair of women's pants."[25] One can only speculate why he was sent into the prison dressed in this unusual attire, but it can be assumed that it was not for his protection. Moreover, he was denied access to a physician regarding necessary prescription medication.[26]

Many LGBTQ rodeo cowboys and cowgirls were raised in Christian families, and they were taught that homosexuality was a sin. The truth about the disease did not stop religious and political conservatives from stigmatizing gay men as being carriers of HIV and a threat to their communities.[27] In major cities, clergy faced questions about their faith and their pastoral duty toward those who were sick. San Francisco's Catholic Charities spokesperson Joseph Zwilling responded to these questions by stating that the Catholic Church still viewed homosexuality as a sin, "but we also see a real need of Christian charity and kindness to those who are suffering."[28] However, Christian extremists broke with larger religious institutions. In Clayton, Missouri, the Central Presbyterian Church congregation voted to withdraw from the Presbyterian group after eight months of deliberation. The church affiliated with a more conservative group, the Evangelical Presbyterian Church, because of their harsher stance on social issues such as homosexuality and AIDS.[29]

Religious extremists called for the quarantine of gay men, especially those infected with AIDS. Conservative evangelical ministers often referred to AIDS as a "gay flu" and showed little sympathy for the afflicted. In editorials written for the St. Louis *Globe-Democrat*, White House speechwriter Pat Buchanan said: "The poor homosexuals—they have declared war against nature, and now nature is exacting an awful retribution."[30] Buchanan went on to demand that gay men be prohibited from food-handling occupations. The Reverend Jerry Falwell, leader of the Moral Majority political organization, argued that homosexuality violated nature's law and explained, in a fire-and-brimstone diatribe, that "God establishes all of nature's laws. When a person ignores those laws, there is a price to pay."[31] Groups like the Pro-Family Christian Coalition launched petition drives to stop gay rodeo events. (The group is not to be confused with the Christian Coalition founded by Pat Robertson in 1987.) Coalition chairman Daniel Hansen argued, "The gathering menaces the public by threatening to spread AIDS."[32] In 1984 Reno Gay Rodeo president Phil Ragsdale condemned these religious extremists, saying: "It is pathetic that these so-called 'good Christians' feel that only their rights are right."[33]

Many IGRA athletes and fans were Christians who were displeased with the messages coming from the pulpit. A group of LGBTQ evangelicals formed Evangelicals Concerned and released a statement responding to Falwell's comments that AIDS was "a definite form of the judgment of God upon a society."[34] Evangelicals Concerned argued: "God does not use disease to punish. . . . [We are] deeply troubled to see the language and convictions of our faith manipulated to attack us and our community, and to further alienate us from our heterosexual neighbors."[35] The AIDS crisis could not have emerged at a worse time. The LGBTQ community, post–1969 Stonewall riots, had made significant social progress in the United States, only to once again experience ostracism because of ignorance and hate.

Magazines like *Rolling Stone* and *Newsweek* began publishing articles attempting to humanize HIV-positive gay men. These articles offered facts about HIV/AIDS and the people living with it, to counter the many community media outlets that provided only a hysterical mixture of misinformation and bigotry. On August 2, 1983, *Newsweek*'s cover read: "Gay America: Sex, Politics and the Impact of AIDS," with two HIV-positive gay men shown on its cover. *Newsweek* went on to publish more articles about gay men, HIV/AIDS, and homophobia. Readers learned more about the painful and horrific reality that AIDS patients endured in their final days of life, including stories of men dying alone after their families had turned them away. *Newsweek* also reported that men in their thirties attended more funerals each month than their elderly grandparents. Three weeks after *Newsweek* released "Gay America," readers commented on the article. Ron Asher said, "It is both refreshing and comforting to see the subject covered by *Newsweek* in a factual article anchored by compassion."[36] However, other readers condemned the LGBTQ community. Terri Gustin of Syracuse, Kansas, blamed gay men for contracting the virus, closing her letter with: "Sorry, fellas—but you asked for it."[37] People like Gustin, who were ignorant about HIV/AIDS, still outnumbered those who understood the virus.

The Gallup organization conducted polls surveying Americans about homosexuality and AIDS in 1982 and 1983. In 1983, 58 percent of those surveyed answered that homosexuality was not acceptable. This number had increased from 51 percent the previous year. The 1983 results illustrated a trend indicating that respondents were less accepting of homosexuality as an "alternative lifestyle." This trend possibly correlated with a growing awareness of AIDS among those surveyed. When asked in 1982 if they had heard of AIDS, 77 percent answered "yes," and by 1983, 91 percent answered "yes" to the same question. When asked whether they believed that if they encountered someone who was HIV positive, they would be likely to contract the disease, 41 percent thought that it was possible or that they were unsure (1983). Finally, 76 percent of the respondents answered that they did not have any friends or acquaintances who were "homosexuals."[38] In a letter to the editors of *Newsweek* about the final question, reader Bill Williams of Chicago stated: "The 76 percent of respondents to your poll who said they had no friends or acquaintances who are homosexual are almost certainly mistaken. They may think that, but almost everyone in America has someone in his or her circle of acquaintances—doctor, lawyer, teacher, coworker, fellow church member—who is gay or lesbian, whether openly so or not. Appearances may be deceiving, but we are everywhere."[39] As more LGBTQ people came out, mainstream Americans became aware of people in their own social circles who did not identify as heterosexual or with their assigned gender at birth. This humanization was important in convincing more Americans to call for funding and research into HIV/AIDS. However, Republican president Ronald Reagan continued to deny that the country had a growing public health crisis, demonstrating a clear failure of leadership on the issue.

By September 1985, 13,074 people had been diagnosed with HIV in the United States, and 6,611 had died. Reagan had still not asked Congress to address the deadly disease, nor had he mentioned AIDS in any public statement. With a rising death toll and the so-called leader of the free world failing to treat HIV/AIDS as a major health crisis, Reagan abdicated leadership during the emerging pandemic. Reagan knew that his base was Christian, conservative, middle-class, and white, and his priority during his presidency was not marginalized groups. In his first few years of office, Reagan reduced Medicaid expenditures by more than 18 percent, and "under Reagan, life-expectancy-at-birth of black Americans decreased."[40] And Reagan slashed the Department of Health and Human Services budget by 25 percent. Moreover, the wealthiest Americans saw a 9 percent gain of wealth, and the poorest Americans experienced a 9 percent loss of wealth between 1982 and 1985.[41] The Reagan administration ignored the LGBTQ community's call to provide federal support for research into the virus. This denial appeased Reagan's conservative base, who believed AIDS to be a disease that afflicted the morally corrupt. They thought that social distancing from gay men was necessary, even though the CDC had reported that casual contact did not contribute to the spread of HIV:

The occurrence of AIDS cases among homosexual men, IV drug abusers, persons with hemophilia, sexual partners of members of these groups, and recipients of blood transfusions is consistent with the hypothesis that AIDS is caused by an agent that is transmitted sexually or, less commonly, through contaminated needles or blood. . . . There has been no evidence that the disease was acquired through casual contact with AIDS patients or with persons in population groups with an increased incidence of AIDS. AIDS is not known to be transmitted through food, water, air, or environmental surfaces.[42]

Religious conservatives followed their faith over science, and Reagan chose politics over compassion.

It was difficult for LGBTQ rodeo cowboys and cowgirls to accept that Republican leaders denied resources for AIDS awareness and research. Many were from conservative towns and were registered Republicans. Eventually, in September 1985, President Reagan's advisers set up a press conference so that he could address the American public about the fear of AIDS, the misinformation that casual contact spread the disease, and the fact that the disease affected communities beyond those that his base deemed morally corrupt. Dr. Anthony Fauci, the leading expert on infectious diseases during the 2020 COVID-19 pandemic, became the director of the National Institute of Allergy and Infectious Diseases in 1984. Fauci advised every president on infectious diseases from Reagan to Donald Trump. In a briefing before his address to the nation, Reagan read documents provided by health scientists, such as Fauci, confirming that "as far as our best scientists have been able to determine, [the] AIDS virus is not transmitted through casual or routine contact." However, when a reporter asked about casual contact, Reagan walked back the message he had given in his speech and said, "yet medicine has not come forth unequivocally and said, 'This we know for a fact that, uh, it is safe.' And until they do, I think we just have to do the best we can with this problem. I can understand both sides of this problem."[43] This divisive statement further stigmatized an HIV-positive diagnosis, and the conservative Reagan continued to deny scientific funding for HIV/AIDS research, allowing thousands more to die before he left office.

The LGBTQ community was aware that Reagan did not have a plan to fund research into HIV/AIDS. Thirty-nine-year-old Victor Bender of Manhattan made an emotional plea to Congress: "I beg my president to care. I beg my president to be moved. I beg my president to act. . . . There is one man residing in Washington, at 1600 Pennsylvania Avenue, who to my knowledge has never once mentioned the word AIDS in public."[44] Bender wanted the world to know that U.S. federal government officials had turned their backs on the country's citizens. A CBS camera crew had learned that an HIV-positive person would be addressing Congress, and they had refused to cover the story. Another team replaced soundperson Boris Grgurovic and cameraperson Frank Viskup. A representative for CBS stated: "The crew members did not know there would be an AIDS victim present, and no one is forced to do anything if they feel that being in close proximity is dangerous."[45] The story was reported not only in major newspapers like the *New York Times* but by newspapers in smaller cities, like the *Cedar Rapids* (IA) *Gazette*, contributing to public fear about HIV-infected people. An internist at the AIDS clinic at St. Luke's–Roosevelt Hospital in New York testified in 1985 that, over the coming five years, AIDS would kill more young Americans than were killed in the Vietnam War during the course of a decade.[46] As conservative Republican leaders such as Reagan did little to nothing to help the LGBTQ community, the AIDS stigma spread across the country, and people who were ignorant about the disease became increasingly homophobic.

## IGRA'S RESPONSE TO AIDS

IGRA cowboys and cowgirls were left to fight the virus largely through their own efforts. In 1982 the Colorado Gay Rodeo Association (CGRA) was the first to turn inward and use their fundraising efforts for the benefit of the LGBTQ community rather than national organizations like the Muscular Dystrophy Association, stating: "We, as an association, feel MD is a worthwhile charity. However, we feel that particular charity is already well funded. And, we feel that each gay community has its own needs, which often times are overlooked."[47] In addition to the CGRA changing course with its philanthropy, local businesses advertised their fundraising efforts for those diagnosed with AIDS. The Aladdin Theater on East Colfax Avenue in Denver presented a live performance of the musical *Godspell*, directed by Robert Morise. Curtains opened at 8:00 p.m. on June 10, 1983, and general admission was twelve dollars. Theater organizers stated, "Our own need . . . in our own time . . . A benefit for AIDS."[48] By 1984 every regional gay rodeo had joined in the effort to combat AIDS.

The CGRA's 1983 rodeo program advertised a fundraising event for AIDS-related charities. In addition to philanthropy, the Rocky Mountain

The Riderless Horse

Regional Rodeo program recognized the importance of getting tested for other sexually transmitted infections: "Get tested during SAFEWEEK at your favorite gay bar or bath. Help 'clean up' Colorado!!!"[49] By 1988 all of the IGRA regional rodeo programs had addressed HIV/AIDS. The program for the 1988 IGRA Finals announced that money raised would go to the Reno Suicide Hotline Prevention and Crisis Center, the Nevada AIDS Foundation, Hospice House, Aid for AIDS of Nevada, and the American Foundation for AIDS Research. Moreover, the program included a half-page advertisement for an AIDS hotline: "Fight fear with facts; 329-AIDS; In the war against AIDS, ignorance is the enemy; Information is the best defense; If you have questions, the Nevada AIDS Foundation has answers."[50]

During November 2–4, 1984, Texas hosted its first gay rodeo at the Roundup Rodeo Grounds in Simonton, Texas, forty minutes west of Houston. The Texas Gay Rodeo Association (TGRA) followed CGRA's lead, stated that its purpose was "solely to raise money for qualified (preferably gay) charities," and listed its previous fundraising efforts in cooperation with the CRGA for the KS/AIDS Foundation, the Montrose Clinic, the Montrose Counseling Center, the Montrose Guest Recovery House, and Gay Switchboard Houston.[51] In the years that followed, dozens of IGRA-affiliated associations formed, and they all raised money for at least one HIV/AIDS-related charity.

In San Diego, realtors Dominick Fiume and Sharen Gibson advertised in the Golden State Gay Rodeo program in 1990 that they were donating a portion of their commissions to the San Diego AIDS Project. The project itself printed a public service message in the same program with a cartoon drawing of a Superman-like character, Safer Sex Dude, flying with a cape and holding a condom. His message was: "Hey rodeo fans! Have fun at the gay rodeo! Remember that drug and alcohol use can impair your judgements in sexual situations" (fig. 19).[52] These advertisements, and the awareness of HIV they helped generate, saved lives.

The IGRA family lost many friends and partners to AIDS. Interviewees recall it as a painful chapter in their lives. Tommy Channel explained: "There was so much death surrounding us in our circle. It was a sad time

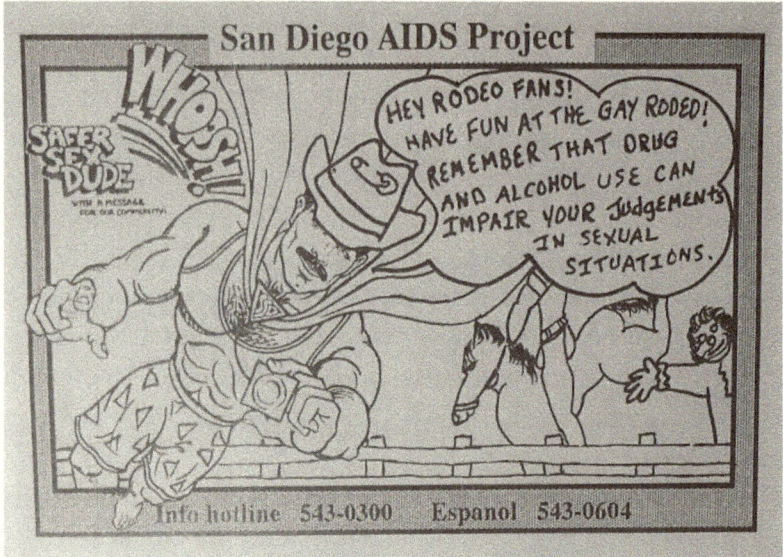

Fig. 19. "Safer Sex Dude," San Diego AIDS Project, safer sex advertisement. 1990 Golden State Gay Rodeo program. Credit to Frank Harrell and the International Gay Rodeo Association Archives, gayrodeohistory.org.

to be alive . . . you never knew what was on the other end of a phone call."[53] During interviews for this book, many respondents became emotional when discussing these darkest of times for the LGBTQ community, with one saying that he rarely goes back in time to those memories because sadness and loss occurred on almost a daily basis. Channel agrees, but he believes that it is important to remember everyone, the names and faces of those who were lost, and not the darkness and despair.

IGRA 2017 Hall of Fame inductee Laura Lee Laykasek, known simply as Laura Lee to her rodeo family, recalls the inhumane treatment of patients dying of AIDS in hospitals. Laura Lee had lost many of her friends to AIDS. When a victim passed, she watched nurses collect items from that patient's room. Dressed in full gowns and masks, nurses gathered everything, from sheets and pillowcases to family picture frames and cards, just about anything the patient might have touched. These items were collected and burned shortly after that. In 1984 Laura Lee entered the first TGRA rodeo in Simonton, Texas, where she won her first All-Around Cowgirl title and buckle. She then won back-to-back Ms. TGRA titles in 1985 and 1986 and toured Texas to raise money for HIV/AIDS-related charities, among others. In an interview, Laura Lee confessed that she had gotten into the IGRA because her friends were dying.[54]

Discrimination against gay men increased as the media shared misinformation about the transmission of the virus. In smaller cities and towns across the country, newspapers reported details that indirectly identified community members who had died of AIDS. In Wisconsin, the *Janesville Gazette* reported the first known AIDS-related death in the neighboring town of Beloit. The article revealed that Beloit Health Department officials had questioned people who knew the man and had reported the information to the *Gazette*. The man was identified to address "concerned citizens."[55] The Houston, Texas, biweekly LGBT publication *Montrose Voice* reported that 25 percent of local hospital residents and interns believed "it would be ethical to turn away AIDS patients if a choice were given, and half believe there should be such a choice."[56] In Reno, an ambulance service became the target of ridicule. The AIDS Ambulance Service earned its name from the specific service it provided. At every gay rodeo, an ambulance would be stationed nearby for any unfortunate accident or any spectator who became dehydrated in the hot summer sun. The AIDS Ambulance Service worked at the Nevada Regional Gay Rodeo for eight consecutive years and bore the brunt of many AIDS-related jokes.

It was not uncommon during the 1980s to hear jokes such as these: "What does G.A.Y. stand for?" with the answer "Got AIDS Yet?"; "What disease do gay crocodiles get? Gator-aids"; and "What is the medical definition of AIDS? A disease that turns fruits into vegetables."[57] Gay men were marginalized further from society because of these ignorant attempts at humor. The stigma dehumanized these men in greater society, leading people from across the country and from various religious faiths to believe erroneously that this was a gay pandemic. In one political cartoon, a woman declared, about AIDS: "It affects homosexual men . . . Thank goodness it hasn't spread to human beings yet."[58] And the employees of the AIDS Ambulance Service were the targets of ridicule and discrimination. Another ill-mannered joke that surfaced in Reno asked: "Why is Reno the only city with a gay rodeo? Because they're the only city with an AIDS ambulance."[59] The service's employees learned to be ready for such behavior, and some prepared clever follow-up responses: "A man walked up to the uniformed ambulance attendant in a local supermarket and said, 'Do you have AIDS?' To which the attendant replied, 'YES, we're the West Coast distributors!'"[60] Stories such as these were published in the 1984 Reno Regional Rodeo program with the explanation that the AIDS virus "is in no way a laughing matter and the 'jokes' and ridicule that have resulted for both victims and this business are senseless."[61] Nationally, gay men became the targets of numerous painful jokes as they witnessed the agonizing deaths of their lovers and friends.

Residents of Fallon, Nevada, in Churchill County, where the 1988 Finals were scheduled to take place, responded with fear and hate. Their ignorance about HIV and AIDS led them to seek legal action to prevent the gay rodeo from coming to their county. For gay rodeo organizers, the fight proved to be dangerous, as protests led to threats to their liberty and safety.[62] The LGBTQ magazine *First Hand Events* reported on the legal challenge in Churchill County. Readers of the magazine were informed of the suppression of civil liberties, but otherwise the general public remained unaware. That year, 1988, was to be the second year that gay rodeo contestants gathered for a national finals event. They were met by citizens and political figures of Churchill County, who protested and worked to prevent the LGBTQ community from hosting their western pride celebration. David Lantry, a rancher, had agreed to host the October 19–23 IGRA Finals. Shortly after noon on Wednesday, October 19, the Churchill County sheriff's office served a temporary restraining order, ordering Lantry to appear in court at 3:00 p.m. to argue why the rodeo should continue. Lantry appeared in the Fallon courthouse and convinced Judge Archie Blake to postpone the case until the following day to allow IGRA lawyers time to make the sixty-mile trip from Reno. District Attorney Kevin Pasquale "swore to the media that if the courts did not grant his restraining order, he would himself see that the rodeo did not take

The Riderless Horse

place in Fallon."[63] The following day, bigotry prevailed. The story made the local newspaper's front page, galvanizing many residents to fight against hosting a gay rodeo. The commotion in the courtroom bordered on violence. One man in attendance shouted that Fallon would become known as the "fruit bowl capital."[64] The only resident to speak in support of the gay rodeo was Ed Anderson. Anderson had been born in Nevada and raised in Winnemucca, and he was a resident of Reno. This ally, who had a gay son, stated in the courtroom: "I feel like a social worker at a KKK rally. . . . I probably had some of the same fears a lot of you have today [when he learned that his son was gay]. . . . I don't want to see an exercise in homophobia and hatred. My God to the left is different than yours to the right. He is more compassionate and forgiving." However, heckling from the crowd followed, and an anonymous attendee shouted that there was only one God, and that Ed should go home if he knew what was best for him. Shortly after that, the judgment was delivered. Lou Thomas, writing for *First Hand Events*, described the scene:

> The hearing began at ten o'clock . . . and lasted until 2:15 p.m. Most of that time was spent in the badgering of Lester Krambeal, president of the Silver State Gay Rodeo Association (SSGRA), the host group to the IGRA finals. Finally, a packed courtroom listened intently as Judge Blake solemnly pronounced that, based on a string of technicalities, he had found in favor of the district attorney. . . . And so it was that the 1988 IGRA Finals Rodeo was not permitted to take place. Bigotry had once again reared its ugly head in redneck country. Repression was once again allowed to hold sway in the land of the free and the home of the brave.[65]

The 1988 IGRA Finals were canceled. Discrimination like this galvanized LGBTQ rights activists in the West, and publications like *First Hand Events* and *The Advocate* published stories about civil rights violations.

*First Hand Events* recorded an interview with District Attorney Pasquale. Pasquale had argued that a restraining order was necessary to protect "public moral safety." When asked what official law the rodeo organizers were violating, Pasquale declined to answer. He went on to say that residents had concerns with pollutants like noise and dust, and that the number of people attending could disrupt traffic and be a burden on law enforcement. However, SSGRA representatives had met with the sheriff, who confirmed that the town was prepared and that he did not anticipate any significant problems. Pasquale raised concerns about the availability of water and sanitation, but organizers had ordered sanitation facilities and were prepared to have drinking water available. Pasquale was aware that Lantry's property had often been used for rodeo, but the word "gay" with "rodeo" was dangerous to the community. When asked about homophobia and violence, Pasquale reminded the reporter about the comments people in the courtroom had made about gay men, AIDS, and the threat of violence. His final words were telling to the reporter, and to posterity: "I think your observations are as good as mine on that [violence]. You saw the people in the courtroom. Right or wrong . . . I say there will be confrontation."[66] If the legal challenge had been unsuccessful in shutting down the gay rodeo in Fallon, community members planned on forming a group to dissuade the event organizers—in other words, a lynch mob, using tactics like the KKK intimidation and violence examined in chapter two.

Celebrations at gay rodeos during the late 1980s and throughout the 1990s included memorials and ceremonies for the lives lost to AIDS. Rodeo programs began paying tribute to IGRA family members who had died of this disease. One of the first memorials was at the 1989 IGRA Finals for Ron Jesser, who had succumbed to AIDS three years earlier in October 1986. Jesser, discussed in chapter six, was remembered for his legendary photograph that was eventually featured in fifty-six newspapers, and likely more. His smile was remembered as engaging during the best of times and the worst. The CGRA created the Ron Jesser Memorial Award "for dedication and sportsmanship."[67] The dedication closed with the following statement: "The Ron Jesser House has served as a temporary hospice for AIDS patients in Denver, and the Colorado AIDS Project has used Ron Jesser's determination to live, as an inspiration in their counseling programs. We know that Ron's spirit, as well as many other gay rodeo contestants, is here wishing for a safe, fun, and successful Finals Rodeo."[68]

The following year, the January Roadrunner Regional Rodeo in Phoenix dedicated the event to honor Dale A. Williams, who had passed away at the age of thirty-nine.[69] In April, the first-ever People's Regional Rodeo, hosted by the Tri-State Regional Rodeo (TSRR) in Cincinnati, was dedicated to forty-one-year-old Diamond Dan Bloomer: "Danny believed that life was a party and always made everyone feel that life was rosy."[70] The Golden State Gay Rodeo honored forty-seven-year-old Clif Howe. Survived by his lover, mother, daughter, and grandchildren: "We love you, and will miss you Cliffie."[71] As the years continued, dedications and memorials became a common theme. The 1991 Zia Regional Rodeo, held in Albuquerque, dedicated the event to all of the lives that had been touched by a loss due to AIDS.[72] Finally, the 2002 Diamond State Gay Rodeo Association (DSGRA) remembered the lives lost to HIV/AIDS, breast cancer, hatred, and terrorism, with a full-page ad that featured the Twin Towers of New York City, less than one year after the September 11th terrorist attacks.[73]

In its inaugural rodeo program, the Alberta Rockies Gay Rodeo Association (ARGRA) remembered three Atlantic States Gay Rodeo Association cowboys who had passed after their fight with AIDS.[74] Barry Jack Doe, thirty-nine years old, had passed away in January 1994, five months before the association he helped create hosted its first rodeo. His favorite charity was the Children's Wish Foundation. The foundation's leaders were so fond of Doe, and all the support he had generated for the children, that they recognized his efforts with a memorial plaque, which they gave to his longtime companion, Bill O'Connell. Cowboy Dwayne Douglas Little, who died at age thirty-seven, was remembered for his compassion to his neighbors and to animals: "He never found calving in January to be work. . . . Dwayne's compassion for humanity was experienced by many. He was never too busy to get to the aid of a neighbor or friend."[75] And Brian Edward Wharrie, who passed away at the age of thirty-three at Calgary General Hospital on January 6, 1994, had had a dream that his rodeo family worked to make come true. Wharrie wanted people living with HIV to have teddy bears to cuddle for comfort. His family set up a fund, the Bear Fund, "to realize Brian's dream."[76]

In addition to the memorials, some LGBTQ people wanted to share their HIV-positive status to end the stigma associated with the disease. Miss IGRA 1993, Chili Pepper, mentioned her HIV-positive status. Neither her drag persona, Chili Pepper, nor his rodeo cowboy identity, Tony Valdez, hid this information and they were proud to be openly gay. When asked about coming out, Valdez said, "Come out? I don't remember ever being in."[77] Following suit, Chili Pepper's HIV-positive status was not going into the closet, either. She had had a long history with gay rodeo and courageously announced her HIV diagnosis at a time when some people were ashamed of that status:

> In 1987, when I tested positive for HIV, I was hard pressed to set goals. Royalty competition has empowered me to challenge the virus in a positive way. The unconditional love and support from IGRA members has forever placed a brilliant and "positive" star on your crowns and has truly touched my heart's center. I would like to thank 5th Street Station of Austin for their sponsorship and continued support. Proudly representing over 8,000 IGRA members in 1993 as Miss IGRA has empowered me to reach beyond my goals . . . it has allowed me to touch my dreams.[78]

Chili Pepper raised thousands of dollars to support HIV/AIDS causes and is a major focus of this book's conclusion. The quest for a cure is a fight to find a weakness in the virus, and gay rodeo cowboys and cowgirls made this their leading philanthropic cause. Little did Phil Ragsdale know in 1976 that his dream of creating a gay rodeo in Reno would later provide a resource that the LGBTQ community desperately needed.

## CONCLUSION

The 1994 IGRA Finals dedicated the rodeo event to all those living with AIDS, cancer, and other medical conditions. The organizers' tribute included a quotation from Theodore Roosevelt, who believed in the ideals

The Riderless Horse

of hard work and "manly strife."[79] Roosevelt, a North Dakota cattleman, revered the cowboy of the American West: "On cow ranches, or wherever there is breeding stock, the spring round-up is the great event of the season."[80] As police commissioner of New York City, Roosevelt appointed recruits based on their qualifications rather than on political expediency. He later received a commission in a volunteer unit for the Spanish-Cuban-American War of 1898—the First Volunteer Cavalry. Of the one thousand available positions, Roosevelt "filled a majority of places with cowboys, hunters, and prospectors of the West and Southwest, men who bore the closest resemblance to his fabled backwoodsman."[81] He described these men as a "splendid set . . . with weather-beaten faces, and eyes that looked a man straight in the face without flinching. . . . There could be no better material for soldiers than that afforded by these grim hunters of the mountains, these wild rough riders of the plains."[82] In 1899 Roosevelt gave a speech in Chicago titled "A Strenuous Life," summing up what he believed should be the moral character of American citizens. In his speech, he argued against men living a complacent life. Historians credit Roosevelt with saving the sport of American football. He was critical of those attempting to ban the sport, saying, "The sports especially dear to a vigorous and manly nation are always those in which there is a certain slight element of risk. . . . It is mere unmanly folly to try to do away with the sport because the risk exists."[83] The rodeo men and women who fought the battle with AIDS embody the "strife" that Roosevelt revered. In the 1984 IGRA Finals Rodeo program, Roosevelt is quoted in their dedication:

It is not the critic who counts, nor the man who points out where the strong man stumbles, nor where the doer of deeds could have done them better. On the contrary, the credit belongs to the man who is actually in the arenas—whose vision is marred by the dust and sweat and blood; who strives valiantly; who errs and comes up again and again; who knows the great devotions, the great enthusiasms; who at best knows in the end the triumph of high achievement. However, if he fails, at least he fails while daring greatly so that his place shall never be with those cold and timid souls who know neither victory nor defeat.[84]

The program concludes: "It is these people that we salute!"[85] The IGRA community saved lives. While many lives were lost, members saved lives through education and open dialogue about the virus and mental health concerns associated with loss of friends and rodeo family members. Editors of queer-identifying publications shared letters, and that chronicled the crisis. And, when much of the world lacked support for HIV-positive philanthropies, poems like this one, in the June 19, 1987, *Out Front* magazine, galvanized members of the gay rodeo and other organizations to take action.

> There is a plague upon the land
> Where every love is in God's hands
> It sneaks, it stalks, it kills its prey
> And then lives on to come our way
>
> And when it comes, our strength it kills
> And then our minds, our souls, our wills
> Then when death's near, not far away
> It takes the life, then hides away
>
> And now the new, not a surprise
> Not only "we" catch "God's demise"
> It strikes the world in shole not part
> Then takes us all not one it parts
>
> When hearts are broken, people fear
> How many will it take this year?
> Along with fear comes hate and pain
> And those it strikes now feel the rain

Be young or old, gay or straight
The plague not pounce, it hesitates
And when it comes, it creeps right in
Then sends us up to God again

When will it End? Not soon, I fear
It takes us all, it's made that clear
It kills, it maims, it has no "clan"
God spare us all and save the land[86]

Messages like this helped unite people to fight discrimination and to support those who were afflicted with the virus.

# Conclusion

A Sustainable Future

I don't want to be seen as a victim. I want to be seen as victorious.

—Tony Valdez, a.k.a. Miss Chili Pepper

There is an expression dating back to world war i: "a man may be down, but he's never out!"[1] This is true of the gay rodeo community since the 1970s. Throughout this book, I have shared stories of discrimination and hate; of physical abuse and the cowardly murder of a collie puppy; of the fight for survival from a virus that took the lives of young rodeo contestants, their friends, and their lovers; and of legal battles against community leaders who attempted to prohibit the use of public property for events that included LGBTQ people. Gay rodeo attendance has declined significantly since its early 2000s peak. The IGRA and member associations are not attracting younger generations of fans, contestants, or volunteers. Sustainability relies on the hard work and effort of board members, volunteers, and royalty members. The World War I expression is not a cliché; rather, it is a rallying cry to maintain the tradition of gay rodeo for years to come.

One of the finest examples of this determination is the 1988 Rocky Mountain Regional Rodeo. In this book, readers learned about Phil Ragsdale's difficulty getting a stock contractor to provide animals for the first Reno Gay Rodeo in 1976, and John King's struggle to find an arena organizer willing to lease out property for his Rocky Mountain event in 1983. A few years later, King and the Colorado Gay Rodeo Association demonstrated that they did not need mainstream rodeo arenas or the approval of those who owned and operated them. The 1988 Rocky Mountain

Regional Rodeo was held in the parking lot of the Regency Hotel in Denver. Organizers were not sure if they could secure an arena, because this was during the height of the AIDS panic and society's fear of a "gay cancer" intensified anxiety. Located where Interstate 25 and Interstate 70 meet, the hotel is now student housing for local universities, but in 1988 CGRA rodeo members brought in truckloads of dirt to transform a parking lot into a rodeo arena. Organizers Wayne Jakino and John Beck were steadfast about building their own arena. Trucks made dozens of trips, taking more than a week to bring in all the dirt. And on July 1, 1988, co–Grand Marshals Carol Hunt and Bob Engel were able to say, "Let's Rodeo!" in the first and only LGBTQ-built rodeo arena in history.[2]

Stealing a line from the 1989 film *Field of Dreams*, "If you build it, they will come," Tommy Channel shared a story about the 1988 Rocky Mountain Regional Rodeo, and how CGRA members created their rodeo arena near downtown Denver.[3] Jakino wanted the gay rodeo to be in the city, near places frequented by the LGBTQ community. Channel explained that, after selecting the Regency Hotel, the trucks had to bring enough dirt to raise the ground level by at least twelve inches. Additionally, they put up fencing and built horse stalls. People staying at the Regency could look down from their hotel room windows and watch the rodeo competition. Rather than hosting the rodeo outside the city limits, "it was a huge statement for the city" to have gay rodeo so visible.[4]

What started in Reno in 1976 became a recurring rodeo event where the LGBTQ community could have a safe place to have fun, celebrate their roots as gay cowboys and cowgirls, and raise money through the imperial court system for charity. "Let's Rodeo!" is a phrase heard at mainstream and gay rodeos. The expression means "to have fun, enjoy the rodeo, and root for your favorite cowboy or cowgirl."[5] "Let's Rodeo" can happen only if there is a group of tenacious individuals who come together with a common goal and sufficient love to unwaveringly keep gay rodeo moving forward. Not only are IGRA board members, judges, volunteers, and royalty teams responsible for the year-long effort it takes to fundraise and produce a gay rodeo, but they are the reason gay rodeo continues today. The CGRA is the longest continuously running gay rodeo association in the world, celebrating its fortieth anniversary in 2021. It held annual Rocky Mountain Regional Rodeos from 1983 until the COVID-19 global pandemic forced the postponement of the 2020 event to July 10–12, 2021.

This conclusion examines how board members, judges, volunteers, and royalty teams each contributed to the decades of gay rodeo success, the role played by philanthropic generosity, and the international spectacle gay rodeo became for the LGBTQ community. Michael Vrooman explained that organizations function best when royalty, board members, and contestants all work together and, in some cases, when their duties overlap. "When it's truly working at its best is when all three are crossing over. Royalty should be volunteering or competing in the arena . . . boards of directors should be helping with the royalty . . . everyone should be crossing over. It should be a circle, not a pyramid with corners."[6] Moreover, Vrooman believes that the most successful royalty members are those who immerse themselves in everything gay rodeo, assuming more than the single role of royalty. And the integrity of the institution is of utmost importance.

Judges for gay rodeo take their jobs seriously and exemplify the integrity of the IGRA. Gay rodeo is often referred to as a family, but when judges are in the arena, they remain unbiased, attempt to conceal their emotions, and stick with their task of implementing the rules. During a rodeo weekend, it is not uncommon for some competitors to go out to dinner and have a few drinks, but it is less common to find judges scooting their boots at Charlie's and consuming shots of tequila. The job requires broad shoulders because judges are dealing with personalities, adrenaline, and a financial outcome. At the end of the day, judges are a lot harder on themselves than anyone who may accuse them of making a bad judgment call. Judges are a subset of the IGRA family because they spend so much time together, with their own set of challenges.

Judging is an important part of any rodeo, and, just like in the professional circuit, gay rodeo judges are certified for the sport. Historian and gay rodeo judge Roger Bergmann first attended the Reno Gay Rodeo in 1981, and later the first two Golden State Gay Rodeos in Los Angeles, in

1985 and 1986. Bergmann admitted that he mainly went to watch a little of the rodeo and do a lot of dancing. As he entered the dance hall on Friday night in 1986 in Los Angeles, he had to walk past the contestants' registration desk first. As he approached, he noticed a sign recruiting people to be trained as certified rodeo judges. Bergmann explained:

> Growing up in Montana, I had always gone to the annual Northwest Montana Fair and Rodeo. I always tried to guess what score the contestants were going to receive and thought I had a good idea of what I needed to learn. I signed up, and instead of dancing, I spent the weekend watching the entire rodeo and learning what to watch for and how to score. I traveled to the Denver and Oklahoma City rodeos later in the year to continue the training. At the Oklahoma City rodeo, I was allowed to enter a few events as a contestant, but then rush back to practice my judging ability. I competed in chute dogging, steer riding, and goat dressing, but did not do well enough to place in any of the events. Over the next few years, I also competed in steer decorating and the wild drag race. I won a few ribbons, but never won the coveted buckle.
>
> Well, if I wasn't a great contestant, I did become a well-appreciated rodeo judge. The first rodeo I judged was the November 1986 Texas Gay Rodeo in Dallas. I had a great weekend, and that was the start of judging over one hundred rodeos over the next seventeen years.[7]

In addition to judges, an integral component of the longevity of gay rodeo is royalty. Royalty candidates earn an opportunity to represent their regional association through intense fundraising. A commitment of nearly two years, and a lifetime of philanthropy for many of these people, culminates with a competition at World Finals for the title of Miss, Mr, Ms, and MsTer IGRA. They compete against each other for titles, sashes, and crowns, but they come together as a family. The gay rodeo community celebrated at the County Line, an LGBTQ+ night club, with Aurora Gayheart (Michael Andrew Martinez Arenas) when she was crowned Miss IGRA 2024. However, tragedy struck when Michael's husband, Thomas Devlin, passed away in his sleep hours later. Many in attendance, including this author, enjoyed watching the two celebrate the royalty honor. His royalty family stuck by him in the months that followed. His friend Jonathan Roman, Mr. ASGRA (Atlantic States Gay Rodeo Association) 2024, traveled to Spain with Michael weeks later. For many IGRA members, the family and support that develops is nothing short of a miracle.

Royalty teams function as bridges between the sport and the LGBTQ community, and they even educate the general public. Priscilla Toya Bouvier, also known as Paul Vigil, selected as Miss Gay Rodeo Association 2019, explained the importance of royalty and gay rodeo:

> Royalty has been a big part of my involvement with gay rodeo. Tessi [Tim Smith], Miss IGRA 1994, was the first person of the royalty program that I met. Royalty has a long history within gay rodeo, from the Reno rodeo days to currently. We are in charge of fundraising, community outreach, and education for gay rodeo. It's our responsibility to educate the public and raise money for the IGRA and our charities. There are four different categories within royalty: Miss (drag queen), Mr. (biological man), Ms. (biological female), and MsTer (drag king).[8]

The MsTer category was not officially added until 2005.[9] The titleholders, along with first and second runners-up, make up the royalty team. Even with all these responsibilities, Vigil believes that some competing athletes don't respect the royalty teams' contribution to gay rodeo: "There seems to be a divide between the contestants and the royalty team. Not all, but a lot of contestants see royalty as a nonvalue to the IGRA and gay rodeo."[10] Divisions like this, if they exist, need to be mended for the future success of gay rodeo. Vigil went even further to explain that the first gay rodeo would not have happened without the tireless work of the royalty team in Reno, affirming that they continue to be the ones out in communities promoting regional associations and educating the general public about gay rodeo. Following a year of virtually no gay rodeos, the 2021 Rocky Mountain Regional Rodeo was a successful event, and the fundraising at Charlie's in Denver, led by manager Brenden Sullivan and CGRA vice president Paula Scogal, was a primary reason for the accomplishment.

Royalty members are tasked with the challenge of promoting gay rodeo, and they often accomplish this using their own funds. Desirey Benavides is a transgender woman. However, she prefers to identify simply as a woman: "Well, I mean, I had my surgeries, so I am a female, but I mean I still am part of the transgender community. So, people ask, yes, I am transgender. Though I don't, I don't try to label myself as being transgender because you spend $35,000 plus to become a female, it's what you wanted to do so [that's] what I want to tell people."[11] Benavides explained how challenging it is to be a royalty member because they must travel to rodeos to represent their association, but they do it largely at their own expense.[12]

Acting as royalty takes a significant commitment. As Vrooman explained, people often fulfill this role for a minimum of three years. First, many IGRA associations require aspiring royalty to be contestants for a year, while demonstrating commitment by raising a specific amount of money or attending a certain number of events. If a contestant wins their local association's title, then they commit to a year-long job representing that IGRA chapter by engaging in community outreach and fundraising. Then, in the third year, the representative attends the international competition, hoping to win the international title. If they win that title, the representative has a year-long commitment to attend multiple gay rodeos with the unwritten expectation that they are committing to the IGRA mission statement: "to promote the country and western lifestyle through rodeo events."[13] Vrooman explained that many royalty winners do not start as rodeo people, but through this journey they become rodeo people. He recognized their importance because they can apply their strength, which is their ability to project public confidence with community outreach and fundraising. "They add that balance to what is considered 'horse people' or contestants."[14] And this is where rodeo contestants and royalty complete each other.

Michael Vrooman remembered when he first met Ron Roldan at Charlie's in Denver in 1993. Roldan was Mr. CGRA 1993 and noticed that Vrooman was new to Denver, so through his kindness he explained the royalty program and paid for Vrooman's CGRA membership. It is generosity like this that exemplifies the gay rodeo family; as Vrooman said, "That pretty much speaks to how just about everyone was, which is why it felt like home."[15] When it comes to carrying out the duties of royalty, Vrooman might be one of the most successful at it. As of 2020 he had been involved in gay rodeo for twenty-seven years. His titles include Mr. CGRA 1995 and Mr. IGRA in 1996. He moved to Chicago and joined the Illinois Gay Rodeo Association (ILGRA), where he was also known as Miss Harley Quinn, winning the title Miss ILGRA 1999 and later Miss IGRA 2000. His association affiliations include Colorado, Illinois, Nevada, and New Mexico. Vrooman has served as a rodeo director and an assistant rodeo director, so it is fitting for this concluding chapter to include his words on royalty involvement: "Wearing a sash and a crown doesn't make you royal. It's the hard work, and kindness, and good deeds that you do. That feeling, that's what should make you feel royal."[16]

Vrooman recalled that at his first gay rodeo in Denver in 1993, he walked into the arena during the Grand Entry and noticed Chili Pepper, Miss IGRA 1993, staring down at him from her horse and buggy. When he heard her say, "Hey, hey you! You walk like a girl in the dirt!" Vrooman felt humiliated.[17] But Vrooman has remained friends with Chili Pepper to this day, and he said that the heckling was "fuel to his fire."[18] Vrooman later claimed many royalty titles and was briefly known as the "sash queen"; he is also credited with creating the "spirit stick." In Albuquerque in 1996, at the IGRA Finals, as Vrooman stepped down from his Mr. IGRA title, he took a piece of wood from an old staircase and fashioned a spirit stick, sanded and painted red, black, and white, which are the IGRA colors. The royalty team of each year's winning association is responsible for securing the spirit stick, which can be stolen at any time by a competing association. In the event it is stolen, the only way to retrieve it is to meet the demands of the person or group that took possession of the spirit stick. These demands are in the form of fundraising for the IGRA.

When a competing IGRA regional association steals the stick, it is returned to the rightful owner only after the latter successfully meets fundraising demands made by the association that stole the stick. Vrooman stated, "If you leave [the stick] unattended, it is free game. That's why people attach it to themselves with handcuffs. . . . It's meant to be light-hearted, [and] although some people have tended to be a little vicious, we gently remind them that that is not the task."[19] Vrooman shared one of his favorite stories of spirit stick theft. It took place at the IGRA convention in Long Beach, California, in 1999. Illinois had possession of the spirit stick, and the reigning Ms. Illinois went to the restroom with the stick and hung it on the coat hanger on the bathroom stall door. Someone in the bathroom recognized the sound it made banging against the stall door, reached over, took it, and ran out to the convention floor for everyone to see. The following day, the party who had captured the stick went to a handmade soap store and asked the owner to donate scrap pieces that could not be sold. They soon returned to the convention with more than two hundred pieces of soap. Illinois representatives were tasked with selling these individual pieces of soap at the convention, throughout the day, to reclaim the spirit stick. Vrooman laughed and said that the episode was in good fun, "and they kept it clean, literally. . . . You just can't manhandle it. I mean, you have to find a way that it's vulnerable."[20]

Vrooman said that the idea of the spirit stick came from his time as a cheerleader in high school and college. In that context, the stick was a mini trophy that people could earn by showing great spirit or support. At the 1996 IGRA Finals, Vrooman awarded the spirit stick to a deserving IGRA association as a sort of traveling trophy. At the end of the rodeo year, the association holding the spirit stick would pass it on to another association that they believed embodied the overall spirit of working with royalty teams, locally or internationally, in fundraising, community outreach, and hospitality efforts. Vrooman believes that the practice continues today because people need this kind of recognition. He believes that it is unique to the IGRA, and that many other sporting organizations do not adequately recognize these types of efforts.

This philanthropic nature continues today. During the 2020 COVID-19 pandemic, for example, gay rodeo philanthropist Tre Brewbaker used social media to raise money for the North Star Gay Rodeo Association. Brewbaker created a fantasy NASCAR event where, for a donation, a person earned a driver and car for the NASCAR Cup Series race at Darlington, South Carolina. He hosted a Facebook Live drawing for car numbers. Following the May 17, 2020, event at Darlington, winners received an assortment of prizes. Brewbaker's idea was ingenious. During the pandemic, nearly all live sporting events were canceled, so even people who were not NASCAR fans tuned in to see if they had won. The night before the race, Brewbaker posted his thanks to everyone who had supported his fundraiser, which earned, to his surprise, $500.[21]

Royalty fundraising efforts were important during the 1980s and 1990s. The LGBTQ community was one of the demographics most impacted by the AIDS pandemic, and the least supported by the Ronald Reagan administration and the George H. Bush administration. Miss Mae (Phil Fikel), a member of the Missouri Gay Rodeo Association (MGRA), fought for a cure for AIDS through her performances, which raised money during gay rodeo events as well as at many other venues. Miss Mae was thrilled to learn that gay rodeo associations submitted documents to be archived at the Autry Museum of the American West in Los Angeles, and she provided her written recollections of the history of the MGRA. Her sense of humor is immediately apparent when reading her interview about the history of MGRA posted on the IGRA website: "I hope no one expects this [interview] to be historically accurate or complete. After twenty years of vodka, mind erasers, and Pucker, I have only one functioning brain cell left . . . and I have to share that one with Mandy Barbarell. Luckily, I have custody this week."[22] Mandy Barbarell (Andrew Goodman) was a dear friend of Miss Mae's. Goodman recalled Miss Mae's dedication to fundraising through drag performances: "Miss Mae was extremely proud of two things (not counting her vodka): that she had attended each and every IGRA convention and that she had never done drag for anything other than a fund-raiser."[23] Miss Mae recalled in her closing remarks about the MGRA that it was not always about fun and games.

Her lifework in gay rodeo was raising money for charities to fight HIV/ AIDS: "Each year this disease that we have been fighting for twenty years takes away some beloved member of our community. My fervent prayer is that someday I will be able to retire the pumps, wigs, and corset because a cure [for] AIDS has been found. I have certainly enjoyed this little trip down memory lane. As I always say, it's not over until the fat lady sings—do I feel a song coming on? So, let's rodeo."[24] Unfortunately, the IGRA lost Miss Mae to a fatal heart attack on Monday, October 5, 2009, at the age of fifty-seven.

When examining royalty and philanthropy at gay rodeo, Tony Valdez (Miss Chili Pepper) is an icon. To call her a "celebrity" is being modest. Chili is a fighter. Drag queens were among the most courageous warriors in the fight for LGBTQ rights and the fight against AIDS. In full drag, they cannot disappear into a closet. They are on full display, unlike some of the gay rodeo men, who are sometimes overlooked because of their straight-acting appearance, or gay rodeo women, whose identity might be dismissed by referring to them as tomboys. If approached by protesters or worse, drag queens stand proud of who they are and what they represent. And Chili is loved by many within the IGRA family. Chili Pepper shared with me her 1992 IGRA Rodeo Finals program, and it looked more like a prom queen's high school yearbook. Filled with congratulatory messages and signatures, the program clearly demonstrates the respect that this artist and philanthropist has earned. Steven Haines wrote, "Hey, Hot Stuff! Congrats on the buckle!! You are the highlight of every rodeo for Kerry & I. Love, Steven." Billy Dee Smith Jr. wrote that Chili was the "love of the rodeo." And competitor Miss Kitsy McKinley (Chris Anderson-Kramer) began with a play on Pepper's stage name with "Miss Picante" but went on to recognize her talent: "What can I say? You [wore] me out; actually, you just give me a run for my money."[25]

Social scientist Toby Marotta told journalists from *Newsweek* that AIDS was not forcing gay political activists to run back into the closet because the disease was "bad public relations"; rather, "the AIDS crisis is drawing American homosexuals together with a new and sober unity of purpose—and virtually to a man, gay leaders speak of a 'new maturity' that is replacing the last decade's mood of pansexual excess."[26] In an interview, Tony Valdez explained how members of the rodeo royalty raised money for local charities to support HIV/AIDS patient organizations. It took dedicated people like Valdez and many others to lift the spirits of those fighting the virus and opportunistic infections.

An HIV-positive status came with a social stigma. While the stigma affected some gay men with concerns about dating, how to tell their families, and what society might think of them, the gay rodeo community discussed the topic openly and raised awareness. Moreover, disclosing a positive status was a powerful statement that worked to eliminate ignorance about the virus. Valdez described the moment he learned he was HIV positive. During 1986–1987, Valdez and his roommate participated in an HIV/AIDS research study at the University of Texas. Every three to six months, they went to the research clinic to get tested. On the day Valdez's test came back positive, he knew without being told as the nurse sat down with him. She was distraught and shaking as she confirmed the diagnosis. Valdez reached out to hold her hand and comforted her, saying, "Oh, girl, I'm gay."[27] Sexually active gay men in the 1980s read the papers that referred to AIDS as a "gay plague," and, as research provided a better understanding of how the disease was actually transmitted and suggested ways to protect oneself from infection, some men, like Valdez, prepared for the worst.

Valdez explained that he never wanted to be seen as an AIDS victim; rather, he wanted to be "victorious." Being victorious means winning a contest or struggle and earning a sense of victory or fulfillment. Valdez has accomplished all of this in his nearly forty-year participation in gay rodeo. As Miss Chili Pepper, she has won many IGRA competitions, and as Tony Valdez, he has been successful in the rodeo arena. It was what Valdez accomplished in life through gay rodeo and royalty that truly defines this amazing person as victorious. Like many royalty members, her philanthropic and fundraising efforts largely gave back to the LGBTQ community as the AIDS crisis struck gay rodeo communities. In Dallas, Miss Chili Pepper raised money through her performances, and with help from the Texas Gay Rodeo Association (TGRA) she funded the

Revlon Apartments. The housing project became a place for AIDS patients who were without a home or the resources they needed to survive. People diagnosed with HIV/AIDS often lost their homes because of their inability to work and pay bills, and discrimination led to the eviction of many who rented housing. For some men, telling their family they were HIV positive coincided with coming out as gay. This delayed a show of compassion from some family and friends as they learned how to understand this revelation.[28] Valdez funded an apartment with the money he raised as Chili Pepper. He painted the interior and put up western-themed wallpaper. For his efforts, Valdez was rewarded with a letter from an AIDS patient who lived in the building, who thanked him for a place to live and die with dignity. Les Pannell, one-quarter Cherokee Indian, thanked Valdez and described Revlon Apartments #210 as a "miracle come true," recognizing Valdez as "a very special person" to his "friends and loved ones" (fig. 20).[29] Not only did people recognize Valdez for his support, but his care and compassion are clearly demonstrated in archived advertisements for fundraisers. Valdez helped with the TGRA's Chuckwagon Program, a benefit for the AIDS Resource Center Food Pantry. An advertisement for the benefit lists needed items such as soup, rolls of bathroom tissue, toothpaste, saltines, cans of fruits and vegetables, and shampoo. Attached to the advertisement was a handwritten message from Valdez: "Let's show our friends that we care. Please bring your donations to bowling on Monday, March 25. Easter basket themes and other creative boxes may brighten up their holiday weekend. For more info contact Chili Pepper (Tony Valdez)."[30] His desire to not only provide these supplies to AIDS patients but to dress up the packages to bring a little cheer was a compassionate touch on the part of this lifelong philanthropist.

The following year, as Miss Chili Pepper prepared her résumé in her bid to become Miss IGRA 1992, she reflected on her work with the Revlon Apartments: "On a personal note, I am planning on continuing my hard work at AIDS Services of Dallas. I find the physical work of redecorating the apartments quite rewarding, and the visits with the residents keep my vision on track and my accomplishments meaningful."[31] Today, the

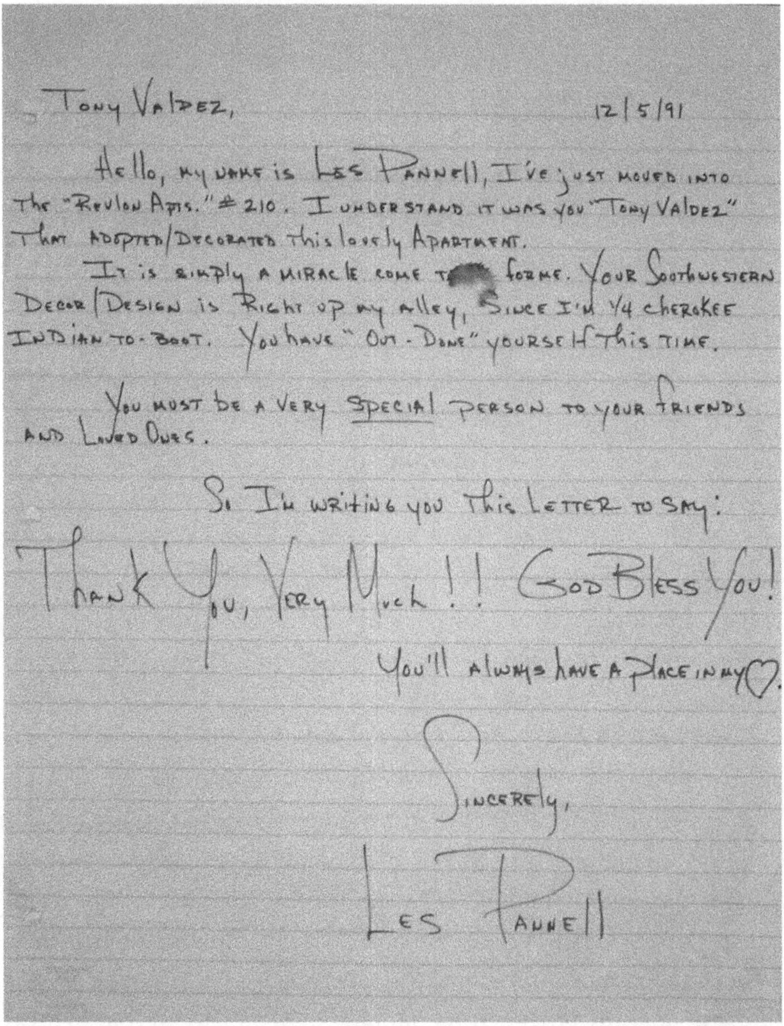

Tony Valdez,                                    12/5/91

Hello, my name is Les Pannell, I've just moved into
The "Revlon Apts." #210. I understand it was you "Tony Valdez"
That Adopted/Decorated this lovely Apartment.
       It is simply a miracle come t[...] for me. Your Southwestern
Decor/Design is Right up my alley, Since I'm 1/4 Cherokee
Indian-to-Boot. You have "Out-Done" yourself This Time.

       You must be a very Special person to your friends
And Loved Ones.

              So I'm writing you This Letter to say:

Thank You, Very Much!! God Bless You!

                     You'll Always have a Place in my ♡.

                            Sincerely,

                            Les Pannell

Fig. 20. Letter from Les Pannell to Tony Valdez, from Tony Valdez's personal collection of gay rodeo memorabilia.

Revlon Apartments, part of AIDS Services of Dallas, continues to provide homes for families working through the many challenges of living with HIV/AIDS. Its slogan is, "Living with AIDS begins with a place to live."[32] In 1992 Valdez and the Texas Gay Rodeo donated $67,471.81 to the NAMES Project in Fort Worth, the Women's Shelter of Corpus Christi, Casa de

Esperanza in Houston, the AIDS Relief Ministry of San Antonio, and twenty-three other charities.[33]

Gay rodeo has drastically decreased in attendance numbers and frequency of rodeos staged since the 1990s. Royalty, board members, judges, and volunteers are tasked with saving this significant segment of LGBTQ history and culture. Nobody is certain why gay rodeo now attracts fewer participants and fans than in earlier decades. Is the answer cultural, communal, or political? Culturally, country music is not as popular in the 2020s among mainstream Americans as it was a few decades earlier, as discussed in chapter four. Today, country singers are not topping the pop charts as Garth Brooks and Shania Twain once did, when they and other popular singers made anything "country" appear attractive. In the twenty-first century, Taylor Swift, who began as a country singer, albeit not fully embraced by her peers in that genre, abandoned that identity and catapulted into the pop music scene, becoming one of the most recognizable celebrities globally while forsaking her country roots. Has the country-loving LGBTQ community joined her? Or is the answer more political? By the early 2000s, liberalism in politics embraced the civil rights of LGBTQ people while rejecting conservative Republican ideals advocating same-sex marriage bans, gay conversion therapy, and so-called religious freedom bills, which result in discrimination against LGBTQ people under the guise of Christian beliefs. These positions are reaffirmed at the Republican National Convention every four years. That is not to say that gay rodeo lost conservative members; many rodeo participants stay true to conservative beliefs in government and spending policy, accepting heterosexual-identifying conservatives' lack of full support for LGBTQ people in the process. Historically, marginalized group members have used the phrase "sell-outs" when members of a group abandon their peers and seek inclusion in the dominant group. Maybe they are complicit with mistreatment of their larger group because individual inclusion, at any cost, is much easier than fighting for greater equality. Or is it that broader society and younger generations equate rural and country with conservative and anti-LGBTQ? I was interviewed for an article in *The Strategist* by Jenna Milliner-Waddell, "What to Wear to Look Like: A Cowboy." It was not surprising to read an anonymous comment that read: "Why is this even a thing? I can't imagine a lot of people who read NY *Magazine* want to walk around looking like [Donald] Trump supporters." The misinformed reader equated Wrangler jeans and cowboy boots with conservatism. This assumption makes anything country seem unattractive to the same group of people who once flocked to country bars in New York City because it was in fashion. And some have suggested that gay rodeo brought the LGBTQ community together in the fight against HIV/AIDS. While there is still need for more research in preventing and treating AIDS and support for people who are HIV positive, younger generations today did not have the heartbreaking experience of watching many of their friends slowly waste away or attending dozens of funerals each year for those same friends. Thus, gay rodeo was a way to honor their memory.

Such factors may have contributed to the loss of support for gay rodeo, but another factor is even more powerful and significant—acceptance. As the twenty-first century progresses, so too does greater acceptance of LGBTQ people. In the 1980s many Americans believed that they did not personally know an LGBTQ person, or they would not admit that they did. However, in 2021, it is difficult to find anyone who can honestly say that they do not know an LGBTQ person, or for a student in a large school district to claim not to have any LGBTQ classmates. Social change and acceptance have led to a new world for LGBTQ people. Someday, establishments once known as gay bars could become obsolete and unnecessary because queer-identifying people will not need to rely on an LGBTQ-marked establishment to socialize. This is the change that Phil Ragsdale hoped for, and in the end its fulfillment might be the reason that gay rodeo, too, becomes a relic, preserved only in the pages of books such as this one.

During the late 1990s, the Grand Entry ceremony at gay rodeos resembled the Parade of Nations during the opening ceremony of the Olympic Games. But instead of contingents from different nations, each IGRA member association entered the arena representing its organization and home state with pride. Tommy Channel referred to it as the Parade of

States: "Every rodeo association or organization in the local community had an entry in that foot parade. . . . Sometimes this thing would go on for forty-five minutes. . . . It was a western gay pride."[34] Each organization entered the arena with their flag or banner, and the rodeo announcer introduced each group to the spectators. Channel explained that organizations took great pride in the "foot parade."

In 1992 the Atlantic States Gay Rodeo Association held its second Atlantic Stampede Rodeo in Washington DC. In its rodeo program, organizers recognized that this was the first time the IGRA had held an event east of the Mississippi River. The following year, organizers wanted to make a political statement about the recent inauguration of President Bill Clinton, evolving attitudes in U.S. society regarding acceptance of the LGBTQ community, and the hundreds of thousands of LGBTQ people who had marched in the nation's capital. Rodeo organizers made a plea for inclusion rather than segregation of LGBTQ people in mainstream society: "Why this need for separate gay events like gay rodeos and the Gay Olympics? Why can't we simply assimilate into existing 'straight' events? Hopefully one day we can, not having to make an implicit distinction between homosexual and heterosexual, gay and straight. But until that acceptance and understanding comes, we have the right—and duty—to exercise our many gifts and talents without denying any part of our person."[35]

The goals of the gay liberation movement have changed over time—so much so that some gay liberation activists struggled with the idea of same-sex marriage because they fought for the right to be different and not conform to heteronormative social rules. That was the purpose of the gay "liberation" movement. They created their own spaces and places for gathering—social groups, sporting clubs, and religious congregations. But in the twenty-first century, inclusion, not assimilation, of the LGBTQ community in politics and sport is occurring.[36] In 2020 Pete Buttigieg, the openly gay mayor of South Bend, Indiana, had a legitimate shot at earning the Democratic Party's nomination for president, and later he was named the secretary of transportation by President-Elect Joe Biden. Sarah McBride, Taylor Small, and Stephanie Byers were elected as the first transgender state legislators for their respective states. In sport, Scott Frantz, an openly gay NCAA Division I football player at Kansas State University, completed his collegiate career with an invitation to play with many of the best college football seniors in the Hula Bowl on January 26, 2020. The same year, on National Coming Out Day, October 11, the National Football League announced its support for openly LGBTQ athletes with a video that included high-profile players like Rob Gronkowski making statements such as "We got you."[37] Social progress and change happen when pioneers such as members of the IGRA fight for acceptance and inclusion. The pain, the anger, and their will to succeed paved the way for generations of LGBTQ people to live in a world where they can count on greater support rather than vilification. Even if gay rodeo one day is no longer staged, these gay liberationists have succeeded by creating a cultural phenomenon that made sport in society a more inclusive space.

# Notes

### Introduction

Epigraph: Wade Earp, personal interview by Nicholas Villanueva Jr., Santa Fe, New Mexico, June 30, 2019.

1. Greg Tinsley, personal interview by Nicholas Villanueva Jr., Little Rock, Arkansas, April 26, 2019.
2. Marcus, *Making Gay History*, 165.
3. Wooden and Ehringer, *Rodeo in America*, 212.
4. Bruce, *Pride Parades*, 2.
5. Michael Vrooman, personal interview by Nicholas Villanueva Jr., Zoom, July 30, 2020.
6. Vrooman, interview.
7. Vrooman, interview.
8. Amy Griffin, personal interview by Nicholas Villanueva Jr., Zoom, July 31, 2020.
9. Downs, *Stand by Me*, 6.
10. Compton, "Queer Eye on the Gay Rodeo," 230.
11. Wooden and Ehringer, *Rodeo in America*, 214.
12. "The Reno Gay Rodeo—Known Internationally as 'The National Reno Gay Rodeo,'" *National Reno Gay Rodeo*, 1982 Program, page 6, International Gay Rodeo Association Archives, gayrodeohistory.org.
13. Scofield, *Outriders*, 138.
14. Griffin, interview.
15. Reiner, *The Princess Bride*.

### 1. A Rodeo to Call Their Own

Epigraph: "The Reno Gay Rodeo—Known Internationally as 'The National Reno,'" Comstock Gay Rodeo Association, *National Reno Gay Rodeo*, 1982 program, page 6, program property of Tony Valdez.

1. Democratic Underground, "Dallas Dudes."
2. Kelefa Sanneh, "Singing Loudly and Carrying a Big Flag," *New York Times*, February 16, 2006, E1.
3. Keller and Jones, "Brokeback Mountain," 22–23.
4. Jacobs, "Cinema Aphrodiso"; Us Weekly Staff, "30 Most Romantic Movies of All Time"; IMDbPro, "Romantic Drama."

5. BBC News, "Nelson Releases Gay Cowboy Song."

6. Bob Schiffer and Sharyn Alfonsi, "Music/Gay Cowboy Song," CBS Evening News, February 15, 2006, Vanderbilt University Television News Archive, no. 821907.

7. International Gay Rodeo Association, "The History of Gay Rodeo." International Gay Rodeo Association Archives, gayrodeohistory.org.

8. Packard, *Queer Cowboys*, 1–2.

9. Packard, *Queer Cowboys*, 1–2.

10. Packard, *Queer Cowboys*, 1–2.

11. Villanueva, "A Rodeo to Call Their Own."

12. Adams, *Western Words*, 172.

13. Pearson and Haney, "The Rodeo Cowboy as an American Icon," 17–18.

14. Le Coney and Trodd, "Reagan's Rainbow Rodeos," 171–72.

15. Brian Rogers, "Pride in the Saddle Starts in Nevada," *The History of Gay Rodeo in Nevada*, International Gay Rodeo Association Archives, gayrodeohistory.org.

16. Anderson, *In the Game*, 45. Anderson is drawing from the work of sociologist Brian Pronger, *The Arena of Masculinity*; the notion of hegemonic masculinity challenges the gay male perspective on masculinity because it argues that femininity replaces masculinity, and gay cowboys challenge this notion.

17. Sublette, "Cowboys Are Frequently, Secretly Fond of Each Other."

18. Blazina, *The Cultural Myth of Masculinity*, 69.

19. Johnson, *Just Queer Folks*, 3.

20. Johnson, *Just Queer Folks*, 3.

21. Blank, *Straight*.

22. Chauncey, *Gay New York*, 89.

23. Anderson, *21st Century Jocks*, 205.

24. Anderson, *21st Century Jocks*, 205.

25. Singal, "The Phenomenon of 'Bud Sex'"; see also, Silva, "Bud-Sex."

26. Feasey, *Masculinity and Popular Television*, 98.

27. Johnson, *The Lavender Scare*, 108–12; Dean, *Imperial Brotherhood*, 95–96.

28. "Perverts Called Government Peril," *New York Times*, April 19, 1950, 25.

29. Boysen et al., "Mental Health Stereotypes about Gay Men," 69.

30. Boysen et al., "The Mental Health Stereotype about Gay Men," 331.

31. "Reno Rodeo Features Gays," *Elyria* (OH) *Chronicle-Telegram*, August 6, 1979, 6.

32. "Reno Rodeo Features Gays," 6.

33. "Rocky Mountain Regional Rodeo!" *Quest: The Voice of the Gay Community*, July 1990, page 26, International Gay Rodeo Association Archives, gayrodeohistory .org.

34. "Rocky Mountain Regional Rodeo!"

35. "The Reno Gay Rodeo—Known Internationally as 'The National Reno Gay Rodeo,'" Comstock Gay Rodeo Association, *National Reno Gay Rodeo*, 1983 program, page 20, International Gay Rodeo Association Archives, gayrodeohistory.org.

36. "The Reno Gay Rodeo—A Local Event for Charity Known as 'The National Reno Gay Rodeo,'" Comstock Gay Rodeo Association, *National Reno Gay Rodeo*, 1980 program, page 5, International Gay Rodeo Association Archives, gayrodeohistory.org.

37. "The Reno Gay Rodeo—Known Internationally as 'The National Reno,'" Comstock Gay Rodeo Association, *National Reno Gay Rodeo*, 1982 program, page 6, program property of Tony Valdez.

38. "Mr., Ms., Miss National Reno Gay Rodeo Contest," Comstock Gay Rodeo Association, *National Reno Gay Rodeo*, 1984 program, page 9, International Gay Rodeo Association Archives, gayrodeohistory.org.

39. "Gay Rodeo Raises Funds for Charity," *Reno Evening Gazette*, August 26, 1977, 2.

40. Herek, "Beyond 'Homophobia,'" 7.

41. Kimmel, *Manhood in America*, 155–56.

42. Kibelstis, "Preventing Violence against Gay Men and Lesbians," 27.

43. Levin and Nolan, *The Violence of Hate*, 56.

44. David Renier, interview with Rebecca Scofield, Duncans Mills, California, September 10, 2016, Voices of Gay Rodeo, Oral Histories of the International Gay Rodeo Association, University of Idaho, http://www.voicesofgayrodeo.com.

45. "He Stands Out as a Different Buckeroo," *Kokomo* (IN) *Tribune*, May 21, 1981, 22.

46. Ragsdale's reference here is to the homophobic culture of rural men. However, the term "redneck" is used at times in this book as a cultural identifier of rural people and not as a derogatory reference. Within the gay rodeo, there are many men and women who identify as "redneck," who are not homophobic and are referencing a pride they have in their country lifestyle.

47. Bill Steinauer, "Rodeo at Washoe County Fairgrounds This Weekend Is Not for Everyone," *Reno Evening Gazette*, August 19, 1977, 15.

48. Steinauer, "Rodeo at Washoe County Fairgrounds," 15.

49. Anderson, *21st Century Jocks*, 40.

50. Miller, *Out of the Past*, 141–42.

51. Lee Gould, "Anita Dances a Jig; Gay Rights Law Repealed," *Reno Evening Gazette*, June 8, 1977, 20.

52. Marcus, *Making Gay History*, 258–59.

53. "Anita Belted with Fruit Pie," *Albert Lea Tribune*, October 16, 1977, 2.

54. Calendo, "Gay Rodeo," 33.

55. "Gays Attack New Movie," *Medicine Hat News* (Alberta, Canada), February 8, 1980, 18.

56. Downs, *Stand by Me*, 4.

57. Downs, *Stand by Me*, 191–92.

58. Brian Rogers, "Pride in the Saddle Starts in Nevada," *The History of Gay Rodeo in Nevada*, International Gay Rodeo Association Archives, gayrodeohistory.org.

59. "The Reno Gay Rodeo—A Local Event for Charity Known as—'The National Reno Gay Rodeo,'" Comstock Gay Rodeo Association, *National Reno Gay Rodeo*, 1980 program, page 5, International Gay Rodeo Association Archives, gayrodeohistory .org.

60. Hunt, "West of the Closet, Fear on the Range," 141.

61. Hunt, "West of the Closet, Fear on the Range," 141.

62. Comstock Gay Rodeo Association, *National Reno Gay Rodeo*, 1982 program, page 20, International Gay Rodeo Association Archives, gayrodeohistory.org.

63. "To: Participants in the National Reno Gay Rodeo," Comstock Gay Rodeo Association, *National Reno Gay Rodeo*, 1982 program, page 4, International Gay Rodeo Association Archives, gayrodeohistory.org.

64. "Reno Ex-Gay Ministry Preaches Forgiveness," *Nevada State Journal*, July 24, 1977, 1.

65. "Reno Ex-Gay Ministry Preaches Forgiveness," 1.

66. Hunt, "West of the Closet, Fear on the Range," 137.

67. Linehan, *Such Were Some of You*, 14.

68. Stuart, "Social Cognition," *Discourse & Society*, 65.

69. "Gay Rodeo 'Bad PR,' Governor Says," *Orange County Register* (Santa Ana, CA), March 28, 1981, 21; and "Gay Rodeo Ban Receives More Support," *Santa Fe New Mexican*, March 26, 1981, 57.

70. "Gay Rodeo 'Bad PR,' Governor Says," 21.

71. Canaday, *The Straight State*, 21–22.

72. "Gay Cowpokes Plan August Rodeo," *Lawrence* (KS) *Journal-World*, May 21, 1981, 6.

73. Fellows, *Farm Boys*, 304–9.

74. Fellows, *Farm Boys*, 304–9.

75. Fellows, *Farm Boys*, 304–9.

76. Streitmatter, *From "Perverts" to "Fab Five"*, 50.

77. Marcus, *Making Gay History*, 255.

78. "Gay Rodeo Protested," *Santa Fe New Mexican*, August 6, 1983, 4.

79. "Scientists Charge Prejudice Is Delaying AIDS Research," *Hutchinson* (KS) *News*, June 4, 1985, 9.

80. Miller, *Out of the Past*, 451.

81. "Mr., Ms., Miss National Reno Gay Rodeo Contest," Comstock Gay Rodeo Association, *National Reno Gay Rodeo*, 1983 program, page 16, International Gay Rodeo Association Archives, gayrodeohistory.org.

82. "TGRA," Texas Gay Rodeo, 1986 program, page 15, International Gay Rodeo Association Archives, gayrodeohistory.org.

83. "In Memoriam: Phil Ragsdale," International Gay Rodeo Association Archives, gayrodeohistory.org.

84. "We Support Animal Rights," *Eighth Annual IGRA Finals Rodeo*, 1994 program, page 31, International Gay Rodeo Association Archives, gayrodeohistory.org.

85. "IGRA History," *Quest: Tenth Annual Rocky Mountain Regional Rodeo Official Program*, 1992 program, pages 39–40, International Gay Rodeo Association Archives, gayrodeohistory.org.

86. "Rodeo Programs," *IGRA History*, gayrodeohistory.org.indexprograms.htm.

87. "Schedule of Events," *Heartland Regional Rodeo*, 1997 program, page 7, International Gay Rodeo Association Archives, gayrodeohistory.org.

88. Jeffrey McCasland and Philip Lister, email message to author, October 27, 2019.

89. "This Is Where Your Money Went in 1991," *Yeeee Haaa! The Ninth Annual TGRA Rodeo*, 1992 program, page 2, International Gay Rodeo Association Archives, gayrodeohistory.org.

90. Judith Halberstam, "Not So Lonesome Cowboys," 201.

## 2. Rough Riding

Epigraph: Tom Morganthau, Vincent Coppola, John Carey, Nancy Cooper, and George Raine, "Gay America in Transition: A Turning Point Has Been Reached, and AIDS May Mean the Party Is Over," *Newsweek*, August 8, 1983, 33.

1. Don Kulick, "Can There Be an Anthropology of Homophobia?" 21.

2. Dervisbegovic, "Bosnia Imam Thanks God for Virus Cancelling Pride March."

3. Constance R. Sullivan-Blum, "'It's Adam and Eve, Not Adam and Steve,'" 48.

4. Rhuaridh Marr, "Church Leader Who Blamed Pandemic on Gay Marriage Tests Positive for COVID-19," *Metro Weekly* (Washington DC), September 8, 2020.

5. Luther and Davidson, *Loving Sports When They Don't Love You Back*, 83.

6. Luther and Davidson, *Loving Sports When They Don't Love You Back*, 84.

7. Zeigler, "Outsports' Asshole of the Year: Tony Dungy."

8. Jane Dalton, "Homophobic Pastor Says LGBT+ People Should Be Killed: 'As Much as God Loves, God Hates,'" *The Independent*, June 14, 2019.

9. Dalton, "Homophobic Pastor."

10. Dalton, "Homophobic Pastor."

11. Hayes Hickman, "Knox Prosecutors Find No Potential Bias in Remaining Cases Involving Anti-LGBTQ Detective," *Knoxville* (TN) *News Sentinel*, October 1, 2019.

12. Jack Morgan, personal interview by Nicholas Villanueva Jr., Zoom, July 25, 2020.

13. Coski, "The Confederate Battle Flag," 195.

14. Coski, "The Confederate Battle Flag," 195.

15. Coski, "The Confederate Battle Flag," 196. Dixiecrats were part of a short-lived political party, an offshoot of the Democratic Party formally known as the States' Rights Democratic Party, which participated in the 1948 presidential election.

16. Coski, "The Confederate Battle Flag," 196.

17. Mitchell, *Ghosts of Ole Miss*.

18. Amber Phillips, "Here Are 12 Other Times Donald Trump Vilified Illegal Immigrants," *Washington Post*, July 1, 2015; Harriet Agerholm, "Donald Trump Tweets 'Pocahontas' Racist Slur about Senator Elizabeth Warren," *The Independent*, November 3, 2017; and Edward Browne, "Trump Sparks Outrage by Calling Coronavirus 'China Virus' AGAIN in 'Patriotic' Tweet," *Daily Express* (London), July 21, 2020.

19. Villanueva, "Land of the Free?" 12.

20. Tarver, "Bigger than Football," 220.

21. Coakley, *Sport and Society*.

22. Coakley, *Sport and Society*, 11.

23. Will Higgins, "Owners Who Refused Cake for Gay Couple Close Shop," *USA Today*, February 27, 2015.

24. Sheerin, "Matthew Shepard."

25. Anderson, *21st Century Jocks*, 2.

26. Calendo, "3 Gay Cowboys," 77.

27. "'Gay Rodeo' Undisturbed," *Press-Telegram* (Long Beach CA), August 23, 1977, 12.

28. "'Gay Rodeo' Undisturbed," 12.

29. "'Gay Rodeo' Undisturbed," 12.

30. Calendo, "3 Gay Cowboys," 31.

31. Anonymous #1, personal interview by Nicholas Villanueva Jr., Rocky Mountain Regional Rodeo, Denver, Colorado, July 6, 2019.

32. "Robert Eichberg, 50, Gay Rights Leader" (obituary), *New York Times*, August 15, 1995, B-7.

33. Eichberg, *Coming Out*, 40.

34. Michael Vrooman, personal interview by Nicholas Villanueva Jr., Zoom, July 30, 2020.

35. Roger Bergmann, personal interview by Nicholas Villanueva Jr., IGRA Finals, Phoenix, Arizona, October 27, 2019.

36. Bergmann, personal interview.

37. Bergmann, personal interview.

38. Ghaziani, "The Closet," 72.

39. Bergmann, personal interview.

40. Bergmann, personal interview.

41. Bergmann, personal interview.
42. Bergmann, personal interview.
43. Bergmann, personal interview.
44. Bergmann, personal interview.
45. Bergmann, personal interview.
46. Denes and Afifi, "Coming Out Again," 301–2.
47. Bergmann, personal interview.
48. Paul Vigil, personal interview by Nicholas Villanueva Jr., Zia Regional Rodeo, Santa Fe, New Mexico, June 30, 2019.
49. Vigil, personal interview.
50. Jeffrey McCasland and Philip Lister, email message to the author, October 27, 2019.
51. Jeffrey McCasland and Philip Lister, email message to the author, October 27, 2019.
52. Hansen, "For Gay Competitors."
53. Hansen, "For Gay Competitors."
54. Hansen, "For Gay Competitors."
55. Hansen, "For Gay Competitors."
56. Hansen, "For Gay Competitors."
57. Hansen, "For Gay Competitors."
58. John King, interview with Rebecca Scofield, Denver, Colorado, July 8, 2017, Voices of Gay Rodeo, Oral Histories of the International Gay Rodeo Association, http://www.voicesofgayrodeo.com.
59. King, interview with Rebecca Scofield.
60. Anthony Lumpkins, interview with Court Fund, Dallas, Texas, May 1, 2020, Voices of Gay Rodeo, Oral Histories of the International Gay Rodeo Association, http://www.voicesofgayrodeo.com.
61. "Gay Rodeo Ban Receives More Support," *Santa Fe New Mexican*, March 26, 1981, B-8.
62. "Gay Rodeo Ban," B-8.
63. King, interview with Rebecca Scofield.
64. Jill Jorden, "Tense Aftermath to Banned Gay Rodeo: Churchill Officials Keep Watch at Fallon Ranch," *Reno Gazette-Journal*, October 23, 1988, 1.
65. Jorden, "Tense Aftermath to Banned Gay Rodeo," 1.
66. John Beck, personal interview by Nicholas Villanueva Jr., Santa Fe, New Mexico, June 30, 2019.
67. Markowitz, "The Most Dangerous Gay Man."
68. Markowitz, "The Most Dangerous Gay Man."
69. Coakley, *Sport and Society*, 635.
70. Kyle Wagner, "In Gay Rodeo, Women Can Compete with the Big Boys—and Big Bulls," *Westword* (Denver), January 6, 2016.

71. Bergmann, personal interview.

72. Bergmann, personal interview.

73. Bergmann, personal interview.

74. Bergmann, personal interview.

75. Bergmann, personal interview.

76. Amy Griffin, personal interview by Nicholas Villanueva Jr., Zoom, July 31, 2020.

77. John Beck, personal interview by Nicholas Villanueva Jr., Santa Fe, New Mexico, June 30, 2019.

78. Sadiyah Ali, "Throwback Thursday: The KKK in Nebraska," *Daily Nebraskan* (Lincoln), October 18, 2018; and Jim McKee, "KKK Groups Formed in Nearly a Dozen Nebraska Cities in the 1920s," *Lincoln* (NE) *Journal Star*, August 22, 2010.

79. "Parades Celebrate Gay Pride," *Hutchinson* (KS) *News*, June 30, 1986, 8.

80. "Chicago Klan Confrontations Continue," *Salina* (KS) *Journal*, June 30, 1986, 12.

81. "Chicago Klan Confrontations Continue," 12.

82. "Chicago Klan Confrontations Continue," 12.

83. Jerry Mitchell, "Congressional Honor Sought for Freedom Summer Martyrs," *Clarion-Ledger* (Jackson MS), February 4, 2014.

84. Large, "Long Journey Ahead," 121–22.

85. Beck, personal interview.

86. Beck, personal interview.

87. Beck, personal interview.

88. Beck, personal interview.

89. Beck, personal interview.

90. Beck, personal interview.

91. Beck, personal interview.

92. Beck, personal interview.

93. Reid, "The Brokeback Cowboys of Ohio's Gay Rodeo."

94. "John Beck," IGRA Hall of Fame, International Gay Rodeo Association Archives, gayrodeohistory.org.

95. Andrew Joseph, "Nebraska Regent Wants Football Players Kicked Off the Team for Anthem Protests," *USA Today*, September 27, 2016.

96. Joseph, "Nebraska Regent Wants Football Players Kicked Off."

97. Tynes and Johnson, "Emails Show a Nebraska Regent was 'Embarrassed.'"

98. Morgan, personal interview.

## 3. Gay Rodeo Programs

Epigraph: "From IGRA president Candy Pratt," *World Gay Rodeo Finals*, 2018 program, page 6, International Gay Rodeo Association Archives, gayrodeohistory.org.

1. Patrick Terry, interview with Rebecca Scofield, Albuquerque, New Mexico, October 21, 2017, Voices of Gay Rodeo, Oral Histories of the International Gay Rodeo Association, http://www.voicesofgayrodeo.com.

2. The absence of this archive is recognized by the author. In place of this archive of primary sources, the author relied heavily on newspaper and magazine articles, the digital archive of rodeo programs, and personal interviews.

3. The absence of this archive is recognized by the author. In place of this archive of primary sources, the author relied heavily on newspaper and magazine articles, the digital archive of rodeo programs, and personal interviews.

4. Michael Vrooman, personal interview by Nicholas Villanueva Jr., Zoom, July 30, 2020.

5. "A Message from the Founder and Director," *Fourth Annual Reno Gay Rodeo*, 1979 program, page 1, International Gay Rodeo Association Archives, gayrodeohistory .org.

6. "CB Club Reno Baths," *Fourth Annual Reno Gay Rodeo*, 1979 program, back cover, International Gay Rodeo Association Archives, gayrodeohistory.org.

7. "Reno Gay Directory," *Fourth Annual Reno Gay Rodeo*, 1979 program, page 9, International Gay Rodeo Association Archives, gayrodeohistory.org.

8. "The Place to Meet a Man's Man," *Roadrunner Regional Rodeo*, 1989 program, page 24, International Gay Rodeo Association Archives, gayrodeohistory.org.

9. "Rope 'em and Ride 'em," *Twelfth Annual Rocky Mountain Regional Rodeo*, 1994 program, page 27, International Gay Rodeo Association Archives, gayrodeohistory.org.

10. "Hey Buddy . . . We Have It All," *San Francisco Bay Area Regional Rodeo '95*, 1995 program, pages 16, 19, International Gay Rodeo Association Archives, gayrodeohistory .org.

11. "Welcome to the Rocky Mountain Regional Rodeo," *2000 Rocky Mountain Regional Rodeo*, 2000 program, page 16, International Gay Rodeo Association Archives, gayrodeohistory.org.

12. "Ride 'em, Cowboy," *Windy City Rodeo 2005*, 2005 program, page 25, International Gay Rodeo Association Archives, gayrodeohistory.org.

13. "Man-Maid House Cleaners," *Great Plains Regional Rodeo*, 1996 program, page 18, International Gay Rodeo Association Archives, gayrodeohistory.org.

14. "We Want to Be Your Travel Agent," *National Reno Gay Rodeo*, 1982 program, page 18, International Gay Rodeo Association Archives, gayrodeohistory.org.

15. "We Want to Be Your Travel Agent," 20.

16. "RSVP Country Western Thanksgiving Mexican Riviera Gay Cruise," *L.A. Rodeo '93*, 1993 program, page 4, International Gay Rodeo Association Archives, gayrodeohistory.org.

17. "Escape to Vallarta," *Canadian Rockies International Rodeo*, 1999 program, page 14, International Gay Rodeo Association Archives, gayrodeohistory.org.

18. "Entertainment," *Canadian Rockies International Rodeo*, 2000 program, page 13, International Gay Rodeo Association Archives, gayrodeohistory.org.

19. Steele, *Banned from California*, 316; *Roundup* is used throughout this book for consistency because it was on a majority of the covers and is the final version of the name. The magazine began as *Round Up—The Gay Western and Rodeo Magazine* in 1993. The name changed to *Roundup—The Gay and Lesbian Western Magazine* in 1995. In the endnotes, the name is the one associated with the title used on the cover of the cited document.

20. "Cowboy Up! Cowgirl Up!" *Rodeo in the Rock*, 2001 program, page 9, International Gay Rodeo Association Archives, http://gayrodeohistory.org.

21. "Frank Harrell," IGRA Hall of Fame, International Gay Rodeo Association Archives, gayrodeohistory.org; Voices of Gay Rodeo, Oral Histories of the International Gay Rodeo Association, http://www.voicesofgayrodeo.com.

22. Terry, interview with Rebecca Scofield.

23. "Welcome to Our Court," *Yeeee Haaa! Ninth Annual TGRA Rodeo*, Rocky Mountain Regional Rodeo, 1992 program, page 32, International Gay Rodeo Association Archives, gayrodeohistory.org.

24. "Welcome to Our Court."

25. "Roundup Mailbag," *Roundup: The Gay and Lesbian Western Magazine*, no. 5, 4 (August 1995).

26. "Roundup Mailbag."

27. "How to Be a Real Cowboy," *Guide Magazine*, Rocky Mountain Regional Rodeo, 1985 program, page 30, International Gay Rodeo Association Archives, gayrodeohistory .org.

28. "Why Go Anywhere Else? PRESTIGE FORD," *17th Annual TGRA Rodeo*, 2000 program, page 32, International Gay Rodeo Association Archives, gayrodeohistory.org.

29. Cowboy drag refers to a person who culturally appropriates western cowboy style and clothing by purchasing hats, boots, shirts, jeans, and a large belt buckle, but who does not live on a ranch or herd cattle, and who cannot claim to have grown up on a farm. This is a performance that allows them an opportunity to look like Hollywood's romanticized western cowboy.

30. Roosevelt, *The Strenuous Life*.

31. Vrooman, interview.

32. "Rodeo Lingo," *Roadrunner Regional Rodeo*, 1989 program, page 41, International Gay Rodeo Association Archives, gayrodeohistory.org.

33. "Rodeo Lingo," 41.

34. "Rodeo Lingo," 41.

35. "Rodeo Lingo," 41.

36. Calendo, "3 Gay Cowboys," 77.

37. "A Taste of Country . . . in the City," *Windy City Rodeo*, 2004 program, page 24, International Gay Rodeo Association Archives, gayrodeohistory.org.

38. "A Taste of Country . . . in the City," 24.

39. "So Many Men . . . So Little Time . . . ," *Fourth Annual Reno Gay Rodeo*, 1979 program, page 3, International Gay Rodeo Association Archives, gayrodeohistory.org.

40. "Debra Danburg," *First Annual Texas Gay Rodeo*, 1984 program, page 13, International Gay Rodeo Association Archives, gayrodeohistory.org.

41. "George Greanias," *First Annual Texas Gay Rodeo*, 1984 program, page 14, International Gay Rodeo Association Archives, gayrodeohistory.org.

42. "Eleanor Tinsley," *First Annual Texas Gay Rodeo*, 1984 program, page 15, International Gay Rodeo Association Archives, gayrodeohistory.org.

43. "Why, Only Budweiser Beer," Comstock Gay Rodeo Association, *National Reno Gay Rodeo*, 1982 program, page 20, International Gay Rodeo Association Archives, gayrodeohistory.org.

44. "Official N.R.G.R. Beer," *National Reno Gay Rodeo*, 1980 program, page 4, International Gay Rodeo Association Archives, gayrodeohistory.org.

45. "Bud Light," *Rocky Mountain Regional Rodeo*, 2006 program, back cover, International Gay Rodeo Association Archives, gayrodeohistory.org.

46. "Budweiser, This Beer's for You!!" *National Reno Gay Rodeo*, 1984 program, page 14, International Gay Rodeo Association Archives, gayrodeohistory.org.

47. "Parker's Western Wear: A 'Real' Part of the History of Reno!!," *National Reno Gay Rodeo*, 1984 program, page 13, International Gay Rodeo Association Archives, gayrodeohistory.org.

48. "About This Program," *First Annual Gay Rodeo, an AIDS Benefit*, 1989 program, page 4, International Gay Rodeo Association Archives, gayrodeohistory.org.

49. "Intolerance Just Doesn't Fly," *CGRA 2000 Rocky Mountain Regional Rodeo*, 2000 program, page 8, International Gay Rodeo Association Archives, gayrodeohistory.org.

50. "United Is Rising," *Rocky Mountain Regional Rodeo*, 1999 program, page 6, International Gay Rodeo Association Archives, gayrodeohistory.org.

51. "Before You Book Your Next Flight," *Rocky Mountain Regional Rodeo 21*, 2003 program, page 3, International Gay Rodeo Association Archives, gayrodeohistory.org.

52. "American Airlines Salutes the Colorado Gay Rodeo Association," *Rocky Mountain Regional Rodeo 22*, 2004 program, page 8, International Gay Rodeo Association Archives, gayrodeohistory.org.

53. "Lowest Scheduled Fares from Denver," *Guide Magazine*, Second Annual Rocky Mountain Regional Rodeo, 1984 program, page 29, International Gay Rodeo Association Archives, gayrodeohistory.org.

54. "Stella Parton," *First Annual Texas Gay Rodeo*, 1984 program, page 18, International Gay Rodeo Association Archives, gayrodeohistory.org.

55. Charles Faber, "National Reno Gay Rodeo and in the Saddle," *The Advocate*, September 16, 1982, 22.

56. Faber, "National Reno Gay Rodeo and in the Saddle," 22.

57. Louis A. Diiorio, "Names and Faces," *Boston Globe*, June 27, 1982, 1.

58. "Rivers to Be Grand Marshal for Gay Rodeo," *Walla Walla* (wa) *Union-Bulletin*, June 27, 1982, 12.

59. "Stars to Serve Rodeo," *Port Arthur* (tx) *News*, June 27, 1982, 2a.

60. "Gay Rodeo Planned," *Blytheville* (ar) *Courier News*, June 29, 1982, 9.

61. "The American Civil Liberties Union . . . It's for Everyone," *National Reno Gay Rodeo*, 1983 program, page 11, International Gay Rodeo Association Archives, gayrodeohistory.org.

62. "Congratulation rmrr," *Guide Magazine*, Second Annual Rocky Mountain Regional Rodeo, 1984 program, page 38, International Gay Rodeo Association Archives, gayrodeohistory.org.

63. "G.I.A. Gay Indians of America," *National Reno Gay Rodeo*, 1984 program, page 14, International Gay Rodeo Association Archives, gayrodeohistory.org.

64. "St. Paul's United Methodist Church," *Guide Magazine*, Rocky Mountain Regional Rodeo, 1986 program, page 26, International Gay Rodeo Association Archives, gayrodeohistory.org.

65. "The Leading Cause of Unsafe Sex Is Treatable," *Guide Magazine*, 1987 program, page 25, International Gay Rodeo Association Archives, gayrodeohistory.org.

66. "The Caremark Connection," *Yeeee Haaa! The Ninth Annual tgra Rodeo*, 1992 program, page 15, International Gay Rodeo Association Archives, gayrodeohistory.org.

67. "The Caremark Connection," 18.

## 4. "Riding with Pride"

Epigraph: "He, She & ??," *Roundup: The Gay Western and Rodeo Magazine*, no. 2 (Fall 1993), from Tony Valdez's personal collection of gay rodeo memorabilia.

1. Bill Steinauer, "Rodeo at Washoe County Fairgrounds This Weekend Is Not for Everyone," *Reno Evening Gazette*, August 19, 1977, 15.

2. Jack Morgan, personal interview by Nicholas Villanueva Jr., Zoom, July 25, 2020.

3. Morgan, personal interview.

4. "Letters of Support," *Rodeo in the Rock*, 1994 program, page 4, International Gay Rodeo Association Archives, gayrodeohistory.org.

5. "Little Rock Holds First Gay Pride Parade," *Jackson* (tx) *Sun*, October 8, 2013, YouTube, https://www.youtube.com/watch?v=iaaeb5mzbz8.

6. "Little Rock Holds First Gay Pride Parade."

7. "Little Rock Holds First Gay Pride Parade."

8. Reno Gay Page, "'Gay' Pride Has a History in Western Nevada."

9. "Gay Parade Sparks Protest," *Ottawa* (KS) *Herald*, June 18, 1990, 2; and "Gays March in Wichita," *Garden City* (KS) *Telegram*, June 18, 1990, 3.

10. "1996 Rodeo Director," *First Annual Big Sky Regional Rodeo*, 1996 program, page 2, International Gay Rodeo Association Archives, gayrodeohistory.org.

11. "A Texas Tradition Rodeo," *Texas Gay Rodeo Association*, 2019 program, cover, International Gay Rodeo Association Archives, gayrodeohistory.org.

12. "Some Info on the Rodeo Facility," *First Annual Texas Gay Rodeo*, 1984 program, International Gay Rodeo Association Archives, gayrodeohistory.org.

13. Adam Taylor, "How a 10-Gallon Hat Helped Heal Relations between China and America," *Washington Post*, September 24, 2015.

14. Ed Martinez, "First Texas Gay Rodeo Held at Simonton," *Houston Star*, 20 (November 9, 1984): 1, International Gay Rodeo Association Archives, gayrodeohistory .org.

15. Martinez, "First Texas Gay Rodeo Held at Simonton," 1.

16. Channel, Tommy, personal interview by Nicholas Villanueva, Jr., Zoom, November 11, 2020.

17. "The Second Gay Rodeo and Dance Festival," *Golden State Gay Rodeo Association*, 1984 program, inside cover, International Gay Rodeo Association Archives, gayrodeohistory.org.

18. In September 2020, the Northalsted Business Alliance announced that they were dropping the name "Boystown" and renaming the neighborhood with a more inclusive identifier. A petition for the name change argued: "The Castro, Greenwich Village, West Hollywood, and many more LGBTQ neighborhoods exist for all intersections of queer identity. Chicago's is the only gendered nickname." Venkatraman, "Chicago's LGBTQ Neighborhood Dropping 'Boystown' Nickname."

19. Michael Vrooman, personal interview by Nicholas Villanueva Jr., Zoom, July 30, 2020.

20. Channel, personal interview.

21. "ASGRA: The First Year," *Atlantic Stampede: Atlantic States Gay Rodeo Association*, 1992 program, page 32, International Gay Rodeo Association Archives, gayrodeohistory.org.

22. "ASGRA: The First Year," 32.

23. "Dedication," *Atlantic Stampede: Atlantic States Gay Rodeo Association*, 1993 program, page 1, International Gay Rodeo Association Archives, gayrodeohistory.org.

24. "Windy City's Illinois Gay Rodeo," 1994 program, page 33, International Gay Rodeo Association Archives, gayrodeohistory.org.

25. At its first official rodeo in 1994, the Alberta Rockies Gay Rodeo Association (ARGRA) advertised as Alberta Gay Rodeo Association (AGRA). It somehow did not recognize that AGRA represented Arizona Gay Rodeo Association. The official name change to ARGRA occurred at the 1994 IGRA convention later that year.

26. *Canadian Rockies International Rodeo*, 1994 program, page 4, International Gay Rodeo Association Archives, gayrodeohistory.org.

27. "Political Messages from Afar," *Canadian Rockies International Rodeo*, 1995 program, page 2, International Gay Rodeo Association Archives, gayrodeohistory.org.

28. "History of North Star Gay Rodeo Association," *North Star Regional Rodeo*, 1994 program, pages 30–31, International Gay Rodeo Association Archives, gayrodeohistory .org.

29. *North Star Regional Rodeo*, 1996 program, page 34, International Gay Rodeo Association Archives, gayrodeohistory.org.

30. "Frank Harrell," IGRA Harrell Hall of Fame, International Gay Rodeo Association Archives, gayrodeohistory.org.

31. In 1995 "Mr. CGRA," Michael Vrooman, created the Spirit Stick from a piece of a staircase. It was sanded and painted red, black, and white, which are the IGRA colors. The royalty team of each year's winning association is responsible for keeping the Spirit Stick secure. It can be stolen at any time by competing associations. In the event it is stolen, the only way to retrieve it is to meet the demands of the person or group that took possession of the Spirit Stick. These demands are in the form of fundraising for the IGRA.

32. "Welcome Y'all!," *Southern Spurs Rodeo: Southeastern Gay Rodeo Association*, 1999 program, page 5, International Gay Rodeo Association Archives, gayrodeohistory.org.

33. "Two Stepping with Heart," *Roundup: The Gay and Lesbian Western Magazine*, no. 4 (June 1995): 31, International Gay Rodeo Association Archives, gayrodeohistory.org.

34. "Two Stepping with Heart," 31.

35. "Two Stepping with Heart," 31.

36. "Two Stepping with Heart," 31.

37. "What a Trump Presidency Means for the LGBT Community."

38. Liam Stack, "Mike Pence and 'Conversion Therapy': A History," *New York Times*, November 16, 2016.

39. Amy Russo, "Alabama Mayor Advocates for 'Killing' of LGBTQ Community on Facebook," *Huffington Post*, June 4, 2019.

40. "A Denver Welcome!" *Guide Magazine*, Second Annual Rocky Mountain Regional Rodeo, 1984 program, page 8, International Gay Rodeo Association Archives, gayrodeohistory.org.

41. Dave W. Dunlap, "Congressional Bills Withhold Sanction of Same-Sex Unions," *New York Times*, May 17, 1996.

42. "A Colorado Welcome," Quest: For a Positive Lifestyle, *Sixth Annual Rocky Mountain Regional Rodeo*, 1988 program, page 19, International Gay Rodeo Association Archives, gayrodeohistory.org.

43. "A Colorado Welcome," 19.

44. Texas Gay Rodeo Association, *Fifth Annual Texas Gay Rodeo*, 1988 program, page 13, International Gay Rodeo Association Archives, gayrodeohistory.org.

45. Coney and Trodd, "Reagan's Rainbow Rodeos," 168.

46. Roger Bergmann, personal interview by Nicholas Villanueva Jr., Phoenix, Arizona, October 27, 2019.

47. Bergmann, personal interview.

48. Bergmann, personal interview.

49. Bergmann, personal interview.

50. "The Reno Gay Rodeo," *Comstock Gay Rodeo Association*, 1982 program, page 5, International Gay Rodeo Association Archives, gayrodeohistory.org.

51. "The Reno Gay Rodeo—A Local Event for Charity Known as—'The National Reno Gay Rodeo,'" Comstock Gay Rodeo Association, National Reno Gay Rodeo, 1980 program, page 5, International Gay Rodeo Association Archives, gayrodeohistory .org.

52. "The Reno Gay Rodeo," *Comstock Gay Rodeo Association*, 1982 program, page 5, International Gay Rodeo Association Archives, gayrodeohistory.org.

53. "Welcome, Cowboys and Cowgirls!! To the Eighth Annual National Reno Gay Rodeo and Country Fair," *National Reno Gay Rodeo*, 1983 program, page 5, International Gay Rodeo Association Archives, gayrodeohistory.org.

54. "Wade Earp," IGRA Harrell Hall of Fame, International Gay Rodeo Association Archives, gayrodeohistory.org.

55. Wade Earp, personal interview by Nicholas Villanueva Jr., Santa Fe, New Mexico, June 29, 2019.

56. Calendo, "Gay Rodeo: Wild Times in Reno," 32.

## 5. Riding, Roughstock, and Camp Events

Epigraph: John Beck, personal interview by Nicholas Villanueva Jr., Santa Fe, New Mexico, June 30, 2019.

1. Fredriksson, *American Rodeo*, 21–22.

2. "Roping Events," *Rodeo in the Rock*, 2013 program, page 20, International Gay Rodeo Association Archives, gayrodeohistory.org.

3. Faderman and Timmons, *Gay L.A.*, 159–62.

4. Liz Galst, "Sacred Cows: Gay Rodeos Are Appearing in Increasing Numbers across the Country, But So Are the Animal Rights Activists Who Want Them Shut Down," *The Advocate*, July 27, 1993, 48.

5. Galst, "Sacred Cows," 48.

6. Galst, "Sacred Cows," 48.

7. Frank Harrell, International Gay Rodeo Association Event Descriptions, "Team Roping," IGRA, http://gayrodeohistory.org/EventDescriptions.htm, accessed October 1, 2019.

8. "We Support Animal Rights," *Eighth Annual IGRA Finals Rodeo*, 1994 program, page 31, International Gay Rodeo Association Archives, gayrodeohistory.org.

9. Frank Harrell, personal interview by Nicholas Villanueva Jr., Santa Fe, New Mexico, June 30, 2019.

10. Wicklund, Foster, and Roy, "Getting Back on the Horse," 657.

11. Conger, "Getting Wrecked."

12. Conger, "Getting Wrecked."

13. "Horse Sense," *Rodeo in the Rock*, 2002 program, page 24, International Gay Rodeo Association Archives, gayrodeohistory.org.

14. "Horse Sense," 24.

15. Belson, "N.F.L. Agrees to Settle Concussion Suit for $765 Million."

16. Frank Harrell, International Gay Rodeo Association Event Descriptions, IGRA, http://gayrodeohistory.org/EventDescriptions.htm, accessed June 19, 2019.

17. Frank Harrell, International Gay Rodeo Association Event Descriptions, IGRA, http://gayrodeohistory.org/EventDescriptions.htm, accessed June 19, 2019.

18. Bakken and Farrington, *Encyclopedia of Women in the American West*, 6.

19. Bakken and Farrington, *Encyclopedia of Women in the American West*, 7.

20. Coakley, *Sport and Society*, 15.

21. "Chute Dogging," *International Gay Rodeo Association Finals Rodeo*, 1989 program, page 28, International Gay Rodeo Association Archives, gayrodeohistory.org.

22. Frank Harrell, "Chute Dogging," *International Gay Rodeo Association Event Descriptions*, IGRA, http://gayrodeohistory.org/EventDescriptions.htm, accessed October 1, 2019.

23. Bruce Casey, personal interview by Nicholas Villanueva Jr., Facebook Messenger, October 4, 2019.

24. "Twenty years' yesterday, October 2, 1999, I watched this man die before my eyes," October 3, 2019, Gay Rodeo Contestant Facebook group, https://www.facebook.com/groups/196989460337229.

25. John Beck, personal interview by Nicholas Villanueva Jr., Santa Fe, New Mexico, June 30, 2019.
26. "International Gay Rodeo Association: Breaking Stereotypes," IGRA, http://www.igra.com/sterotypes.htm, accessed October 1, 2019.
27. Sean Bugg, Will O'Bryan, and Doug Rule, "13 Camp Films Everyone Should See," *Metro Weekly* (Washington DC), February 22, 2012.
28. Sontag, *Notes on "Camp"*, 1.
29. Sontag, *Notes on "Camp"*, 31.
30. Erika W. Smith, "Ahead of the Met Gala, Remember: 'You Can't Have Camp without Queer'"; *Fashion*, May 2, 2019, https://www.refinery29.com/en-gb/2019/05/231566/camp-fashion-gay-culture-drag-lgbtq-history.
31. Frank Harrell, "Event Descriptions," IGRA, http://gayrodeohistory.org/EventDescriptions.htm, accessed June 19, 2019.
32. Harrell, "Event Descriptions."
33. Wes Givens, personal interview by Nicholas Villanueva Jr., Phoenix, Arizona, October 27, 2019.
34. Givens, personal interview.
35. Anderson, "Why a Gay Rodeo? Why Not!"
36. Anderson, "Why a Gay Rodeo? Why Not!"
37. Anderson, "Why a Gay Rodeo? Why Not!"
38. Anderson, "Why a Gay Rodeo? Why Not!"
39. Anderson, "Why a Gay Rodeo? Why Not!"
40. Bruce, *Pride Parades*, 63.
41. Bruce, *Pride Parades*, 63.
42. Bruce Casey, personal interview by Nicholas Villanueva Jr., Facebook Messenger, October 4, 2019.
43. Matt Story, personal interview by Nicholas Villanueva Jr., Santa Fe, New Mexico, June 30, 2019.
44. Pawel Orlinski, personal interview by Nicholas Villanueva Jr., Golden, Colorado, July 5, 2019.
45. Arsenaux, "Ride 'em Cowboy!" 76.

## 6. Masculine Capital

Epigraph: Sontag, *Notes on "Camp"*, 9.
1. Compton, "Queer Eye on the Gay Rodeo," 231.
2. Levine, "'It's Raining Men,'" 29.
3. Kimmel, *Manhood in America*, 184.

4. Compton, "Queer Eye on the Gay Rodeo," 230.

5. Anderson, *In the Game*, 23–26.

6. Cindy Boren and Michael Errigo, "Carli Lloyd Says of Kicking in the NFL: 'I Definitely Could Do It,'" *Washington Post*, August 28, 2019.

7. Kimmel, *Guyland*, 207.

8. Brinson, "Chris Long Didn't Appreciate ESPN's Michael Sam Shower Segment."

9. "NFL Celebrates National Coming Out Day 2020," https://www.nfl.com/videos/nfl-national-coming-out-day-2020, accessed October 13, 2020.

10. "Parade Was Too Butch for Some WSU Graduates," *Chronicle* (Centralia/Chehalis WA), July 18, 1996, C4.

11. "Parade Was Too Butch for Some WSU Graduates," C4.

12. "Welcome Rodeo Fans & Contestants," *Rocky Mountain Regional Rodeo*, 1998 program, page 19, International Gay Rodeo Association Archives, http://gayrodeohistory.org.

13. Arsenaux, "Ride 'em Cowboy!" 75.

14. "Wild Cow Milking: 'Working Together,'" Comstock Gay Rodeo Association, National Reno Gay Rodeo, 1980 program, page 22, International Gay Rodeo Association Archives, gayrodeohistory.org.

15. "Wild Cow Milking: 'Working Together,'" 22.

16. Hunt, "West of the Closet, Fear on the Range," 137.

17. Matt Story, personal interview by Nicholas Villanueva Jr., Santa Fe, New Mexico, June 30, 2019.

18. LeCompte, *Cowgirls of the Rodeo*, 26.

19. Kimmel, *Guyland*, 45–46.

20. Anderson, Magrath, and Bullingham, *Out in Sports*, 123.

21. Kimmel, *Guyland*, 56.

22. Coakley, *Sport and Society*, 198.

23. Florencio Ramirez, "Title IX," *GPSolo* 27, no. 1 (January–February 2010): 17.

24. Sage, Eitzen, and Beal, *Sociology of North American Sport*, 121.

25. Sage, Eitzen, and Beal, *Sociology of North American Sport*, 169.

26. Sage, Eitzen, and Beal, *Sociology of North American Sport*, 169.

27. Women's Sports Foundation, "History of Title IX"; Grove City College v. Bell was a U.S. Supreme Court case that applied Title IX to private schools, even if they refused direct federal funding, because students received federally funded scholarships.

28. Scofield, *Outriders*, 138.

29. Scofield, *Outriders*, 138. See also Feirstein, *Real Men Don't Eat Quiche*; and Henley, *The Butch Manual*.

30. Scofield, *Outriders*, 139.
31. Coney and Trodd, "Reagan's Rainbow Rodeos," 167.
32. "Ron Jesser," IGRA Hall of Fame, International Gay Rodeo Association Archives, gayrodeohistory.org.
33. "Ron Jesser."
34. "Contestants," *Rocky Mountain Regional Rodeo*, 1984 program, page 39, International Gay Rodeo Association Archives, http://gayrodeohistory.org/1982/ProgramReno.htm.
35. "Ron Jesser."
36. "Model Search: Takin' It Off for Charity!" *Palm Springs Gay Rodeo*, 2012 program, page 8, International Gay Rodeo Association Archives, gayrodeohistory.org.
37. Blazina, *The Cultural Myth of Masculinity*, 69.
38. "Club Baths," *Comstock Gay Rodeo Association*, 1984 program, page 26, International Gay Rodeo Association Archives, gayrodeohistory.org.
39. "I.T.: In Touch for Men," *Comstock Gay Rodeo Association*, 1984 program, page 35, International Gay Rodeo Association Archives, gayrodeohistory.org.
40. Arsenaux, "Ride 'em Cowboy!" 74.
41. Arsenaux, "Ride 'em Cowboy!" 74.
42. Arsenaux, "Ride 'em Cowboy!" 74.
43. Arsenaux, "Ride 'em Cowboy!" 74.
44. Calendo, "Gay Rodeo: Wild Times in Reno," 27–29.
45. Calendo, "Gay Rodeo: Wild Times in Reno," 27–29.
46. Calendo, "Gay Rodeo: Wild Times in Reno," 29.
47. "The Ranch," IGRA *Finals Rodeo*, 1990 program, page 16, International Gay Rodeo Association Archives, http://gayrodeohistory.org.
48. Scofield, *Outriders*, 160.
49. Jeffrey McCasland and Philip Lister, email message to the author, October 27, 2019.
50. Paul Vigil, personal interview by Nicholas Villanueva Jr., Zia Regional Rodeo, Santa Fe, New Mexico, June 30, 2019.
51. Mike Nichols, dir., *The Birdcage*; Movie Clip, "Walking Like John Wayne."

## 7. Our Chosen Family

Epigraph: "Ken Pool," *Diversity City*, July 2002, 39, International Gay Rodeo Association Archives, gayrodeohistory.org.
1. "The History of Sheena," IGRA Hall of Fame, International Gay Rodeo Association Archives, gayrodeohistory.org.
2. "The History of Sheena."

3. Patrick Terry, interview with Rebecca Scofield, Albuquerque, New Mexico, October 21, 2017, Voices of Gay Rodeo, Oral Histories of the International Gay Rodeo Association, University of Idaho, http://www.voicesofgayrodeo.com.

4. Patrick Terry, interview with Rebecca Scofield.

5. "Breaking Barriers, Building Bonds at Rodeo"; McNight covered "Stand By Your Man," originally written by Tammy Wynette.

6. Anderson, *21st Century Jocks*, 25.

7. Coakley, *Sport and Society*, 442.

8. Brian Sims, personal interview by Nicholas Villanueva Jr., April 20, 2017.

9. "Cowboy Up!," IGRA *Finals Rodeo*, 2001 program, page 5, International Gay Rodeo Association Archives, http://gayrodeohistory.org.

10. Mosbacher and Yacker, dir., *Training Rules*.

11. Devon Garcia, personal interview by Nicholas Villanueva Jr., Zoom, December 13, 2020.

12. Michael Vrooman, personal interview by Nicholas Villanueva Jr., Zoom, July 30, 2020.

13. "Country Thursdays," *Rocky Mountain Regional Rodeo*, 1998 program, page 23, International Gay Rodeo Association Archives, http://gayrodeohistory.org.

14. "Spurs," *LA Rodeo*, 1992 program, page 2, International Gay Rodeo Association Archives, http://gayrodeohistory.org.

15. "The Brick Bar," *Ninth Annual TGRA Rodeo*, 1992 program, page 31, International Gay Rodeo Association Archives, http://gayrodeohistory.org.

16. "Hanky Codes," IGRA Harrell Hall of Fame, International Gay Rodeo Association Archives, gayrodeohistory.org.

17. Anonymous HIV-positive interviewee, personal interview by Nicholas Villanueva Jr., Zia Regional Rodeo, Santa Fe, New Mexico, June 30, 2019.

18. Davis, "HIV/AIDS: The Litmus Test for Love," 210.

19. "Mavericks: A Gay Cowboy Club," *Bay Area Regional Rodeo*, 1993 program, page 44, International Gay Rodeo Association Archives, http://gayrodeohistory.org.

20. Lisa Levitt, "Gay Cowpokes Plan August Rodeo," *Lawrence* (KS) *Journal-World*, May 21, 1981, 6.

21. Levitt, "Gay Cowpokes Plan August Rodeo," 6.

22. Jeffrey McCasland and Philip Lister, email message to the author, October 27, 2019.

23. Jeffrey McCasland and Philip Lister, email message to the author, October 27, 2019.

24. Jeffrey McCasland and Philip Lister, email message to the author, October 27, 2019.

25. Jeffrey McCasland and Philip Lister, email message to the author, October 27, 2019.

26. Jeffrey McCasland and Philip Lister, email message to the author, October 27, 2019.

27. Candy Pratt, interview with Rebecca Scofield, Duncans Mills, California, September 10, 2016, Voices of Gay Rodeo, Oral Histories of the International Gay Rodeo Association, University of Idaho, http://www.voicesofgayrodeo.com.

28. Pratt, interview with Rebecca Scofield.

29. Pratt, interview with Rebecca Scofield.

30. Paul Vigil, personal interview by Nicholas Villanueva Jr., Zia Regional Rodeo, Santa Fe, New Mexico, June 30, 2019.

31. "Male America Cards for Men," *National Reno Gay Rodeo*, 1983 program, page 35, International Gay Rodeo Association Archives, http://gayrodeohistory.org.

32. Smith, *Encyclopedia of AIDS*, 347.

33. Vrooman, interview.

34. Amy Griffin, personal interview by Nicholas Villanueva Jr., Zoom, July 31, 2020.

## 8. The Riderless Horse

Epigraph: David Black, "The Plague Goes Public," The Plague Years: A Chronicle of AIDS, the Epidemic of Our Times; The Eighties Club: The Politics and Pop Culture of the 1980s, file:///Users/nicholasvillanuevajr./Documents/Professional%20items/Books/Rainbow%20cattle%20company/The%20plague%20goes%20public%22.webarchive.

1. "Ceremony of the Riderless Horse," *LA Rodeo*, 1992 program, page 41, International Gay Rodeo Association Archives, http://gayrodeohistory.org.

2. National Public Radio, "AIDS Patients Now Living Longer, But Aging Faster."

3. Scaccia, "Facts about HIV."

4. Morganthau et al., "Gay America in Transition," 30.

5. Bruce, *Pride Parades*, 63.

6. Bruce, *Pride Parades*, 62–63.

7. Rompalo and Handsfield, "Overview of Sexually Transmitted Diseases in Homosexual Men," 6.

8. Victoria A. Harden, *AIDS at 30: A History* (Washington DC: Potomac Books, 2012), 6.

9. Morganthau et al., "Gay America in Transition," 30.

10. Harden, *AIDS at 30*, 1.

11. Harden, *AIDS at 30*, 1.

12. "Club CB Reno Baths," *Reno Gay Rodeo*, 1979 program, back cover, International Gay Rodeo Association Archives, http://gayrodeohistory.org.

13. Steve's Bathhouse, "The Story of Steve's Bathhouse," 2021.

14. "2 Fatal Diseases Focus of Inquiry: Rare Cancer and Pneumonia in Homosexual Men Studied," *New York Times*, August 29, 1981, L-9.

15. Cran and Barker, dirs., *The Age of* AIDS.

16. Cran and Barker, dirs., *The Age of* AIDS.

17. Cran and Barker, dirs., *The Age of* AIDS.

18. Highberg, "The (Missing) Faces of African American Girls with AIDS," 4.

19. Maurice Carroll, "State Permits Closing of Bathhouses to Cut AIDS," *New York Times*, October 26, 1985, 1.

20. Evelyn Nieves, "San Francisco Is Urged to Allow Secluded Sex in Bathhouses," *New York Times*, May 29, 1999, A-1.

21. Jack Morgan, personal interview by Nicholas Villanueva Jr., Zoom, July 25, 2020.

22. Morgan, personal interview.

23. Lou Thomas, "The Shame of Fallon," *First Hand Events*, no. 2, 1989, 66–68, International Gay Rodeo Association Archives, http://gayrodeohistory.org.

24. Health Resources and Services Administration, "Who Was Ryan White?"

25. "Gay Prisoner Gets Pink I.D. Bracelet," *Out Front*, June 19, 1987, 30.

26. "Gay Prisoner Gets Pink I.D. Bracelet," 30.

27. Lawrence K. Altman, "Clues Found on Homosexuals' Precancer Syndrome," *New York Times*, June 18, 1982, B-8.

28. Fred Bayles, "Clergy Mixed in Response to Crisis over AIDS Disease," *Alton* (IL) *Telegraph*, September 14, 1985, E-5.

29. "Church Votes to Withdraw from Presbyterian Group," *Alton* (IL) *Telegraph*, September 14, 1985, E-5.

30. Jerry Schwartz, "AIDS Panic Shakes Lives of Likely Victims," *Lawrence* (KS) *Journal-World*, June 29, 1983, 30.

31. Bayles, "Clergy Mixed in Response," E-5.

32. "Protesters Try to Stop Gay Rodeo," *Odessa* (TX) *America*, August 7, 1983, 14A.

33. "A Message from the Desk of the President," *Reno Gay Rodeo*, 1984 program, page 5, International Gay Rodeo Association Archives, http://gayrodeohistory.org.

34. "Gay Christians Condemn Falwell's Statement about AIDS," *Santa Ana* (CA) *Register*, July 16, 1983, C-11.

35. "Gay Christians Condemn Falwell's Statement," C-11.

36. "Letters: Gay America," *Newsweek*, August 22, 1983, 7.

37. "Letters: Gay America," *Newsweek*, August 22, 1983, 7.

38. Morganthau et al., "Gay America in Transition," 33.

39. "Letters: Gay America," *Newsweek*, August 22, 1983, 7.

40. Olivia Campbell, "Here's What Happened When Reagan Went After Healthcare Programs."

41. Olivia Campbell, "Here's What Happened When Reagan Went After Healthcare Programs."

42. Centers for Disease Control and Prevention, "Current Trends Update."
43. Philip Boffey, "Reagan Defends Financing for AIDS," *New York Times*, September 18, 1985, B-7.
44. "AIDS Victim Begs Feds to Help," *Cedar Rapids (IA) Gazette*, September 14, 1985, 12-C.
45. "AIDS Victim Begs Feds to Help," 12-C.
46. "AIDS Victim Begs Feds to Help," 12-C.
47. "The Birth of the First Annual Rocky Mountain Regional Rodeo," *Rocky Mountain Regional Rodeo*, 1983 program, page 16, International Gay Rodeo Association Archives, http://gayrodeohistory.org.
48. "The Birth of the First Annual Rocky Mountain Regional Rodeo."
49. "Tired of 'Catching' VD?" *Rocky Mountain Regional Rodeo*, 1983 program, page 30, International Gay Rodeo Association Archives, http://gayrodeohistory.org.
50. "Fight the Fear with Facts," *Rocky Mountain Regional Rodeo*, 1988 program, page 8, International Gay Rodeo Association Archives, http://gayrodeohistory.org.
51. "TGRA," *First Annual Texas Gay Rodeo*, 1984 program, page 8, International Gay Rodeo Association Archives, http://gayrodeohistory.org.
52. "San Diego AIDS Project," *Golden State Gay Rodeo Association*, 1990 program, page 15, International Gay Rodeo Association Archives, http://gayrodeohistory.org.
53. Tommy Channel, personal interview by Nicholas Villanueva Jr., Zoom, November 11, 2020.
54. Laura Lee Laykasek, personal interview by Nicholas Villanueva Jr., Santa Fe, New Mexico, June 30, 2019.
55. "Beloit Man AIDS Victim," *Janesville (WI) Gazette*, February 16, 1985, 2-B.
56. "Some Doctors Want Option of Turning Away AIDS Patients," *Out Front*, July 21, 1987, 30.
57. Black, "The Plague Goes Public."
58. Black, "The Plague Goes Public."
59. "A.I.D.S. vs. AIDS," *Reno Gay Rodeo*, 1984 program, page 18, International Gay Rodeo Association Archives, http://gayrodeohistory.org.
60. "A.I.D.S. vs. AIDS."
61. "A.I.D.S. vs. AIDS."
62. Thomas, "The Shame of Fallon," 66.
63. Thomas, "The Shame of Fallon," 66.
64. Ann Diggins, "County Wants to Stop Gay Rodeo," *Lahontan Valley (WI) News and Fallon Eagle Standard*, October 20, 1988, 1.
65. Thomas, "The Shame of Fallon," 66.
66. "I Say There Will Be Confrontation," *First Hand Events*, no. 2, 1989, 67, International Gay Rodeo Association Archives, http://gayrodeohistory.org.

67. "Dedication," *Rodeo 1989 Finals*, 1989 program, page 4, International Gay Rodeo Association Archives, http://gayrodeohistory.org.

68. "Dedication," *Rodeo 1989 Finals*.

69. "The 1990 Roadrunner Regional Rodeo Is Dedicated to Dale A. Williams," *Arizona Gay Rodeo Association*, 1990 program, page 3, International Gay Rodeo Association Archives, http://gayrodeohistory.org.

70. "The People's Rodeo Is Dedicated to the Memory of 'Diamond Dan' Bloomer," *Tri-State Gay Rodeo Association*, 1990 program, page 5, International Gay Rodeo Association Archives, http://gayrodeohistory.org.

71. "In Memory," *Golden State Gay Rodeo Association Rodeo*, 1990 program, page 16, International Gay Rodeo Association Archives, http://gayrodeohistory.org.

72. "Silence = Death," ZIA *Regional Rodeo*, 1991 program, page 1, International Gay Rodeo Association Archives, http://gayrodeohistory.org.

73. "In Memoriam," *Rodeo in the Rock*, 2002 program, page 19, International Gay Rodeo Association Archives, http://gayrodeohistory.org.

74. At its first official rodeo, the Alberta Rockies Gay Rodeo Association (ARGRA) advertised as Alberta Gay Rodeo Association (AGRA) and somehow did not recognize that AGRA represented Arizona Gay Rodeo Association. The official name change to ARGRA occurred at the 1994 IGRA convention later that year.

75. "In Memory Of," *Canadian Rockies International Rodeo*, 1990 program, page 25, International Gay Rodeo Association Archives, http://gayrodeohistory.org; Frank Harrel noted on the website: "Notice the association acronym of AGRA. When Canada's first association was seated at convention, somehow they missed the fact their acronym was exactly the same as Arizona. This was changed to ARGRA at the 1994 convention."

76. "In Memory Of," *Canadian Rockies International Rodeo*.

77. Tony Valdez, personal interview by Nicholas Villanueva Jr., Chicago, December 4, 2019.

78. "IGRA Royalty 1993," IGRA *Finals Rodeo*, 1993 program, page 9, International Gay Rodeo Association Archives, http://gayrodeohistory.org.

79. Roosevelt, *The Strenuous Life*.

80. Allen, *Rodeo Cowboys in the North American Imagination*, 15.

81. Gerstle, *American Crucible*, 27.

82. Gerstle, *American Crucible*, 27.

83. Miller, *The Big Scrum*, 132–33.

84. "Dedication," IGRA *Finals Rodeo*, 1991 program, page 1, International Gay Rodeo Association Archives, http://gayrodeohistory.org.

85. "Dedication," IGRA *Finals Rodeo*.

86. "Touch, Known, and Loved," Gregory James Pope, *Out Front*, June 19, 1987, 4.

## Conclusion

Epigraph: Tony Valdez, personal interview by Nicholas Villanueva Jr., Chicago, December 4, 2019.

1. Salvation Army, Home Service Fund Campaign, May 19–26, 1919.
2. "Grand Marshals: Rocky Mountain Regional Rodeo!" *Quest: The Voice of the Gay Community*, July 1988, 21, International Gay Rodeo Association Archives, http://gayrodeohistory.org.
3. Tommy Channel and David Hill, personal interview by Nicholas Villanueva Jr., Zoom, November 11, 2020.
4. Channel and Hill, personal interview.
5. "Rodeo Lingo," *Roadrunner Regional Rodeo*, 1990 program, page 38, International Gay Rodeo Association Archives, http://gayrodeohistory.org.
6. Michael Vrooman, personal interview by Nicholas Villanueva Jr., Zoom, July 30, 2020.
7. Roger Bergmann, personal interview by Nicholas Villanueva Jr., IGRA Finals, Phoenix, Arizona, October 27, 2019.
8. Paul Vigil, personal interview by Nicholas Villanueva Jr., Zia Regional Rodeo, Santa Fe, New Mexico, June 30, 2019.
9. Scofield, *Outriders*, 239.
10. Vigil, interview.
11. Desirey Benavides, interview with Rebecca Scofield, Palm Springs, California, May 17, 2017, Voices of Gay Rodeo, Oral Histories of the International Gay Rodeo Association, University of Idaho, http://www.voicesofgayrodeo.com.
12. Desirey Benavides, interview with Rebecca Scofield.
13. Vrooman, interview.
14. Vrooman, interview.
15. Vrooman, interview.
16. Vrooman, interview.
17. Vrooman, interview.
18. Vrooman, interview.
19. Vrooman, interview.
20. Vrooman, interview.
21. Tre Brewbaker, Facebook, June 9, 2020, https://www.facebook.com/tbrew82.
22. "Miss Mae," In Memoriam, http://gayrodeohistory.org.
23. "Miss Mae."
24. "Miss Mae."

25. IGRA Finals program, 1992, from Tony Valdez's personal collection.

26. Morganthau et al., "Gay America in Transition," 33.

27. Tony Valdez, personal interview by Nicholas Villanueva Jr., Chicago, December 4, 2019.

28. Isensee, *Love between Men*, 139.

29. Letter from Les Pannell to Tony Valdez, December 5, 1991, from Tony Valdez's personal collection of gay rodeo memorabilia.

30. Chuckwagon Program advertisement, from Tony Valdez's personal collection of gay rodeo memorabilia.

31. Miss Chili Pepper, Tony Valdez, 1992 Miss IGRA Royalty Form 3, résumé, from Tony Valdez's personal collection of gay rodeo memorabilia.

32. "Living with AIDS Begins with a Place to Live," aidsdallas.org, accessed December 6, 2019.

33. "This Is Where Your Money Went in 1991," *Ninth Annual TGRA Rodeo*, 1992 program, page 2, International Gay Rodeo Association Archives, http://gayrodeohistory .org.

34. Tommy Channel, personal interview by Nicholas Villanueva Jr., Zoom, November 11, 2020.

35. "Dedication," *Atlantic Stampede Gay Rodeo*, 1993 program, page 1, International Gay Rodeo Association Archives, http://gayrodeohistory.org.

36. Jobin-Leeds, *When We Fight We Win*, 20–21.

37. NFL Communications, "NFL Celebrates LGBTQ+ History Month."

# Bibliography

## Archives

International Gay Rodeo Association Archives, gayrodeohistory.org.

International Gay Rodeo Association Institutional Archives, 1982–2009, Autry National Center, Los Angeles, California.

Vanderbilt University Television News Archive, Vanderbilt University, Nashville, Tennessee.

## Oral Histories and Personal Interviews

Scofield, Rebecca. Voices of Gay Rodeo. Oral Histories of the International Gay Rodeo Association, University of Idaho. http://www.voicesofgayrodeo.com. Includes interviews with the following:

Benavides, Desirey

Bergmann, Roger

Harrell, Frank

Morgan, Jack

Pratt, Candy

Renier, David

Terry, Patrick

## Personal Collections/Archives

Beck, John, "The International Gay Rodeo Association: Facts and Figures from the Years 1983–1999," Information Systems Committee Report on Seventeen Years of Gay Rodeo History, Presented to the 15th IGRA Annual Convention, Long Beach, California, August 1, 1999.

———. Correspondence between Phil Ragsdale and John Hansen, 1982 Contestant Package, June 21, 1982.

## Books, Journal and Magazine Articles, Manuscripts

Adams, Raymond F. Western Words: A Dictionary of the Range, Cow Camp and Trail. Norman: University of Oklahoma Press, 1936.

Allen, Michael. Rodeo Cowboys in the North American Imagination. Reno: University of Nevada Press, 1998.

Altschiller, Donald. *Hate Crimes: A Reference Handbook*. Santa Barbara CA: ABC-CLIO, 2005.

Anderson, Eric. *In the Game: Gay Athletes and the Cult of Masculinity*. Albany: State University of New York Press, 2005.

———. *21st Century Jocks: Sporting Men and Contemporary Heterosexuality*. New York: Palgrave Macmillan, 2014.

Anderson, Eric, Rory Magrath, and Rachael Bullingham. *Out in Sports: The Experience of Openly Gay and Lesbian Athletes in Competitive Sport*. New York: Routledge, 2016.

Anderson, Shelagh. "Why a Gay Rodeo? Why Not!" *Roundup: The Gay and Lesbian Western Magazine*, no. 5 (August 1995): 51.

Arsenaux, Bill. "Ride 'em Cowboy!" *In Touch for Men*, no. 38 (November 1978): 74–77.

Bakken, Gordon Morris, and Brenda Farrington. *Encyclopedia of Women in the American West*. Thousand Oaks CA: Sage Publications, 2003.

Belson, Ken. "N.F.L. Agrees to Settle Concussion Suit for $765 Million." *New York Times*, August 29, 2013.

Black, David. *The Plague Years: A Chronicle of AIDS, the Epidemic of Our Times*. New York: Simon and Schuster, 1985.

Blank, Hanne. *Straight: The Surprisingly Short History of Heterosexuality*. New York: Beacon Press, 2012.

Blazina, Chris. *The Cultural Myth of Masculinity*. Westport CT: Praeger, 2003.

Boag, Peter. *Re-Dressing America's Frontier Past*. Berkeley: University of California Press, 2011.

Boysen, Guy A., Mary Fisher, Michael DeJesus, David L. Vogel, and Stephanie Madon, "The Mental Health Stereotype about Gay Men: The Relationship between Gay Men's Self-Stereotype and Stereotypes about Heterosexual Women and Lesbians," *Journal of Social and Clinical Psychology*, 30, no. 4 (2011): 329–60.

Boysen, Guy A., David L. Vogel, Stephanie Madon, and Stephen R. Wester. "Mental Health Stereotypes about Gay Men." *Sex Roles* 54, nos. 1–2 (January 2006): 69–82.

"Breaking Barriers, Building Bonds at Rodeo: Phil Ragsdale Proves the Old West Belongs to Us All," *Go: Magazine of Great Outdoors Men and Women*, 6 (Fall 1981): 4–6.

Bruce, Katherine McFarland. *Pride Parades: How a Parade Changed the World*. New York: New York University Press, 2016.

Calendo, John. "3 Gay Cowboys." *In Touch for Men*, (January 1981): 27–30, 32–36, 91.

———. "Gay Rodeo: Wild Times in Reno." *In Touch for Men* (January 1981): 33, 77.

Canaday, Margot. *The Straight State: Sexuality and Citizenship in Twentieth-Century America*. Princeton NJ: Princeton University Press, 2009.

Chauncey, George. *Gay New York: Gender, Urban Culture, and the Making of the Gay Male World*. New York: Harper Collins Publishers, 1994.

Coakley, Jay. *Sport and Society: Issues and Controversies*, 13th ed. New York: McGraw-Hill, 2021.

Compton, D'Lane R. "Queer Eye on the Gay Rodeo." In *Gender in the Twenty-First Century: The Stalled Revolution and the Road to Equality*, edited by Shannon N. Davis, Sarah Winslow, and David J. Maume, 222–38. Berkeley: University of California Press, 2017.

Coney, Christopher Le, and Zoe Trodd. "Reagan's Rainbow Rodeos: Queer Challenges to the Cowboy Dreams of the 1980s." *Canadian Review of American Studies* 39, no. 2 (January 2009): 163–83.

Coski, John M. "The Confederate Battle Flag in American History and Culture." *Southern Cultures* 2, no. 2 (Winter 1996): 195–231.

Davis, Herndon L. "HIV/AIDS: The Litmus Test for Love." In *Not in My Family: AIDS in the African-American Community*, edited by Gil L. Robertson IV, 209–13. Chicago: Agate Publishing, 2006.

Dean, Robert D. *Imperial Brotherhood: Gender and the Making of Cold War Foreign Policy*. Amherst: University of Massachusetts Press, 2001.

Denes, Amanda, and Tamara D. Afifi. "Coming Out Again: Exploring GLBQ Individuals' Communication with Their Parents after the First Coming Out." *Journal of GLBT Family Studies* 10, no. 3 (November 2014): 298–325.

Dervisbegovic, Nedim. "Bosnia Imam Thanks God for Virus Cancelling Pride March." *Balkan Insight*, August 7, 2020.

Downs, Jim. *Stand By Me: The Forgotten History of Gay Liberation*. New York: Basic Books, 2016.

Eichberg, Robert. *Coming Out: An Act of Love*. New York: Dutton, 1990.

Faderman, Lillian, and Stuart Timmons. *Gay L.A.: A History of Sexual Outlaws, Power Politics, and Lipstick Lesbians*. New York: Basic Books, 2006.

Feasey, Rebecca. *Masculinity and Popular Television*. Edinburgh: Edinburgh University Press, 2008.

Feirstein, Bruce. *Real Men Don't Eat Quiche: A Guidebook to All That Is Truly Masculine*. New York: Chrysalis Books, 1982.

Fellows, Will. *Farm Boys: Lives of Gay Men from the Rural Midwest*. Madison: University of Wisconsin Press, 1996.

Fredriksson, Kristine. *American Rodeo: From Buffalo Bill to Big Business*. College Station TX: A&M University Press, 1985.

Galst, Liz. "Sacred Cows: Gay Rodeos Are Appearing in Increasing Numbers across the Country, but So Are the Animal Rights Activists Who Want Them Shut Down." *The Advocate*, July 27, 1993, 47–51.

Gauthier, Paula. "Steer and Queers." Master's thesis, University of California, San Diego, 2000.

Gerstle, Gary. *American Crucible: Race and Nation in the Twentieth Century*. Princeton NJ: Princeton University Press, 2001.

Ghaziani, Amin. "The Closet." *Contexts* 16, no. 3 (Summer 2017): 72–73.

Halberstam, Judith. "Not So Lonesome Cowboys." In *The Brokeback Book: From Story to Cultural Phenomenon*, edited by William R. Handley, 190–201. Lincoln: University of Nebraska Press, 2011.

Harden, Victoria A. *AIDS at 30: A History*. Washington DC: Potomac Books, 2012.

Henley, Clark. *The Butch Manual: The Current Drag and How to Do It*. New York: Seahorse Press, 1982.

Herek, Gregory M. "Beyond 'Homophobia': Thinking about Sexual Prejudice and Stigma in the Twenty-First Century." *Sexuality Research and Social Policy* 1, no. 2 (April 2004): 6–24.

Herring, Scott. *Another Country: Queer Anti-Urbanism*. New York: New York University Press, 2009.

Highberg, Nels P. "The (Missing) Faces of African American Girls with AIDS." *Feminist Formations* 22, no. 1 (Spring 2010): 1–20.

Hunt, Alex. "West of the Closet, Fear on the Range." In *The Brokeback Book: From Story to Cultural Phenomenon*, edited by William R. Handley, 137–50. Lincoln: University of Nebraska Press, 2011.

Isensee, Rik. *Love between Men: Enhancing Intimacy and Keeping Your Relationship Alive*. New York: Prentice Hall Press, 1990.

Jimenez, Stephen. *The Book of Matt: Hidden Truths about the Murder of Matthew Shepard*. Hanover NH: Steerforth Press, 2013.

Jobin-Leeds, Greg. *When We Fight We Win: Twenty-First-Century Social Movements and the Activists That Are Transforming Our World*. New York: New Press, 2016.

Johnson, Colin. *Just Queer Folks: Gender and Sexuality in Rural America*. Philadelphia: Temple University Press, 2013.

Johnson, David K. *The Lavender Scare: The Cold War Persecution of Gays and Lesbians in the Federal Government*. Chicago: University of Chicago Press, 2001.

Keller, James R., and Anne Goodwyn Jones. "Brokeback Mountain: Masculinity and Manhood." *Studies in Popular Culture* 30, no. 2 (Spring 2008): 21–36.

Kibelstis, Teresa Eileen. "Preventing Violence against Gay Men and Lesbians: Should Enhanced Penalties at Sentencing Extend to Bias Crimes Based on Victims' Sexual Orientation?" *Notre Dame Journal of Law, Politics and Public Policy* 9, no. 1 (1995): 309–43.

Kimmel, Michael. *Guyland: The Perilous World Where Boys Become Men; Understanding the Critical Years Between 16 and 26*. New York: HarperCollins, 2006.

——. *Manhood in America: A Cultural History*. New York: Oxford University Press, 2006.

Kulick, Don. "Can There Be an Anthropology of Homophobia?" In *Homophobias: Lust and Loathing across Time and Space,* edited by David A. B. Murray, 19–33. Durham NC: Duke University Press, 2009.

Large, Jason. "Long Journey Ahead." *Journal of Bisexuality* 5, nos. 2–3 (2005): 119–26.

LeCompte, Mary Lou. *Cowgirls of the Rodeo.* Urbana: University of Illinois Press, 2000.

Levin, James, and Jim Nolan. *The Violence of Hate,* 4th ed. London: Rowman and Littlefield Publishing, 2017.

Levine, Martin P. "'It's Raining Men': The Sociology of Gay Masculinity." In *Gay Macho: The Life and Death of the Homosexual Clone,* 10–29. New York: New York University Press, 1998.

Levitt, Eugene E., and Albert D. Klassen. "Public Attitudes toward Homosexuality: Part of the 1970 National Survey by the Institute for Sex Research." *Journal of Homosexuality* 1, no. 1 (1974): 29–43.

Limerick, Patricia Nelson. *The Legacy of Conquest: The Unbroken Past of the American West.* New York: W. W. Norton, 1987.

Linehan, Kevin. *Such Were Some of You: The Spiritual Odyssey of an Ex-Gay Christian.* Scottsdale PA: Herald Press, 1979.

Luther, Jessica, and Kavitha Davidson. *Loving Sports When They Don't Love You Back.* Austin: University of Texas Press, 2020.

Marcus, Eric. *Making Gay History: The Half-Century Fight for Lesbian and Gay Equal Rights.* New York: HarperCollins, 2002.

McCall, George J., and J. L. Simmons. *Identities and Interactions: An Examination of Human Associations in Everyday Life.* New York: Free Press, 1966.

McClain, Craig. "Gay Rodeo: Carnival, Gender, and Resistance." Master's thesis, University of New Mexico, 2005.

Miller, John J. *The Big Scrum: How Teddy Roosevelt Saved Football.* New York: Harper Perennial, 2011.

Miller, Neil. *Out of the Past: Gay and Lesbian History from 1869 to the Present.* New York: Vintage Books, 1995.

Morganthau, Tom, Vincent Coppola, John Carey, Nancy Cooper, and George Raine. "Gay America in Transition: A Turning Point Has Been Reached, and AIDS May Mean the Party Is Over." *Newsweek,* August 8, 1983, 30.

Packard, Chris. *Queer Cowboys: And Other Erotic Male Friendships in Nineteenth-Century American Literature.* New York: Palgrave Macmillan, 2005.

Pearson, Demetrius W., and C. Allen Haney. "The Rodeo Cowboy as an American Icon: The Perceived Social and Cultural Significance." *Journal of Cultural History* 22, no. 4 (Winter 1999): 17–21.

Pronger, Brian. *The Arena of Masculinity: Sports, Homosexuality, and the Meaning of Sex.* New York: St. Martin's Press, 1990.

Ramakers, Micha. *Dirty Pictures: Tom of Finland, Masculinity, and Homosexuality.* New York: St. Martin's Press, 2000.

Ramirez, Florencio. "Title IX." GPSolo 27, no. 1 (January–February 2010): 16–19.

Rompalo, Anne, and H. Hunter Handsfield. "Overview of Sexually Transmitted Diseases in Homosexual Men." In *AIDS and Infections of Homosexual Men*, edited by Pearl Ma and Donald Armstrong, 3–11 Boston: Butterworths, 1989.

Roosevelt, Theodore. *The Strenuous Life: Essays and Addresses.* Mineola NY: Dover, 2012.

Sage, George H., D. Stanley Eitzen, and Becky Beal. *Sociology of North American Sport*, 11th ed. New York: Oxford University Press, 2019.

Savin-Williams, Ritch C. *Mostly Straight: Sexual Fluidity among Men.* New York: Harvard University Press, 2017.

Scofield, Rebecca. "'Chaps and Scowls': Play, Violence, and the Post-1970s Urban Cowboy." *Journal of Social History* 26, no. 4 (December 2017): 325–40.

——. *Outriders: Rodeo at the Fringes of the American West.* Seattle: University of Washington Press, 2019.

Silva, Tony. "Bud-Sex: Constructing Normative Masculinity among Rural Straight Men That Have Sex with Men." *Gender & Society* (November 2016): 51–73.

——. *Still Straight: Sexual Flexibility among White Men in Rural America.* New York: NYU Press, 2021.

Smith, Raymond. *Encyclopedia of AIDS: A Social, Political, Cultural, and Scientific Record of the HIV Epidemic.* New York: Routledge, 1998.

Sontag, Susan. *Notes on "Camp."* New York: Penguin Random House, 2018.

Steele, Robert C. *Banned from California—Jim Foshee—Persecution, Redemption, Liberation . . . and the Gay Civil Rights Movement.* Yuma, AZ: Wentworth-Schwartz Publishing Company, 2020.

Streitmatter, Rodger. *From "Perverts" to "Fab Five": The Media's Changing Depiction of Gay Men and Lesbians.* New York: Routledge, 2009.

Stuart, Craig O. "Social Cognition and Discourse Processing Goals in the Analysis of 'Ex-Gay' Rhetoric." *Discourse & Society*, 19, no. 1 (January 2008): 63–83.

Sullivan-Blum, Constance R. "'It's Adam and Eve, Not Adam and Steve': What's at Stake in the Construction of Contemporary American Christian Homophobia." In *Homophobias: Lust and Loathing across Time and Space*, edited by David A. B. Murray, 48–63. Durham NC: Duke University Press, 2009.

Tarver, Erin C. "Bigger Than Football: Fan Anxiety and Memory in the Racial Present." *Journal of Speculative Philosophy* 33, no. 2 (2019): 220–37.

Villanueva, Nicholas Jr. "Land of the Free? Sporting Nationalism and White Privilege in the United States." In *The Athlete as National Symbol: Critical Essays on Sports* in the *International Arena*, edited by Nicholas Villanueva Jr., 9–23. Jefferson NC: McFarland, 2020.

———. "A Rodeo to Call Their Own: LGBTQ Vaqueros and the Gay Rodeo of the American West." In *Decolonizing Latinx Masculinities*, edited by Arturo J. Aldama and Frederick Luis Aldama, 307–325. Tucson: University of Arizona Press, 2020.

Warren, Patricia Nell. *The Lavender Locker Room: 3000 Years of Great Athletes Whose Sexual Orientation Was Different*. Beverly Hills CA: Wildcat Press, 2006.

Wicklund, Alissa, Shayla Foster, and Ashley Roy. "Getting Back on the Horse: Sport-Specific Return to Play in Rodeo Athletes After Concussion Injury." *Journal of Athletic Training*, 53, Iss. 7, (July 2018), 657–661.

Wooden, Wayne S., and Gavin Ehringer. *Rodeo in America: Wranglers, Roughstock, and Paydirt*. Lawrence: University Press of Kansas, 1996.

## Electronic Resources

Avery, Dan. "What a Trump Presidency Means for the LGBT Community." *NewNowNext*. Accessed June 29, 2020. http://www.newnownext.com/what-a-trump-presidency -means-for-the-lgbt-community/11/2016/.

BBC News. "Nelson Releases Gay Cowboy Song." BBC *News*, February 15, 2006. http:// news.bbc.co.uk/2/hi/entertainment/4715822.stm.

Brinson, Will. "Chris Long Didn't Appreciate ESPN's Michael Sam Shower Segment." CBS *Sports*, August 26, 2014. https://www.cbssports.com/nfl/news/chris-long-didnt -appreciate-espns-michael-sam-shower-segment/.

Campbell, Olivia. "Here's What Happened When Reagan Went After Healthcare Programs. It's Not Good." *Timeline*, September 13, 2017. https://timeline.com/reagan-trump -healthcare-cuts-8cf64aa242eb.

Centers for Disease Control and Prevention. "Current Trends Update: Acquired Immunodeficiency Syndrome (AIDS), United States." *Morbidity and Mortality Weekly Report*, September 9, 1983. http://www.cdc.gov/mmwr/preview/mmwrhtml/00000137 .htm.

Conger, Joe. "Getting Wrecked: Brain Injuries Impact Popular Rodeo." *News Four San Antonio*, February 6, 2019. https://news4sanantonio.com/news/local/getting-wrecked -brain-injuries-impact-popular-rodeo-sport.

Democratic Underground. "Dallas Dudes Who Inspired Willie Nelson's Salute to Gay Cowboys Usher in Star-Studded Aetheria Bash." Accessed February 28, 2014. http:// www.democraticunderground.com/discuss/duboard.php?az=view_all&address= 221x48205.

Hansen, Matthew. "For Gay Competitors, A Rodeo to Call Their Own." KQED *News*, March 25, 2014. https://www.kqed.org/news/130353/for-gay-competitors-a-rodeo-to -call-their-own.

Health Resources and Services Administration. "Who Was Ryan White?" Last reviewed October 2016. https://hab.hrsa.gov/about-ryan-white-hivaids-program/who-was-ryan -white.

IMDbPro. "Romantic Drama." *Box Office Mojo*. Accessed March 22, 2016. http://www.boxofficemojo.com/genres/chart/?id=romanticdrama.htm.

Jacobs, Laura. "Cinema Aphrodiso." *Vanity Fair*, August 9, 2014. http://www.vanityfair .com/hollywood/2013/09/25-best-love-story-movies.

Karlan, Sarah, J. Lester Feder, and Michelle Rial. "Here Are the World's Most Popular Dating Apps for Gay Dudes." *BuzzFeed News*, December 17, 2015. https://www .buzzfeednews.com/article/skarlan/here-are-the-worlds-most-popular-hook-up-apps -for-gay-dudes.

Markowitz, Eric. "The Most Dangerous Gay Man in America Fought Violence with Violence." *Newsweek*, January 25, 2018. https://www.newsweek.com/2018/02/02/most -dangerous-gay-man-america-789402.html.

National Public Radio. "AIDS Patients Now Living Longer, but Aging Faster." *NPR Morning Edition*, November 10, 2009. https://www.npr.org/templates/story/story.php?storyId =120249388.

"NFL Celebrates National Coming Out Day 2020." Accessed October 13, 2020. https:// www.nfl.com/videos/nfl-national-coming-out-day-2020.

NFL Communications. "NFL Celebrates LGBTQ+ History Month." October 11, 2020. https://nflcommunications.com/Pages/Rundown/nfl-Celebrates-lgbtq—History-Month .aspx.

Reid, Skyler. "The Brokeback Cowboys of Ohio's Gay Rodeo." *Vice Media Group*, September 22, 2014. https://www.vice.com/sv/article/5gkjxa/the-brokeback-cowboys-of -ohios-gay-rodeo-922.

Reilly, Rick. "Queer Eye for the Sports Guy." *Sports Illustrated*, November 10, 2003. https:// vault.si.com/vault/2003/11/10/queer-eye-for-the-sports-guy.

Reno Gay Page. "'Gay' Pride Has a History in Western Nevada." June 17, 2015. https:// therenogaypage.wordpress.com/2016/06/17/gay-pride-has-a-history-in-western -nevada/.

Scaccia, Annamarya. "Facts about HIV: Life Expectancy and Long-Term Outlook." *Healthline*, updated April 24, 2020. www.healthline.com/health/hiv-aids/life-expectancy.

Sheerin, Jude. "Matthew Shepard: The Murder that Changed America." *BBC News*, October 26, 2018. https://www.bbc.com/news/world-us-canada-45968606.

Singal, Jesse. "The Phenomenon of 'Bud Sex' between Straight Rural Men." *New York Magazine*, December 2016. https://www.thecut.com/2016/12/why-straight-rural-men -have-gay-bud-sex-with-each-other.html.

Smith, Erica W. "Ahead of the Met Gala, Remember: 'You Can't Have Camp without Queer.'" *Fashion*, May 2, 2019. https://www.refinery29.com/en-gb/2019/05/231566/camp-fashion-gay-culture-drag-lgbtq-history.

Steve's Bathhouse. "The Story of Steve's Bathhouse." 2021. https://stevesreno.com/our-story/.

Sublette, Ned. "Cowboys Are Frequently, Secretly Fond of Each Other." *Song Meanings*. Accessed February 28, 2014. http://songmeanings.com/songs/view/3530822107858574657/.

Tynes, Tyler, and Richard Johnson. "Emails Show a Nebraska Regent was 'Embarrassed' by Cornhusker Football Players' Protest." sb *Nation*, October 20, 2016. https://www.sbnation.com/college-football/2016/10/25/13337820/nebraska-cornhusker-football-players-protest-kneel-national-anthem.

Us Weekly Staff. "30 Most Romantic Movies of All Time." *Us Weekly*, February 14, 2012. http://www.usmagazine.com/entertainment/pictures/30-most-romantic-movies-of-all-time-2012102/20669.

Venkatraman, Sakshi. "Chicago's LGBTQ Neighborhood Dropping 'Boystown' Nickname." NBC *News*, September 28, 2020. https://www.nbcnews.com/feature/nbc-out/chicago-s-lgbtq-neighborhood-dropping-boystown-nickname-n1241262.

Women's Sports Foundation. "History of Title IX." August 13, 2019. https://www.womenssportsfoundation.org/advocacy/history-of-title-ix/.

Zeigler, Cyd. "Outsports' Asshole of the Year: Tony Dungy." *Out Sports: Courage is Contagious*, December 30, 2014. https://www.outsports.com/2014/12/30/7465205/tony-dungy-gay-homophobia-michael-sam-2014.

## Films

Cran, William, and Greg Barker, dirs. *The Age of* AIDS. 2 parts. Arlington VA: Public Broadcasting Service, 2006.

Horn, Mitchell, dir. *Gidyup! On the Rodeo Circuit*. Pleasantville NY: Litlhorn, 2005.

Livadary, Matt, dir. *Queens and Cowboys: A Straight Year on the Gay Rodeo*. Go West, 2014.

Mitchell, Fritz, dir. *Ghosts of Ole Miss*. Bristol CT: ESPN Films, 2012.

Mosbacher, Dee, and Fawn Yacker, dirs. *Training Rules: No Drinking, No Drugs, No Lesbians*. San Francisco, CA: Woman Vision Productions, 2009.

Nichols, Mike, dir. *The Birdcage*. Los Angeles CA: United Artists, 1996. Movie clip, "Walking Like John Wayne." YouTube, February 4, 2014. https://www.youtube.com/watch?v=Tmo1r-Gqd50.

Reiner, Rob, dir. *The Princess Bride*. Beverly Hills CA: Act III Communication, 1987.

Spottiswoode, Roger, dir. *And the Band Played On*. USA, 1993.

# Index

*Page numbers in italics indicate illustrations.*

protests (*cont.*)
  against police brutality, 5, 44, 84; at
  pride, 4, 62, 98
public health, 6

Ragsdale, Phil, 1, 10–12, 15, 17, 20, 22–
  24, 26, 30, 35, 36, 56, 58, 71, 72, 86,
  91, 94, 96, 112, 113, 116, 145, 160, 194,
  206, 210, 224; letter by, *115*
Reagan, Ronald, 35; AIDS, 185, 196, 197,
  198, 218; masculinity, 110, 152; Title
  IX, 150
Renier, David, 26, 179
Revlon Apartments, 221–23
Rivers, Joan, 36, 88, *90*, 91
Roosevelt, Theodore, 81, 152, 206, 207
roping events, 53, 118–22, 137, 154, 242
roughstock events, 3, 37, 82, 117–38, 140,
  144–46, 162, 179
*Roundup* magazine, 76–78, 106, 107, 134,
  157, *159*, 161, 171
royalty competition, 13,17, 36, 53, 69, 70,
  78, 87, 206, 210–20, 223
royalty titles: Miss, 28, 30, 36, 53, 78, 94,
  206, 210, 213, 214, 216, 218–21; Mr.,
  78, 214; Ms., 201, 214, 217; MsTer, 78,
  213, 214
RuPaul, 80, 81

sadomasochism (S&M), 162
safe sex, 92, 167, 169, 175, 176, 190;
  advertisement, 200
Save Our Children, 26
Scofield, Rebecca, 8, 12, 26, 55, 151, 152,
  162, 166

sexual freedom, 50, 182, 188
Sontag, Susan, 132, 139
speed events, 14, 37, 53, 118, 126, 145,
  146, 179
sponsorship, 169, 206
steer decorating, 3, 82, 118, 133, 135, 213
steer riding, 82, 112, 117, 118, 130, 131,
  144, 213
Stonewall riots, 2, 17, 24, 25, 57, 80, 108,
  151, 173, 194

terrorism, 42, 59
transgender people, 15, 58, 76, 111, 125,
  173, 215, 226
Trump, Donald, 43, 44, 99, 197, 224
Twain, Shania, 9, 83, 102, 223

United Airlines, 87–88, *89*, 160
*Urban Cowboy* (film), 9
urban cowboy (term), 81, 82, 141
U.S. Supreme Court, 245n27

*Vanity Fair*, 16
vaqueros, gay, 19
Vrooman, Michael, 5, 6, 81, 103, 170,
  212, 215–17

Washoe County, Nevada, 23
Wayne, John, 19, 79, 110, 151, 152, 164
whiteness, 5, 42, 44, 61, 62, 84, 196
wild cow milking, 82, 118, 145
wild drag race, 3, 12, 14, 37, 118, 131–34,
  144, 146, 213
Wrangler jeans, 81, 224

www.ingramcontent.com/pod-product-compliance
Lightning Source LLC
Chambersburg PA
CBHW031538260326
41914CB00039B/2003/J